IT TOOK COURAGE

IT TOOK COURAGE

Eliza Winston's Quest for Freedom

CHRISTOPHER P. LEHMAN

 MINNESOTA HISTORICAL SOCIETY PRESS

The publication of this book was supported
though a generous grant from the
Elmer L. and Eleanor Andersen Publications Fund.

mnhspress.org

The Minnesota Historical Society Press is a member
of the Association of University Presses.

Manufactured in the United States of America

10 9 8 7 6 5 4 3 2 1

⊗ The paper used in this publication meets the minimum
requirements of the American National Standard
for Information Sciences—Permanence for Printed Library
Materials, ANSI Z39.48–1984.

International Standard Book Number
ISBN: 978-1-68134-282-5 (paper)
ISBN: 978-1-68134-283-2 (e-book)

Library of Congress Control Number: 2023950046

CONTENTS

IT TOOK COURAGE

INTRODUCTION

More than a Minnesotan

Eliza Winston is an iconic figure in Minnesota's history. In the summer of 1860, she had the courage to leave her enslavers and pursue her freedom in a state district court, and on August 21, 1860, a judge proclaimed that she was a free woman.

Winston was one of several enslaved people brought by their enslavers from the slaveholding South to the free Northwest during the nation's antebellum era. Wealthy slaveholders enjoyed their vacations away from home without losing the comfort of service from the people they owned; because northern merchants depended on enslavers' spending, the southerners faced no legal consequences for violating the antislavery laws. The US Supreme Court's decision in *Dred Scott v. Sandford* legalized this activity in all US territories, including Minnesota Territory, in March 1857. Fourteen months later, when the new state of Minnesota adopted a constitution that prohibited slavery, its residents continued to welcome enslavers and their captives. Winston was the first person to legally challenge the state's informal continuance of the practice, and she won.

Her victory resulted in no small part from assistance she received from a few residents of Hennepin County, Minnesota.

She complained about her northern enslavement to a free African American woman living in the city of St. Anthony, the community across the river from what would become Minneapolis, who then contacted multiple abolitionists to help Winston become free. After an attempt to sneak her away from the captors' hotel failed, they succeeded in convincing the district judge to issue a writ of habeas corpus. The county sheriff seized Winston and brought her to court, where the judge emancipated her.

Ever since that moment, Eliza Winston's iconic status in the state has had less to do with her character and the details of her enslavement than with the fact of her winning freedom in the North with the help of Minnesotans. She left the state three months after her emancipation, but her local allies recounted their stories of involvement in the affair for decades afterward. As a result, they tended to talk more about themselves than about the person they helped to liberate. Over the generations, Winston evolved into a minor figure in her own story.

Moreover, few people mentioned her outside of Minnesota. Southerners wrote angry editorials about the North's seizing of Winston in late 1860; but after Union troops started killing Confederate troops in April 1861, the North's freeing of one captive became a much less pressing concern. Minnesotans have controlled the historical narrative about her by default.

As for Winston herself, her narrative's construction only partly came from her own words. Three days after her emancipation, she filed an affidavit—a sworn statement, put in writing—with Hennepin County, describing the events before and after her freedom trial. She revealed in her statement that she was thirty years old as of August 1860, and that she had lived in the states of Tennessee and Mississippi before coming to Minnesota. More importantly, she provided some detailed information about her life. She spoke about being enslaved first by a "Mr. Macklemo," his daughter, his son-in-law "Mr. Gholson" of Memphis, and the Christmas family of Mississippi. She recalled the broken promises Gholson and the Christmases made to her. She spoke of her faithful care to all her enslavers and how she hoped it would lead to her freedom. She disclosed her dream of returning to Memphis and working there as a free person.[1]

The affidavit is the longest statement known to have been written by an African American formerly enslaved in Minnesota. Scholars quote or paraphrase extensively from the affidavit when writing about either Winston's life or the practice of slavery in Minnesota. Works drawing from her affidavit follow its example of treating her life before Minnesota as irrelevant to her struggle for liberation. Articles and books mention "Mr. Macklemo" and "Mr. Gholson," but they do not identify them beyond their familial relationship of father-in-law and son-in-law. They do not provide first names for them or information about how they came to acquire Winston.

Most of the literature about Minnesota's relationship to slavery or the state's involvement in the Civil War refers to Winston. Her story exemplifies Minnesota's complex relationship to slavery, because the state's healthy tourism industry required local officials and entrepreneurs to overlook wealthy southern visitors who disobeyed the ban on slavery. With the Panic of 1857, the white-hot Minnesota economy crashed, causing land to lose value, banks and businesses to fail, and entire communities to operate without hard currency. By January 1861, merchants in Winona were issuing "checks" of five to fifty cents to provide customers with change. But southern tourists paid for their purchases in cash. Winston's emancipation also illustrated the sectionalism that had already infected the country and would, within months, explode into war. Her enslavers resented the intrusion into their relationship with her by northerners, and southern newspapers expressed disgust with her enslavers' treatment in what they had assumed was a sympathetic northern state.[2]

Much of the information cited in writings about Winston is from two very different kinds of sources. Her affidavit is her only recorded autobiographical statement. A newspaper article from seventy-four years later recalls the story of her emancipation, but it adds dramatic touches that bore little relevance to Winston's life. The article portrays her as an elderly, hefty mammy prone to cursing—but no primary source describes her in such a manner. Also, although she did not identify her first husband by name, the article calls him "Jim Winston."[3]

Historians have made the best of the limited sources about Eliza Winston's life. William D. Green wrote two articles and two books that reintroduced her story to twenty-first-century consumers of Minnesota's history. As with earlier writers' works, his writings drew significantly from Winston's affidavit. On the other hand, his works resulted from the most thorough historical research on Winston's enslavement and freedom in Minnesota in recent years. He relied not only on newspaper articles from the summer of 1860 but also on monographs that explained the politics of the state at the time, the status of slavery as an informal but very evident practice there, and the conditions of African Americans in Minnesota.

It Took Courage: Eliza Winston's Quest for Freedom explores the years of Winston's enslavement well beyond the information provided in the affidavit and, in doing so, makes her story a national one. Her six weeks of captivity in Minnesota and her seven years with the Christmases before then are only part of her story. Through research into the minimal information the affidavit provided, this book looks at her time with the Gholsons and her early years while "raised" by "Mr. Macklemo." Careful research of newspaper articles, municipal marriage records, and federal census records in Memphis places Eliza's date of birth in 1817 instead of 1830. The documents also reveal that "Mr. Macklemo" was John Christmas McLemore of Nashville, that his daughter was Catherine (Kate) McLemore Gholson, and that his son-in-law was Thomas Yates Gholson of Memphis.

An examination of Winston's claim that McLemore passed her

to his daughter Kate upon the latter's marriage yielded startling information. A couple from Maury County, Tennessee, enslaved Winston for eight years in between McLemore and Kate. Moreover, McLemore did not directly give Winston to the couple. Rather, the sheriff of Davidson County, Tennessee, seized Winston from McLemore in Nashville in 1834 because of the latter's debt, and the couple purchased her at a subsequent auction. Kate was twelve years old in 1834. Research of the seizure revealed that Kate's granduncle arranged for the couple to keep Winston in trust until his grandniece was married. She received her human inheritance one year after her marriage in 1841 to Gholson.

The granduncle who saved Kate's inheritance was Andrew Jackson, the seventh US president. For eight years the nation's leader held a claim to Winston, and the first three of those years took place during his second term in the White House. President Jackson co-owned her while conducting government policies on slavery and Indian removal in the mid-1830s. This book discusses the details and ramifications of Winston's ties to the White House and how that connection influenced the trajectory of her life after 1834.

Further study of McLemore's holding of Winston showed her long presence in Tennessee. She stated in her affidavit that she was thirty years old in 1860, so her birth year would have been 1829 or 1830. But deeds identify her as seventeen years old in 1834 and as a woman—not a girl—in 1842, when she went to the Gholsons' household in Memphis. In addition, McLemore was not Winston's first captor, because he had purchased her from another enslaver in Tennessee in 1822. She was five years old at the time, and she may not have remembered an enslaver before McLemore when she gave her statement thirty-eight years later in 1860. The deed of the 1822 sale lists not only Winston but also her mother, grandmother, siblings, aunt, and uncle. Therefore, elders in the family raised her, and she had siblings as playmates when they were not laboring together. This book looks at the first five years of her life, how her family raised her, and how their absence from her life shaped her.

Many writings about Winston portray her as ignorant of the significance of freedom and needing to be convinced by Minnesotans to pursue liberation. The abolitionists themselves tended to emphasize their own actions, and their detractors blamed them for making Winston a political pawn. Both groups focused on mob actions, rather than Winston's story. This description contradicts her claims that her husband periodically hired her out from Gholson and that the couple enjoyed a partially free marriage. Also, in 1844, the Gholsons permitted Winston to worship without them at a church whose membership included other enslaved people, slave-less European Americans, and free African Americans. She was a member of the church for at least one year, enjoying some sustained agency over an important part of her life. Therefore, she was quite familiar with freedom for almost two decades before seeking her emancipation in Minnesota. This book examines how her church membership affected her life.

Winston's captivity in Minnesota was not an accident. It resulted from deliberate planning by the Christmases and the failure of public and private citizens to prevent the enslavement of people in their free state. The social, economic, and political conditions enabling slavery in Minnesota developed long before 1860. For Winston's entire enslaved life, she lived in states that were considered the American West. During her childhood and young adulthood in Tennessee, Americans referred to that state as the West. When she went to Mississippi in 1853, that state was part of the Southwest. Finally, during her brief time in Minnesota in 1860, she lived in captivity in the Northwest. The westward trajectory of her enslavement was a direct legacy of Indian removal policies and the westward expansion that began in the 1830s under President Jackson. This book explores the different ways she experienced slavery as enslavers took her farther west.

Although the bulk of information about Winston concerns her three months in Minnesota, her enslavement in multiple states makes her story a fundamentally American one. In 1860 the country consisted of only thirty-three states, and she had lived in or traveled past one-third of them by then. Enslavers held her captive in Tennessee, Louisiana, Kentucky, Mississippi, and Minnesota. Each state had its own culture of slavery, and she adjusted to each. She suffered captivity in the cities of Nashville and Memphis, the French-influenced slave market of New Orleans, the free-slave border culture of Louisville, the Deep South plantation life near Vicksburg, and the free-state slavery of the Twin Cities. In addition, her multiple journeys with her enslavers by steamboat along the Mississippi and Ohio Rivers exposed her to even more states.

This book adds to the small but growing historiography of African Americans enslaved by US commanders in chief. In recent years Annette Gordon-Reed's *The Hemingses of Monticello: An American Family* and Erica Armstrong Dunbar's *Never Caught: The Washingtons' Relentless Pursuit of Their Runaway Slave, Ona Judge* have vividly explored the lives of Thomas Jefferson's laborer Sally Hemings and George Washington's captive Ona Judge. Winston shared Judge's willingness to become free without her captor's blessing. However, just as Hemings navigated Jefferson's family dynamics, complicated through his sexual exploitation of her, Winston maneuvered through the relationships of multiple generations of Donelsons—Jackson's family by marriage. Jackson's wife and McLemore's wife and daughter were all Donelsons by birth, and the president saw to it that as long as he lived, Winston would always belong to his wife's kin.

The effort for Winston's emancipation was at root a women's campaign. Winston initiated it, but a free African American woman named Emily Grey organized it. They both relied on assistance from European American women, and the men they contacted followed their lead. Winston's liberation showed the potential for more successful activism from coalitions that crossed boundaries of gender and color.

It Took Courage: Eliza Winston's Quest for Freedom places Hennepin County, Minnesota, in the history of the nation's Underground Railroad (UGRR). Local abolitionists helped Winston hide from her enslavers and proslavery mobs at several places in the county, and each location became a new stop on Hennepin's UGRR. The abolitionists who welcomed and quartered her in those locations consequently became new local "conductors." For the most part, Hennepin's UGRR was a self-contained entity or a local railroad line, concerned mostly with protecting Winston within the county. When one conductor brought her out of the county and onto the route that ultimately took her to Canada, Hennepin County's UGRR joined the more established national one. However, she was the first and only enslaved person to travel from Hennepin County to Canada on the UGRR. After her emancipation, enslavers in the free county quickly returned to slave states with their enslaved people, and the Civil War's eruption seven months later ended the tourism business that had brought unfree laborers like Winston to the county—and to its UGRR.

Winston was much more than simply a Mississippi captive who became free in Minnesota with the help of locals. She remembered the prices her captors paid for her, and she knew the wage for the job she wanted. She made choices for herself whenever possible within her enslavement, whether by joining a church without her enslavers or by becoming literate. Having known free African Americans for much of her life, she sought freedom for herself long before 1860. By meeting slave-less European Americans in church, she saw that some people resembling her enslavers opposed slavery, and that exposure prepared her for her partnerships with abolitionists. This book is about how her pursuit of liberation within the law evolved throughout her enslavement from her solo efforts at manumission to a coalition dedicated to her emancipation. As many African Americans today struggle to receive justice after suffering brutality from law enforcement, her story stands out as a rare example of an African American relentlessly confronting a legal institution of brutality—the institution of slavery—and ultimately winning justice for herself in a court of law.

The first five chapters look at Winston's childhood and early adulthood. Much of the content of these chapters necessarily concerns the lives and actions of her captors and their families. Her enslavers were wealthy and powerful people, and their lives are documented in newspapers, archives, memoirs, biographies, and government documents. But the stories of their lives also provide precious clues to Winston's life. During these years, her enslavers designated her as a "house servant." Her daily work made her a witness to intimate family matters; the Jackson/Donelson family made ownership of her a part of their family interactions. She had to anticipate her enslavers' needs and serve their guests, who acted at the highest levels of American society. She was clearly smart, emotionally adept, and accomplished in her work. "I was never sold," she stated in her affidavit. "I have always been faithful, and no master that I have ever had has found fault with me."

She labored among small populations of household captives. By relying on so few enslaved laborers and restricting her work to the confines of the home, the enslavers directly controlled and influenced the conditions of Winston's enslavement; she provided the labor that supported the significant events in their households. The slaveholders' decisions on how to spend household finances affected her work. For example, when an enslaver struggled to pay for food for his household, Winston had less food to cook for them but also less food to eat. These chapters significantly focus on how the enslavers of her early years constructed the parameters of her captivity via the intimate nature of domestic slavery.

The enslavers' financial decisions also directly affected Winston's family—and determined her proximity to them. She retained her family when her first enslaver Thomas Hopkins sold her with them to John McLemore, whose wife was a member of the powerful Donelson family of Nashville, Tennessee. However, in the quarter century that members of the Donelsons enslaved Winston in Tennessee and Kentucky, they exposed her to some of the cruelest aspects of slavery. The McLemores' financial hardships forced them to sell off several of her acquaintances over the years, and these struggles peaked with a court-ordered liquidation that removed the remaining enslaved people—including Winston and other children, who became her virtual siblings—from the household itself.

The chapters also explore the role of national politics in Winston's captivity. The Donelsons' most famous and most powerful family member was President Andrew Jackson. During his presidency he purchased Winston—but only to ensure that McLemore's crippling debt did not prevent the father from passing the enslaved woman down to his daughter. Jackson laid a claim to Winston from 1834 to 1842, and that period included his second presidential term and most of his years in retirement. He arranged for another Donelson—his grandniece Mary Ann Eastin Polk—to keep Winston during those eight years, and that arrangement forced Winston away from the urban domestic service of her childhood and into labor on a sprawling plantation in rural Tennessee during her early adulthood. Moreover, the president protected his own family's wealth by sacrificing Winston's family, specifically designating her for Kate McLemore Gholson while banishing her virtual siblings miles away to Kate's sister Mary.

On the other hand, Jackson's separation of Winston from the rest of her family gave her more agency in her enslavement. When Kate inherited Winston and brought her to Memphis, the new enslaver granted her new privileges. She received permission to attend church by herself, and the church she chose consisted of a diverse membership—including free African Americans and European Americans without captives. The congregants exposed her to different degrees of slavery and freedom, and she could see how other African Americans shaped their lives according to those degrees. Still, she remained an enslaved person, and the Gholson household's financial problems forced her to leave the church and to relocate with them—to Louisville and then to Nashville—as they sought sources of income.

The next two chapters are about Winston's enslavement beyond the Donelsons. Here the story of her captivity transitions from the conditions her enslavers set for her labor. For the rest of her enslavement, she actively sought more autonomy in her captivity and ultimately pursued complete liberation. After Kate's death in 1848, no Donelson ever owned Winston again. Kate's widower subsequently assumed ownership of Winston, and he gave even more agency to her and put her on a path to freedom. They returned to Memphis, where she had first experienced partial freedom. After relocating there he granted permission for Winston to marry, helped the newlyweds establish their own household, and developed a payment plan for her manumission.

However, Winston's husband died, and Gholson's financial woes forced him to transfer her to a couple on a plantation in rural Mississippi. In the process, she lost her partial freedom and her social network, especially because her new enslaver Mary Phillips Christmas was sickly and demanded Winston's constant presence and full attention. From this point on, the story of her captivity concerns her continued pursuit of total freedom while suffering restrictions placed over her life by Mary and her husband Richard. Winston expected her new owners to fulfill their promise to free her during their trip to Minnesota in 1860, and their refusal only made her more determined to become free in the Northwest.

The next three chapters are about Winston's enslavement in Minnesota and the emergence of her opportunity for freedom. She suffered her captivity in a palatial proslavery sanctuary in St. Anthony, but she enjoyed a brief encounter outside that space with a free African American woman. That woman—Emily Grey—rallied local abolitionists to help Winston, and Grey's meeting at her home with Winston and abolitionist women became the first stop of Hennepin's UGRR. On the other hand, the Christmases learned about the plan to free Winston, kidnapped her, and took her an hour away to Lake Harriet—a much smaller, more rustic proslavery haven. By doing so the couple desperately tried to maintain their enslavement of her in a free state, thus performing slavery as a reactionary illegal act.

The rest of the book is about the end of Winston's enslavement and the role of Minnesota's legal system. A judge issued a writ of habeas corpus for her, sent the local sheriff to apprehend her and bring her to court, and then emancipated her. That verdict changed her life and the lives of the people with whom she interacted. Hennepin's UGRR kept her safe from proslavery mobs who wanted to return her to the Christmases, and the conductors led her to the national UGRR line, which brought her to safety in Canada. Winston briefly became a national symbol of antebellum sectional strife, but the sectional violence and bloodshed of the Civil War soon overshadowed her story. The South forgot about her. With the sudden ending of southern tourism in the North in April 1861, Winston's freedom in Minnesota seven months earlier came to define the state's relationship to slavery for years to come.

≋1
Captive Childhood
in Tennessee

A five-year-old enslaved girl named Eliza stood on a plateau in Warren County, Tennessee, in 1822. Above her were the Appalachian mountaintops. Beyond the edge of the plateau, the caves below beckoned her, and thirty miles north the Cumberland River flowed. Dense forests surrounded her enslaver's plantation. Wherever the girl walked, ran, and romped on the estate's land, her feet touched rich, fertile soil—a rarity on the mostly sandy ground of the Cumberland Plateau.

Eliza Winston's enslaver—Thomas Hopkins—was a fortunate man in owning his plantation in Warren County, Tennessee, but fortune constantly smiled on him. He was born in 1764 into a wealthy family that lived in Virginia by the James River. Boats from the city of Richmond carried indentured servants and enslaved people on the James to other riverside counties, and the Hopkinses' access to the river contributed to their wealth, blessing them with fertile land and a convenient waterway for transporting the goods the family's laborers produced. Thomas's father passed a second plantation to the junior Hopkins when the latter turned thirty years old in 1794. The family also enjoyed powerful political ties. Hopkins's paternal grandfather was a friend of Thomas Jefferson, and Jefferson's first cousin married Hopkins's paternal uncle.[1]

Hopkins acquired captives while building his own wealth. He left Virginia shortly after inheriting his father's plantation, and he then traveled southwest through the Great Appalachian Valley. He settled on the Cumberland Plateau and established the plantation where he eventually enslaved Eliza. He may have brought some of his father's captives with him. The elder Hopkins had held two women named Phebe, and Thomas himself enslaved a little girl by that name. Another of Hopkins's laborers shared the first name of his sister Molly. Born around 1798, the enslaved Molly was Eliza's mother. Phebe and Molly were among the Virginians whose enslavers either sold them away from the state or moved with them to another state. By January 1822 little Eliza was another of Hopkins's captives.[2]

He invested in fertile women, and each childbirth on his plantation raised the value of his estate. Although children under ten years of age and elderly people sold for the lowest prices among the enslaved, the prices of children grew with their maturity, stronger muscles, and—concerning girls—ability to reproduce. Molly gave birth to George at age fifteen, to Matilda at seventeen, to Eliza at nineteen, and to Sally at twenty-one. Each newborn saved the enslaver from having to buy laborers, and Molly's youth and fertility promised to greatly enrich him for years to come. Young motherhood—a common situation among enslaved African American women—was multigenerational in Eliza's family. Her grandmother Judah had given birth at age sixteen to Molly. In 1810, when she was twenty-eight, Judah welcomed Eliza's Uncle Burgis, and Aunt Phebe arrived in 1812. Judah became a grandmother at age thirty-one with George's birth, and she was thirty-five at Eliza's birth.[3]

Adolescents and young adults comprised about half of the plantation's enslaved population. Hopkins constructed a human investment portfolio of significant wealth, and each teenager's transition into adulthood made him richer. In 1820 nineteen of his forty-one captives were between the ages of fourteen and twenty-five. A seller could receive as much as one thousand dollars for just one healthy man in his twenties. Teenagers were about six hundred to eight hundred dollars per person but would soon age into young adults. An enslaved woman named Patsey, thirty-five years old, also lived at the estate with her two children. Her children Alexander and Harriet were the same age as Uncle Burgis and Aunt Phebe, respectively.[4]

Multiple women on the plantation were Eliza's elders, and they possessed wisdom from their experiences as enslaved women and as Hopkins's captives. Eliza likely studied the actions, words, and demeanor of the elder women of her community: Molly, Judah, and Patsey. As enslaved women in Appalachia, they probably performed some field work. Over half of the area's captive women engaged only in field labor, and 15 percent of enslaved domestics received assignments in fields.[5]

Eliza's grandmother Judah had served multiple generations of the Hopkins family. She may have encountered Thomas Jefferson or other members of the Jefferson family—or even, perhaps, the enslaved members the Hemings family, consisting of Elizabeth, her six children (including Sally Hemings), and her grandchild. Judah's service to Hopkins from his boyhood exposed her to his behavioral patterns and personal tastes, thus teaching her how to please him and avoid angering him.[6]

Hopkins never married and never had any children. By age five, Eliza probably observed that her enslaver was the only European American on his plantation. It would have been reasonable for his enslaved children to connect the differences in skin color to the dynamics of human ownership. Hopkins as "white" was the owner, and Eliza and her family and fellow laborers were the "negro" captives. On the other hand, some of Hopkins's laborers had previously belonged to his antislavery brother-in-law Samuel Richardson, who sold his enslaved people to Hopkins on the condition that Hopkins free them upon his death if not earlier. He called his new laborers "Richardson's negroes," and his neighbors knew of their pending free status. Eliza's family likely knew too.[7]

Eliza was three years old in December 1820 when a strikingly handsome man came to the plateau from Nashville to meet with Hopkins. The two men traveled more than two hundred miles to the west, to Obion County on the Mississippi River, where they acquired five thousand acres of land. The stranger's last name sounded like "Macklemo" to little Eliza. In May 1821 he and her enslaver again went to Obion, and they purchased five thousand more acres.[8]

After returning home from Obion, Hopkins concentrated more of his wealth on real estate in Warren County. He chose to sell some of his laborers to acquire the money he required for the local land he wanted, and his choices determined whether he would splinter Eliza's family by selling away any of them—or Eliza herself. The year's planting season had already begun by May, and Hopkins needed his current laborers to finish out the year's work in the fields. January was the usual month for enslavers to buy and sell people, because a new season of growing crops had not yet begun. Enslaved adults like Molly and Judah spent each New Year's Day anxiously hoping to escape the dreaded auction block.[9]

Eliza briefly spent her captivity with two other elders on the plantation. Hopkins purchased another woman named Molly, who was slightly older than Judah, and her thirteen-year-old daughter Aye in 1817 from a man named John Hammons. The senior Molly was born enslaved in 1776, just as the United States declared independence from Britain. Her daughter was thirteen years older than Eliza, a peer of Aunt Phebe and Uncle Burgis. Aye was one of the first light-skinned captives to share a slave community with Eliza, showing the little girl that enslavement did not differ by the amount of melanin in an African American.[10]

The elder Molly and Aye suddenly disappeared from the plateau in early 1821. The seller, John Hammons, unlawfully removed them from Hopkins's estate, transported them south to the state of Alabama, and sold them again. That buyer then sold them to another person. Eliza had never known anyone to have been stolen away, and the removal of the mother and daughter from Hopkins's household showed her that slaveholders did not have total control over their captives while enslaving them. The theft was also the first time she witnessed a bitter truth: when enslavers sent people with brown skin to the Deep South, those exiles never returned.[11]

In January 1822 the handsome man "Macklemo" visited the plantation again. The visitor identified which people he would purchase from Hopkins and for how much money. While there, he probably studied Eliza and the other captives, scanning their bodies for scars from whippings and looking for physical signs of injury or ill health. Hopkins eventually agreed to sell two men, three women, two boys, and four girls to the man for $4,350. Eliza, her mother, her grandmother, her siblings, her aunt, and her uncle were among the acquisitions.[12]

The new owner, John Christmas McLemore, then took Eliza and her family away from Hopkins's plantation—the only home she had ever known. The deed for the sale was one of the first documents to record her existence. Hopkins identified her as "Eliza a negro girl about five years of age." Sellers of enslaved people listed their human merchandise by their first name, age, gender, and color in deeds and county court documents across the country during the antebellum era, and for the remainder of Eliza's enslavement, people recording her existence rarely deviated from mentioning only those attributes.[13]

> The freezing winter mountain winds chilled Eliza's skin during her eighty-mile trip northwest with her family. As frigid air slapped her face, the swaying barren branches on the trees revealed the direction from which the gusts came. The travelers exited Warren County and descended from the Cumberland Plateau, and they then trekked through Middle Tennessee. The muddy East Fork Stones River lay at a close distance.

As the sojourners began to arrive at their destination, their surroundings starkly changed. They encountered a dense, urban
community: Nashville. The city had public areas where European
Americans, free African Americans, and enslaved people all gathered together, watching entertainers and horse races. The enslaved
could walk the city streets as the free people did, but instead of
free papers they carried instructions from their enslavers as to
where they were to go within Nashville.[14]

Eliza and her family eventually reached their new captor's
home and began laboring there. The McLemore estate was a
house full of people—a stark contrast to Hopkins's plantation.
John McLemore, his wife Catherine Elizabeth (Betsy) Donelson
McLemore, and their children, Mary, John Jr., and Andrew Jackson (known as A. J.), comprised the household. Eliza suddenly
had to take orders from a European American woman and from
European American children for the first time. Mary was close
to her in age, and, as they grew up, Eliza would also witness the
enormous differences in their lives.[15]

The McLemores' relatives and dearest friends in the Nashville area were General Andrew Jackson and Rachel Donelson
Jackson, who resided at their massive plantation, the Hermitage.
Rachel was Betsy McLemore's paternal aunt. Thus, McLemore
and Jackson shared a bond of marrying into the Donelson family, albeit in different generations. In 1820 the McLemores had
named their second son after Jackson. There were many other
significant ties: Andrew and Rachel adopted one of the twin sons
of her brother Severn and raised him as Andrew Jackson Jr.;
Andrew and Rachel became guardians of the children of Rachel's
deceased brother Samuel, and one of them—Andrew Jackson
Donelson—became his protégé and personal secretary. The deep
connection between the McLemores and Jacksons made the general a significant presence in Eliza's life.

Eliza met the enslaved people already at the McLemore estate,
which may have included the people Betsy had inherited from

Andrew Jackson
and Rachel Donelson
Jackson. Engraved
by Francis Kearney,
about 1829. *Library
of Congress*

her father. In 1820 the McLemores enslaved eight people, all of them twenty-five years of age or younger. That same year the couple purchased someone else within that age range—"a certain mulatto boy slave named Gabriel about thirteen years of age," as the deed for the sale put it. The McLemores' holdings of people suggested a strategy of buying people who were still growing in value and then removing them immediately after their peak. Also, the McLemore household quartered no free African Americans at all. Eliza lived in a binary environment, in which only color determined one's status, and she did not have the color for freedom.[16]

Barely one month after Eliza's transition to the McLemore estate, she witnessed yet another new event. Betsy gave birth to Catherine (Kate) Donelson McLemore on February 28, 1822. Although enslaved women had birthed babies at Hopkins's plantation, no one with his color had given birth to anyone there. Except for the newest McLemore's pale red skin, she was just like the newborns on the plateau—small, helpless, and crying in between gasps for air.

The McLemores added to their holdings of captives. Six months after Eliza's arrival in Nashville, McLemore purchased a woman named Linda, age twenty-seven, from a resident of Williamson County, Tennessee. The addition of enslaved family units provided more virtual siblings for Eliza. In the following month, Eliza welcomed Patsey and her children from the Hopkins estate. Alexander and Harriet were already over the age of ten when the McLemores purchased them. The next year the McLemores bought a family of eight—the couple Daniel and Rachel, their five children, and their grandchild from their sixteen-year-old daughter Maria, the couple's oldest child. McLemore sold Maria and her child in 1824, but the births of Malinda that year and Julius two years later increased his collection of enslaved people.[17]

McLemore's eye for investment defined his enslavement of Eliza. He worked as a land speculator and a dealer in real estate, and the health of the real estate business determined the house-hold income. In flush times he could afford to buy enslaved people, but in dire times he sold them. The instability of the market made the McLemores' enslaved population fluid, exposing Eliza to frequent transactions involving her fellow captives. Also, by training her and her family for domestic service, the McLemores added to the laborers' financial worth as enslaved people in an urban environment.

McLemore traveled to other counties to see the captives and the land he was considering purchasing. Eliza years later remembered that she was "raised by Mr. Macklemo," but his constant travels reinforced Betsy's authority over her unfree laborers. She was an experienced enslaver, because her parents had held captive at least three dozen people at their home, which they dubbed the Mansion. Her mother—Mary Purnell Donelson—taught them how she wanted them to make the provisions for the Donelsons and for themselves. The younger laborers learned from her and from their elders how to cook and preserve food and how to make clothes and shoes. Betsy, in turn, observed how to supervise the unfree.[18]

General Jackson added to McLemore's responsibilities outside of Nashville. Jackson was elected to the US Senate in 1823, and he relocated to Washington, DC. He immediately made plans to run in the following year's presidential election, and McLemore was part of the scheme. That October, Jackson sold his one-eighth share of the city of Memphis—eleven hundred acres—to McLemore, because the general did not want his business interests to hinder his ultimately unsuccessful campaign. McLemore was an absentee proprietor of Memphis from the start, however, because he was frequently traveling to survey and purchase land in Florida, Alabama, and elsewhere in Tennessee.[19]

When Eliza was ten, McLemore purchased two more people, and this transaction revealed a new dynamic of slavery to her. Before that purchase, her enslavers had brought either an entire family or an individual adult to the household, and she herself had been part of a family purchase. However, in February 1827 McLemore purchased two children from a seller in Shelby County. The older of the juvenile captives—"one negro boy named Trusty of black colour"—was about the same age as Eliza, and the younger—"one negro girl named Mary Ann of black colour"—was only five years old. Eliza was not too young for McLemore to sell her away from her family.[20]

General Jackson ran again for the US presidency in 1828, and McLemore donated to his uncle-in-law's campaign and solicited money from others. "We must go to the whole for the old Hero and the people's cause," he wrote to John Coffee, who had served in the Tennessee militia under Jackson and who had married another of Jackson's nieces. "Now is the time to make the push. I am ready heart & soul to go to my length for him." Jackson won that November, and he remained a close friend to McLemore. Eliza's enslaver had already arranged for a five-week stay in Memphis the previous spring, but Jackson's victory threatened to take McLemore even farther away from her—all the way to Washington.[21]

Betsy had braced herself for her Aunt Rachel to leave the Nashville area for a much longer period than before. Rachel herself had received a heavy barrage of deeply personal criticism during her husband's presidential campaign, and she did not look forward to leaving the comfort of the Hermitage and residing among her critics. But Rachel died two months before her husband's inauguration. Betsy's youngest sister Emily (who was married to Andrew Jackson Donelson—the new president's personal secretary and her own first cousin) and her niece Mary Ann Eastin, who lived at the Hermitage at the time, agreed to accompany the widowed president-elect to the White House and jointly perform the traditional duties of First Lady.[22]

The McLemores' daughter Mary and Eliza both entered adolescence as Jackson took the oath of office in March 1829. For the former, this phase meant preparations for becoming a wife and an enslaver in her own right; for the latter, the teenage years brought continued enslavement and forced labor. Juvenile captives had witnessed this rite of passage among their captors' children for generations. On the other hand, Mary was the oldest child, and neither of Eliza's older siblings George and Matilda had seen a European American juvenile peer mature into the role of an enslaver. Therefore, her siblings could not advise Eliza from experience on how to process the transition.

McLemore's frequent, apparently random buying and selling of his captives gave Eliza little opportunity to maintain relationships with the household's other enslaved people. Two of the laborers in 1830 were born during the 1820s. The families of Judah and Patsey comprised eleven people purchased in 1822 alone. At least half of the estate's enslaved population in 1830 came from those two families. In addition, McLemore bought another person named Gabriel in 1830.[23]

A generational shift also took place throughout the 1820s among the McLemores' captives. In 1820 five laborers were twenty-six or older; by 1830, no McLemore captives were older than thirty-five. In 1820 all eight of the estate's enslaved people were older than Eliza; ten years later she was older than at least two of the household's ten unfree laborers. Eliza's grandmother Judah, as well as Patsey and the couple Daniel and Rachel, all of whom were in their forties when the McLemores acquired them, were gone from the household by 1830. They had decreased in value as they aged. The McLemores had changed their unfree population and owned people who were either growing in monetary value or currently at their most valuable.[24]

Eliza and the other young captives served a growing household. Betsy gave birth to three babies between 1828 and 1832. Eliza's mother and the other enslaved women of nursing age had no relief from the constant arrival of newborns. The women comforted the infants and saw to their needs, which prevented them from taking care of Eliza and the other enslaved children. Then again, with Eliza having reached adolescence, she was old enough to be a mother herself. In 1832 she turned fifteen—the age when her mother, Molly, gave birth to her first child.

Some of the children of the extended Donelson family reached adulthood during this time, and Eliza probably had to serve them too. The McLemores' nephew John Donelson Coffee visited the household while attending the University of Nashville nearby, at least in 1830 and 1831. He called the couple "Uncle McLemore" and "Aunt Betsy." Born in 1815, he was approximately the same age as Eliza and Mary, and he was the first teenage boy Eliza ever served. McLemore sons John Jr. and A. J. also reached adolescence within the next two years.[25]

Jackson continued to influence the McLemore household from the White House. He appointed his friend John Eaton to be secretary of war early in 1829, but Eaton's wife was shunned by Washington society for her alleged sexual promiscuity, and the appointment became controversial. Jackson and McLemore wrote to each other about these events over the next few months. "I knew Eaton was too pure a man to be guilty of acts charged against him," the president told McLemore in September. "I have not been mistaken." McLemore traveled to the White House that fall to discuss the issue with President Jackson in person, and McLemore's absence once again placed Betsy in full supervision of Eliza's labor for several weeks. He returned home in December with no progress made on the controversy.[26]

McLemore was suffering his own scandal by then, chronically indebted to at least one of his two creditors. In a statement to the press, he acknowledged what the general public already knew about his work in surveying and acquiring land grants in the Western District of Tennessee. He noted, "It is known to the public that under the law of 1819, and under subsequent statutes for the entry, . . . I have been largely concerned in locating lands in that quarter for persons in this and other States." He then painfully explained, "Immediately after entry those lands were by law subject to taxes: . . . I have heretofore, to prevent sacrifice of my own interest and to preserve the interest of others, voluntarily paid taxes to an amount every way distressing to myself and injurious to my creditors. In short, I can no longer bear it." He bitterly observed, "[Citizen debtors] seem to have no particular concern about the matter, and I suppose never will, so long as I am silent and continue to pay taxes for them without any remuneration." But he was silent no more, and he announced, "Now be it known that I will in no one case pay the taxes for any one henceforward."[27]

McLemore routinely sold land to pay off his debts, needing $10,000 as of April 1830 to meet immediate demands. His speculative bad luck indebted him when his new city Memphis needed him most. He transferred the city's management to another person and rarely visited it in the first decade after its establishment in 1826. He ultimately realized that he owned more real estate than he could manage. In March 1831 he had his agent begin selling his land in western Tennessee, and the money from those transactions allowed McLemore to address some of his debt, feed his family, and provide for Eliza and the others he enslaved. The president consoled McLemore: "Let me know how you get on with your business, You have my best wishes and shall have my aid if needed, as far as my means will permit." After that year, McLemore's sole major investments in the state were enslaved people, and Eliza continued to adjust to new members of the household.[28]

McLemore was not the only family member to frequently travel from home in the early 1830s. By age fourteen, Mary started traveling apart from her parents. The time away from them allowed her to escape her family's crisis of debt, and her travels left Eliza with one fewer McLemore to serve. In the fall of 1830, Mary went on a trip to Alabama with her twenty-year-old cousin Mary Ann Eastin, who was temporarily away from the White House. Mary also tried to form her own relationship with President Jackson, independent of the one her father enjoyed with him. In Alabama she started working on a present for Jackson—"a beautiful map of the world," as her cousin put it. By June that year, she completed it, and Eastin bragged that it was "said by judges to exceed any thing ever seen in the Typograthical [*sic*] department." Eastin also called her "a very accomplished amiable girl."[29]

Eliza likely encountered the map while working in the McLemore home. The map would have presented to her an illustration of the world and her geographical place in it, perhaps for the first time. Mary's freedom and her family's social prominence provided access to education, including geography. Eliza's enslavement meant that she was exposed to very few environments outside of the households she served, and that is where she would do what learning she could. In addition, Mary's hard work on the map further demonstrated the high regard that Eliza's captors held for President Jackson, and it suggested that Jackson's hold on the McLemore family would continue for at least another generation.

President Jackson took Mary under his wing, and her new level of privilege diverged dramatically from Eliza's life of enslavement. Mary left home late that summer to attend school in Pennsylvania, and Jackson became her pseudo-guardian. He paid a French woman in Philadelphia to give his grandniece music lessons; Mary also learned to play the harp. The president set expectations for his grandniece's behavior while in his company. He wrote to Vice President Martin Van Buren, "Major Donelson and his family have just arrived since I began this letter, with miss Mary Easton [*sic*], and miss McLemore, and I hope, with all those feelings which ought at first to have accompanied them hither—they know my *course*, and my wishes, and I hope, they came to comply with them." Mary behaved well enough for him to invite her for another visit to the White House months later.[30]

McLemore's resilient political stature through the controversy continued to affect Eliza's enslavement. He traveled through Tennessee from August to October 1831, one of the longest stretches that Betsy alone supervised Eliza. In November he arranged for John Branch—a US congressman from North Carolina and a former governor of that state—to visit the house during every day of the politician's visit to Tennessee. The household's enslaved people had to make sure that the McLemores made a good first impression on him, because McLemore wanted the legislator to vote in Congress for Jackson's policies. McLemore worried about Branch's close ties to Jackson's political enemies, but the president's friend optimistically reported to him, "I have seen Governor Branch sinse [sic] his arrival here, and I think him well disposed towards you still."[31]

The McLemores navigated through a health crisis while enduring their financial troubles. An outbreak of cholera spread throughout Tennessee in 1831, and it was especially rampant in Nashville in the late months of the year. Eliza was fortunate to survive the epidemic. She was not yet an adult and not at her peak in strength to resist the disease. Also, the unhealthy diets and substandard medical care that characterized enslavement placed unfree laborers like her at greater risk than their enslavers for severe illness.[32]

In contrast, Mary continued to experience good fortune. As cholera spread toward Philadelphia in early 1832, her granduncle arranged for her to leave the city and move to Washington, DC, in June. Her cousin Mary Ann Eastin married Lucius J. Polk of Maury County, Tennessee, that month at a ceremony in the White House. She immediately left the White House, and Jackson replaced the departing bride with Mary McLemore as a stand-in First Lady. Mary bristled at the authority Aunt Emily Donelson and cousin Mary Coffee—daughter of John Coffee—held in the White House by virtue of their seniority, but the three women hid their discord from the president. Mary could find ways to assert her preferences to people at the highest levels of power in the country; Eliza's enslavement forced her to defer to much less powerful people than the president.[33]

Mary stayed at the White House through 1832 and into the winter of early 1833. Her granduncle sent notices to her family whenever possible. He told his son in October 1832, "To all our connections say to Mr. McLamore [*sic*] & Betsy that Mary is in fine health."[34]

In the fall of 1832, Mary's granduncle was reelected president, and she celebrated his victory. By late November she welcomed relatives to the White House for holiday observances with the president: her cousins Mary Coffee and Mary Ann Eastin Polk, who arrived with her new husband. Months later, on March 4, 1833, Mary McLemore, several Donelson cousins, an aunt, and an uncle observed Jackson's second inauguration.[35]

The following day Mary left the White House with her cousin Mary Coffee, her uncle John Coffee, and Congressman James K. Polk and his wife. They traveled to Nashville and returned to their respective homes. Mary McLemore never fully grew into her role in the White House before her departure. "You want to know whether Cousin Mary is a belle here," Mary Coffee wrote to Mary Ann Eastin Polk. "She is a good deal admired but don't talk enough to be a very great belle here. She is silent as ever." On the other hand, Mary returned home as a more worldly and more educated girl, showing Eliza how opportunities for travel and education could shape someone of her age.[36]

Mary's homecoming did not lessen McLemore's travels away from home, and Betsy's supervision of Eliza remained the sole constant factor of her enslavement. President Jackson's policies concerning land formed the context for McLemore's travels in late 1833. Jackson forced the Choctaw people to leave their homes in Mississippi and move hundreds of miles away to the area that became Indian Territory (and later Oklahoma). They departed in phases between 1831 and 1833, traveling under brutal conditions on what came to be known as the Trail of Tears. The federal government conducted a three-day sale of the vacated land in October 1833. McLemore became a partner of the Chocchuma Land Company, which bought two-thirds to three-fourths of the land at Chocchuma, Mississippi, and then sold it, primarily to planters seeking fertile land. He acquired over seven hundred acres from Chocchuma, Mississippi, in his own name, and he spent his share of his company's profits on his family and his investments—including his captives. As a result, Jackson's Indian removal policies allowed McLemore to reap profits that affected Eliza's enslavement—but also to gamble, which caused other changes.[37]

McLemore's involvement in the Chocchuma Land Company soon aroused suspicion in Tennessee. Congressman James K. Polk heard from an acquaintance, "It is said Mr. McLemore has made a *grand* speculation at the Choctaw Land sales, & it is attempted to implicate Genl. Jackson in the matter." Rumors swirled that McLemore "had some private information from the Executive of the time &c. of sales that gave him the advantage of others," as Polk's friend put it. The controversy had the potential to badly hurt Jackson's seccond term, but the president weathered the storm, politically unscathed.[38]

Meanwhile, Eliza's enslavers did not write to Jackson during 1833. Any information the president received about the McLemores that year came from his son, the Coffees, and William Berkeley Lewis. McLemore was, according to Lewis, "exceedingly oppressed at this time." He was overextended, having trouble paying taxes and retiring debt. Lewis elaborated on McLemore's desperation: "Every body, it is said, to whom he is indebted, is making a push at him, as if afraid he is about to fail." Thus, Jackson continued to provide for McLemore's daughter although taken aback by her lack of correspondence after her recent departure from Washington, DC. He wrote a check in early April 1833, putting forty-four dollars in her bank account. He expressed satisfaction to his son that other close relatives "got relieved from their alarm and incumbrances." The president then sighed, "Would to god my friend Mr. McLamore [*sic*] was also clear."[39]

McLemore looked to enslaved people to relieve him of his mounting debt. He acquired two captives of other enslavers between 1830 and 1833, while those slaveholders struggled to pay off promissory notes. Meanwhile, he partnered with other Nashville residents to co-purchase enslaved people. However, he remained financially insolvent, and in May 1833 he sold a woman for three hundred dollars, removing another of Eliza's elders from the community.[40]

Eliza's constant presence among the McLemores' captives allowed the enslavers to continue their standard activities at their residence, because she had wisdom from years of service there to share with the newer enslaved people. The McLemores entertained some of the most politically powerful people in Washington, DC. During the spring of 1833, Congressman Polk and his wife brought Mary from the White House to the McLemore house, and William Berkeley Lewis, an advisor to Jackson who lived in the White House, paid at least one visit to the family. Polk was chair of the Ways and Means Committee at the time and a loyal Jacksonian Democrat in the House of Representatives. Lewis was part of the president's informal inner circle of advisers.[41]

The McLemores stubbornly refused to let their financial status diminish their social stature, but their defiance strained them. Betsy especially experienced stress, and she must have brought that anxiety to her supervision of Eliza. The McLemores still enjoyed the superficial trappings of their dwindling wealth— their estate, their captives. Lewis wrote to Jackson about a visit to McLemore in April: "I never saw him look better, but Mrs. McLemore has been unwell for some time; altho getting better she still looks badly." She was in a helpless position, merely reacting to the constant petitions from her husband's creditors. She could not stop the household from suffering from financial decisions she did not make. Eliza had seen the women in her own family struggle to lead their families while oppressed by enslavers throughout her childhood, but Betsy's situation presented something different: the vulnerability of a European American woman deprived of her own wealth and of the power to control it.[42]

In 1833 Mary returned to Nashville with her days as an unmarried woman numbered. Mary Coffee had noticed in Washington, DC, that for one man there, "it [was] Miss McLemore he ha[d] taken a fancy to," but nothing progressed from that infatuation. Instead, after coming home, Mary found a suitor in a local doctor named James Walker, and she agreed to marry him. Her fiancé came from a wealthy colonial family, and the marriage raised her social status and improved her financial health.[43]

On February 20, 1834, the McLemore estate hosted the wedding. The event was probably the first such occasion for Eliza to serve, because the bride was the first of the McLemore children to marry. Mary had turned eighteen just four days earlier, yet she became a plantation mistress in her own right by marrying a planter. Eliza was also of marrying age, but marriage for enslaved people simply meant continued captivity with a partner and the enslavement of any children. African American captives throughout the country could not legally marry, and slaveholders routinely ended informal marriages by selling spouses away from each other. Mary's transition to adulthood had started with education and travel and ended in marriage, but Eliza remained as unfree when entering adulthood as during her childhood.[44]

By 1834 yet another generational shift had taken place among the McLemore captives. The McLemores' enslaved population shrank from ten people in 1830 to five. Eliza's mother Molly, aunt Phebe, uncle Burgis, and older siblings George and Matilda were gone—probably before 1830. So were the children of Daniel and Rachel. The oldest unfree laborer was Gabriel, who was twenty-five in 1834. Patsey's daughter Harriet, at age twenty-two, was the second-oldest. In addition, Eliza became the last remaining member of her family to have come to the McLemores from Hopkins. Her younger sister Sally was no longer serving alongside her there.

Eliza lost her mother, her mother's siblings, her own siblings, and people she had known from childhood. She became the third-oldest among the enslaved servants. The only other enslaved person at the McLemore house who had previously served Hopkins was Harriet. By 1834 they had only each other for sharing specific memories and comforting specific hurts that only they understood.

With Molly, Judah, and Phebe gone, none of the family elders who had raised Eliza could help her navigate through her late adolescence. Harriet was merely five years Eliza's senior and barely an adult herself. By and large, Eliza was on her own in making sense of her maturity in enslavement. She was only seventeen and had many years of captivity ahead of her. Soon, however, life as she knew it would radically change.

≈ 2

Enslaved by
President Jackson

Shortly after Mary McLemore's festive wedding, the McLemores and their enslaved laborers suffered a crushing blow. A man named Samuel Meek sued John McLemore in the Circuit Court of Davidson County for money owed. Sometime earlier, the plaintiff had bought 930 acres from Chocchuma Land Company for a total of $1,377.42, and he and McLemore continued to do business together until the latter's debt soured the relationship. Meek won his lawsuit, and he suggested repayment by way of a sale of some of McLemore's property. The court agreed, and County Sheriff Willoughby Williams subsequently dispossessed the McLemores of their carriage, horses, furniture, and captives—including Eliza. The liquidation took place at the McLemore estate in July 1834.[1]

The sale of an enslaver's estate was usually a devastating event. Attendees studied the skin of the enslaved to see if fresh or healed marks from whippings revealed a history of disobedience. Enslaved women and adolescent girls experienced the humiliation of examinations if not molestations of their breasts by potential buyers. A home would be transformed into a land-mark of inhumanity during the sale. The voices negotiating the prices for the captives bounced off the walls of the rooms where the enslaved had worked and grown together. The items that domestic laborers had cleaned, had repaired, and had used when preparing food for the household were all sold away.[2]

This did not happen to the McLemores and to Eliza. The sheriff considered McLemore his "true and trusty friend"; the youngest McLemore child—a son—was named Willoughby. Per-haps because of this friendship, Williams did not publicize the upcoming sale. No notice for it appeared in any newspapers in or near Nashville, and the sale took place at the McLemores' home instead of the county courthouse. Moreover, the sheriff took steps to sell the entire inventory of his friend's seized prop-erty to one person and keep all the items together.[3]

In addition, the sale seems to have been previously arranged by even more powerful friends. Betsy's urbane and friendly nephew-in-law Lucius Polk, a cousin of US Represen-tative (and future president) James K. Polk, attended. His marriage into the Donelson family two years earlier— in the wedding hosted by President Jackson at the White House—continued the family's reputation for attracting men of elite pedi-grees and privilege.[4]

Lucius J. Polk. *Maury County Archives, Columbia, Tennessee*

Polk made the highest bid for all the items in the sale. He paid over four thousand dollars, and Sheriff Williams transferred ownership of the merchandise to him. The McLemores at that moment lost the last of their enslaved people. Moreover, of those captives, none of them included elders in Eliza's family. Rather, as the sheriff put it, Polk bought "the following negroes . . . Malinda 10 years old, Julius 8 years old, Gabriel 25 years old, Harriet 22 years old, Eliza 17 years old." By acquiring the possessions at the auction in mid-July, Lucius Polk had gifts to present to his wife for her twenty-fourth birthday on July 24.[5]

By the time the proceedings ended, the emptied house was a shell, and the McLemores were no longer the people who "raised" Eliza but instead the people who sold her. She had seen her previous enslaver lose control over a couple of captives years earlier because of theft, but the McLemores' forced relinquishing of their enslaved people was a self-inflicted wound resulting from the household's debt.[6]

But Polk was not acting on his own. President Jackson, seeing his Donelson grandnieces at risk, had made a financial arrangement to restore their elite status without entangling himself with their father's finances. He funded Lucius Polk's purchase as sole bidder at the McLemore auction, but he did so with conditions. Polk could continue to own those items but only to manage them for the McLemore family. The president spent two thousand dollars "to redeem the furniture and house servants of John C. McLemore," as he put it. In 1834 Jackson required that the property "be conveyed . . . to a trustee for the use of John C. McLemore & his wife during their life & to their children at their death." Jackson and Polk later amended the arrangement in order for Polk to give the property to the two McLemore daughters after they married, but Polk served as the trustee between 1834 and 1842. According to the deed, the president reserved only "the negro woman Eliza" for Kate, but Mary would receive the other laborers and the furniture. With this stipulation he showed his

Andrew Jackson's memorandum noting his arrangements for the McLemore properties—including Eliza Winston. *Manuscript collection, the Hermitage, Nashville, Tennessee*

willingness to have Eliza suffer permanent separation from the rest of her virtual family for the benefit of his own family's wealth.[7]

The president budgeted two payments of one thousand dollars at six months apart for Polk. For the first installment, Jackson's Nashville neighbor H. R. W. Hill drafted one thousand dollars from the Bank of the United States and sent it to Polk, and on October 31, 1834, the president repaid the draft to the bank. At that moment Eliza became, in part, the property of a sitting US president, and his conditions for the agreement immediately placed her on borrowed time with the McLemore household. Kate was only twelve years old in 1834 and not yet old enough to claim the enslaved woman for herself. Although Eliza suddenly belonged to President Jackson, and the president sent Polk

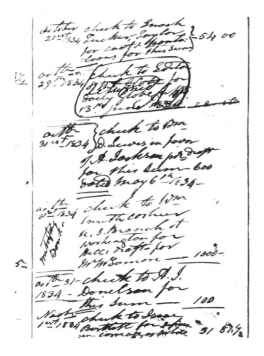

Andrew Jackson's bank book. His entry for October 31, 1834, says, "Washington bank. Check to Wm Smith cashier N[ational] B[ank] Branch at Washington for Hill's draft for MMcLamore—$1,000." The corresponding $1,000 check, made out to "W. Smith" on the same day, reimbursed funds advanced for the purchase of Eliza Winston and the rest of the McLemore estate. *Library of Congress*

funds to subsidize her support, she was enslaved by Polk for the remainder of Kate's childhood.[8]

Jackson's investment in Eliza reflected his concern for his own legacy. After his wife's death he became sick with increasing frequency, and he thought often about the continuation of his name. His attention to his son's business practices and his hosting of his grandniece's wedding at the White House tied his presidency to his legacy. His preservation of inheritances for his McLemore grandnieces fit in that pattern of using the platform of the presidency to provide for the next generation.[9]

The president could afford to buy Eliza for the Polks partly because of the slave labor generating his plantation's wealth. As a major planter from Nashville, he bought and sold multiple people, and he never expressed uncertainty about slavery's morality. In 1830 Jackson held ninety-four people captive there, and even his smaller number of seventy-three enslaved people ten years later kept him among the elites of Nashville. On the other hand, he ran an expensive operation, and the laborers' work barely produced enough money for the plantation to stay financially afloat. His $25,000 annual salary as president enabled him to meet some expenses, but one niece still complained that the president could not afford to buy an enslaved person for her, because the totality of his income covered his massive debt.[10]

> After the sale ended, Eliza and the other enslaved people left the McLemore estate. They traveled sixty miles southwest in the July heat. As soon as the party left Nashville, traces of urbanity disappeared and largely remained absent for the rest of the journey. Public areas in which European Americans, captives, and free African Americans fraternized were few and far between. Fields and plantations replaced the city scenery, and enslaved people worked fields along the travelers' path.

The party arrived at Polk's sprawling plantation, Hamilton Place, near Columbia in Maury County. Magnolia trees stood in front of Hamilton Place, and Greek Revival columns supported the

Rattle and Snap, the Polk family's plantation, in 1936. *Library of Congress*

plantation's two-story brick mansion. The wealth of Eliza's new captors and their ties to the White House virtually guaranteed that President Jackson would continue to affect her enslavement. Polk, unlike McLemore, was not one of Jackson's close friends, but his cousin's support of the Democratic Party and Mary Ann's blood ties to Jackson's late wife attracted the president and his supporters to Hamilton Place as a venue for political events.[11]

Lucius Polk and his three brothers were second-generation planters in Maury County. Hamilton Place was one of four equal portions of land that collectively had originally comprised their father's 5,200-acre plantation, Rattle and Snap. The patriarch had died mere months before Polk acquired the McLemore captives. Consequently, although the McLemore laborers did not share the experiences of the enslaved under the late patriarch,

Eliza and all the other captives at Hamilton Place were adjusting to the newness of Polk's authority over them.[12]

The plantation's enslaved people lived apart from the mansion. Because of Eliza's previous service as a household "servant" for the McLemores, she likely resided among the Polks' domestic captives in the detached kitchen building behind the main house. By seeing to the personal needs of the enslavers, Eliza had to acquaint herself with their traits and idiosyncrasies, just as she had done for the McLemores. On the other hand, the detached kitchen allowed her some physical distance from the Polks' direct supervision, unlike her labor under Betsy's management at the McLemore home. Hamilton Place's unfree domestics prepared food for the Polks in the separate facility during the day and slept there at night. By resting where they cooked, they no doubt encountered scavenging mice, and they certainly received constant exposure to smoke from the oven's fire and steam from boiling water.[13]

Hamilton Place had a back porch in the form of a covered colonnade that connected the big house to the enslaved servants' quarters. Those who worked in the house walked through the colonnade every day of their enslaved lives—to and from the big house, laboring at the discretion of their captors. In winter months the wind whipped around the columns, chilling the enslaved workers to their bones. At least the porch's roof protected them from the brunt of rainfall, snow, hail, and heat. Their fellow captives working in the fields did not have even that protection.[14]

Eliza's enslaved coworkers at Hamilton Place included people of ages similar to those of long-lost family members. Although they could never have replaced her relatives, they could have provided a re-creation of her original family. Her mother Molly had been born around 1798, and one of the plantation's elders—a woman named Kitty—was only one year younger. The Polks' enslaved man Peter was the same age as Eliza's older brother

George. Also, the couple held girls Jane and Letty, both similar in age to Eliza. For the first time in years, Eliza was not merely in the middle between her older and younger siblings and virtual siblings. She had true peers with whom she could perhaps talk about issues of concern to young enslaved women.[15]

Enslavement at Hamilton Place carried a performative element encouraged by the Polks. Even during times of leisure, they expected their captives to entertain them. Lucius Polk's niece remembered years later, "In the 'quarters,' as the negro cabins were called, there was usually a band, which played at night for the 'white folks' to dance." The man she called "Old Master" always started the festivities by hoofing the Virginia reel. The enslaved musicians played such standards as "Jim Crack Corn, I Don't Care" or "Run, N——, Run" or "The Patrolers Will Catch You." The niece recalled that "they would become wildly excited and beat the tambourines over their heads," but to her such behavior was natural for them. As she put it, "Negroes are always fond of music."[16]

The Polks also had a special affinity for old families among their enslaved. Their affection was conditional, hinging on the compliance of the captives to their own exploitation and on the productivity of their labor. Moreover, the enslavers assumed that the fondness was mutual. Polk's niece said, "There was such a kindly feeling on both sides between the owners and their slaves— inherited kindly feelings. . . . Many were descendants of those who had served in the same family for generations." Indeed, some of Eliza's enslaved colleagues were second-generation Donelson captives who had previously lived and worked at the Mansion near Nashville, where Betsy Donelson McLemore grew up. After John Donelson died in 1830, his estate passed down enslaved people to his granddaughter Mary Ann Eastin Polk.[17]

Eliza and the four other enslaved people from the McLemore estate comprised a small portion of Hamilton Place's workforce. About three dozen of Polk's workers were also enslaved, and the remaining four laborers were free African Americans. Eliza had not lived among free African Americans since leaving Hopkins's estate, but, unlike the free family at his plantation, all four of the Polks' free laborers were men. Their presence revealed that wherever Eliza went, African Americans worked only for European Americans. Freedom for African Americans did not necessarily mean self-employment or the end of deference to European Americans.

Mary Ann Eastin Polk carried her accomplishments with great humility. She was witty and sharp but unassuming. An acquaintance marveled at how her "mind naturally possessed of great vigor and dignity" and "education unusually extensive" balanced her "rich and pure loveliness." A sensitive person, she once burst into tears just from overhearing her aunt Emily Donelson argue with someone over an untoward comment at the White House. One person remembered Mary Ann as having "the most winning gentleness and unobtrusiveness" and being "so gentle that . . . she would scarcely have crushed a rosebud." She offered an example to Eliza of how a woman could possess great intellectual power but be circumspect about it—and how a woman could be sensitive to sharp remarks but not to the lives of enslaved people all around her.[18]

Despite moving to a new household, Eliza probably remained in service to newborn babies. The youngest of the eight McLemore children had just outgrown infancy when Sheriff Williams sold the family's enslaved laborers. However, when Eliza arrived at Hamilton Place, Mary Ann had a one-year-old baby and had just become pregnant with her second child. Moreover, she followed her Aunt Betsy's pace, giving birth every other year for the next dozen years. Eliza thus saw no relief from taking care of infants while enslaved by the Polks.

Hamilton Place sheltered more adults than the McLemore home did. Polk asked his brother Leonidas and Leonidas's wife, Frances (Fanny), to leave their home in North Carolina and start a new life in Tennessee, and he invited them to stay at his mansion while their own house was being built. Leonidas and Frances accepted the offer and moved to Hamilton Place in May 1833. They were still there when Eliza arrived the following year. They returned to North Carolina in the fall of 1834 to care for a sister dying of cholera, but after her death they returned to Hamilton Place the following spring and stayed for the next two years. They brought their two children with them, and a third child was born during their stay at Hamilton Place in November 1835—yet another baby for Eliza to serve.[19]

Fanny Polk brought with her a woman she had enslaved since childhood, a woman whom she called Mammy Betsey. Mammy Betsey called her captor "Miss Fanny." As a Polk relative recalled, "Often I have heard her impress on the younger servants the necessity of cultivating good manners, so that, when ladies and gentlemen came in master's and mistress's absence, they might be received with 'credit to the family.'" She had been born in 1800 and thus was one of Eliza's elders among the plantation's captives and likely one of the enslaved people to receive the "aunt" honorific.[20]

Eliza's previous enslaver McLemore had busied himself with politics and speculation, but horses preoccupied Lucius Polk. Hamilton Place quartered several racehorses, which Polk raised on the family land. He co-owned a thoroughbred stable and bred thoroughbreds with his brother Rufus. Captives of the family probably performed the daily drudgery of walking the horses and shoveling manure, and any such enslaved people encountering Eliza during the day brought the strong smell of the stables directly to her. More importantly, Polk's degree of success in selling racehorses partly determined whether he could afford to provide for his family and enslave his laborers.[21]

While Eliza began working at Hamilton Place, President Jackson traveled to his home in Nashville for a summer visit. The president left the White House in late June or early July 1834 and arrived at the Hermitage on August 5, where he stayed until September 10. He had recently fared poorly in health, especially with "affectations of the chest and pulmonary complaints," and his acquaintances worried about his travel. One friend informed him of Vice President Martin Van Buren's concern one week after Jackson's departure: "[He] felt and expressed much anxiety about you, on account of the great distance you had to travel and the inte[n]se hot weather."[22]

Jackson had spent much of the previous winter and spring worried about how his family managed the Hermitage in his absence. He frequently expressed his views about money and thrift to Andrew Jr. He wrote to his son in one case, "Why will you not[,] my d'r Andrew, attend to my admonition about your money matters—never incur debts when you have the money to discharge your contracts, . . . in this instance there was no necessity to have left any unpaid." Moreover, the president considered the purchasing of people to be so important as a means of accumulating and maintaining wealth that he would help in the effort: "You had my advice to buy the girl, and if you had not the means in cash, which I thought you had, you ought to have drew on me, notifying me thereof," he complained.[23]

After the president arrived in Nashville, he visited the McLemores and saw firsthand the state of his friend's estate. Andrew Jr. wanted to purchase real estate from McLemore, but the president warned, "See the land first." He then told Andrew Jr., "I have had some conversation with Doctor Gwinn on the subject of my friend Mr. McLemores [sic] situation. I say to you, in strict confidence, that I find it is worse than I anticipated, and I fear, nay much fear, that William and Stockly [sic] will ultimately be ruined. I therefore conjure you my son to keep clear of indorsements or obligations of every kind, or you may also be ruined."[24]

On October 13, eighteen days before Jackson transferred the first payment for the purchase of the McLemores' enslaved people, a fire destroyed much of the Hermitage. The president's nephew Stockley Donelson told him of the fire and made a point to recognize the hard work of the captives there in trying to extinguish the blaze. "When the fire was first discovered by Charles and Squire, they made ev[er]y effort to get a ladder," Donelson reported. "But none could be found, and there was no other way to get to the roof etc."[25]

Jackson's response to the fire was instructive. He saw the exploitation of his captives as the saving grace of the Hermitage. He instructed Andrew Jr., "Use industry to repair and regain the Loss. Therefore, as the only fund to aid in paying for the Land and repairing the building and other arrangements [is] the cotton crop, I urge you have it carefully taken in, gin'd, baled and sent to markett [sic]." While expecting the enslaved to provide for him, however, he did not have adequate provisions for them. The following week he lamented to his son, "I regret to see that we are without seed wheat and that negroes are without shoes in these heavy frosts, they cannot do half work without shoes." The labor the enslaved people performed while shoeless in the snow helped Jackson pay for the Polks' enslavement of Eliza during her first winter at Hamilton Place.[26]

The president scheduled his second payment of one thousand dollars to the Polks for April 1835. If he wanted them to treat the entrusted laborers as he treated his own captives at the Hermitage, then Eliza may have alternated between house labor and field labor at Hamilton Place. Jackson celebrated his new overseer that spring: "How pleasant to hear that our poor servants are happy and contented with their overseer, and that he feeds and clothes them well and treats them with humanity . . . he now has a set of willing hands, who do their duty cheerfully, and one willing hand is really worth two who only does what labour he is forcibly compelled to perform." If the field workers had too many crops to handle, the overseer was to send the "house servants" alongside them.[27]

Hamilton Place had its largest force of unfree laborers when Eliza arrived, and its size increased during her captivity there. The Polks purchased a mother in her twenties and her three children under ten years old in October 1835, barely one year after acquiring Eliza. They were unusual additions, because the couple rarely increased their enslaved holdings through purchases. The plantation's enslaved population grew from thirty in 1836 to over fifty in 1840, largely through births of enslaved newborns. Eliza had constantly seen her fellow laborers come and go at the McLemore household, but the influx of enslaved babies at the Polks' home repositioned her from one of the plantation's newer captives to one of its more experienced ones.[28]

In early 1836 the Walkers came to Columbia, Tennessee, and dined with the Polks. The event was a reunion of sorts, because it allowed Mary Ann to see her cousin Mary for perhaps the first time since the former's 1832 wedding at the White House. The women had more in common by 1836. They were plantation mistresses through marriages to wealthy individuals, and they had become mothers. Eliza had not seen Mary since the latter's wedding at the McLemore estate. Mary had become educated, married, and a parent within the previous five years, while Eliza remained uneducated, unmarried, childless, and enslaved.[29]

As of March 1836 Eliza's co-owner Andrew Jackson had exactly one year left in his second term as US president. He had already decided not to seek a third term, following the precedent set by the first White House occupant George Washington. Jackson could not wait to leave the White House, and he confided in his grandniece Mary Ann about his restlessness. "I am most looking forward with great anxiety to the 4th of next March," he admitted, "when I will be once more freed from the shackled slavery of office." To him, slavery was figurative. It was not Eliza's actual suffering of forced labor and family dissolution but rather his own constant exposure to the selfish acts of his fellow officials. "I am indeed tired of the scores of corruption and treachery with which I have been surrounded ever since I have been here," he complained.[30]

That August, as Eliza completed her second year at Hamilton Place, the president traveled to that plantation to visit his grand-niece and her children. His visit there was part of his summer vacation to Tennessee, but he spent much of his time speaking publicly in support of the vice president's campaign to succeed him. In addition, the trip allowed Jackson to envision what to expect in his home state upon his permanent return the following March. He arrived at the Hermitage on August 4, accompanied by Andrew Jackson Donelson.[31]

For a dozen years, Eliza had witnessed her enslavers profess-ing Jackson's greatness, and their naming of their children after him exemplified their adoration for him. On the other hand, his physical and emotional health was in decline when he arrived at Hamilton Place. He was an anxious and fatigued man that summer. He looked forward to resuming full-time residency at the Hermitage, but he worried about his niece Emily Donelson's constantly poor health that year. In her illness she chose not to travel with her husband to see Jackson. Meanwhile, the presi-dent's cross-country travels to generate support for Van Buren's presidential campaign produced massive crowds that over-whelmed him. In stark contrast to the handsome and youthful John McLemore and Lucius Polk, Jackson was old and haggard. However, the president's age and weariness did not make him any less of an enslaver, and his brief stay at Hamilton Place demonstrated to Eliza that power over the enslaved manifested itself in various forms.[32]

President Jackson rested at the Hermitage for six weeks that summer, and constant rainfall and blazing heat filled his last few days back in Tennessee. His enslaved laborers consumed his thoughts as he returned to the White House. He lamented to his son on September 22, "The continued fall of rain . . . this with the unusual warmth must be distructive [sic] to our cotton." He instructed Andrew Jr. to keep the captives busy: "If the hands cannot be employed picking out cotton, you ought to have the ploughs running, preparing our meadows for sowing and the colts lotts [*sic*] for Grass as we must change our culture in part from cotton and turn our attention to stock, hemp and perhaps tobacco." The Hermitage should not "depend on the cotton crop entirely, for a support." Selling a diverse array of items increased the plantation's chances for greater revenue.[33]

Martin Van Buren won the presidential contest that fall, and the win was a cause for celebration at Hamilton Place. The victory validated how Jackson had groomed his vice president to succeed him in office, and it showed that the general still held tremendous influence over national politics. The Donelsons thus remained a powerful political family. Mary Ann was well acquainted with the president-elect, having served at the White House during his vice presidency. Van Buren considered her one of his friends. More political events at Hamilton Place for the benefit of the new president loomed for Eliza.[34]

Meanwhile, the rise in political prominence of the Polk family also kept the enslaved servants busy entertaining luminaries. In the fall of 1836, they served Alabama judge and future US senator Sidney C. Posey at the plantation. The Polks' hospitality was a gesture of gratitude for the kindness Posey had recently extended to Polk's first cousin. Supporters for Speaker of the House James K. Polk held a dinner for him in Maury County on September 23. Posey was invited but could not attend. However, three days before the event, he wrote an open letter of praise to the speaker. In the letter Posey lamented the growing support among Tennessee's electorate for the new Whig Party, which had formed in opposition to Jackson's exercise of presidential power. He concluded, "Let her, as Alabama has done, retrace her steps, return to her first love, and adhere to the principles of Andrew Jackson and James K. Polk." The speaker's cousin then hosted Posey at Hamilton Place two weeks later.[35]

Not all occasions were festive for the Polks. As at the McLemore home, Eliza's enslavers at Hamilton Place occasionally went into mourning. In 1836 alone Mary Ann lost two Donelson aunts. Eliza's former enslaver Betsy Donelson McLemore died in July. Before 1834 Betsy had never known a life without African Americans nearby to cater to her, and she did not live for very long after Davidson County's sheriff sold them all away. Also, Emily Donelson passed away at age twenty-nine from a lingering illness. Mary Ann and her youngest aunt had been especially close, for they had served in the White House together from the start of their granduncle's administration in 1829 until Mary Ann's wedding in 1832. Mary Ann was four months away from giving birth at the time of her aunt's death. In memory of her aunt, she named her new child Emily Donelson Polk.[36]

While President Jackson grieved the loss of one of his former stand-in First Ladies, he made sure to provide for his captives at the Hermitage. He shipped gifts to them via his nephew and secretary Andrew Jackson Donelson, who was to pass them along to the overseer for him to distribute among the enslaved of the Hermitage: "I wish the negroes their Hats at christmas, and their Blankitts [sic] as soon as they arrive." The provisions served not only as gifts to the laborers but also as means for the captives to stay warm and labor more efficiently.[37]

With Jackson's retirement and his vice president succeeding him, the Hermitage—and, by extension, Tennessee—became an important location in national politics. People called on Jackson at his home to request meetings about government issues, and they invited him to events. The Polks were among those seeking his favor, thus guaranteeing that his leaving office did not diminish his influence over Eliza's labor. He brought Secretary of the Navy James Kirke Paulding to Hamilton Place on one occasion in either 1839 or 1840. Paulding had published multiple works of literature, which included the nationally popular play *Lion of the West*, which featured a character like Davy Crockett. His book

View of Slavery in the United States supported the institution's existence.[38]

Hamilton Place's unfree labor force had become younger by the time Eliza reached adulthood. On August 31, 1840, Polk bought an adolescent boy named Jack for $650. He was seventeen—the same age Eliza had been at her arrival six years earlier. She knew how it had felt to come to the plantation at seventeen and to be without any family there. By 1840 only one-fourth of Hamilton Place's enslaved laborers were twenty-four or older, and Eliza was among those few elders. After years of looking up to the adults among her fellow captives, she had to become vigilant of the enslaved children looking up to her.[39]

Leonidas Polk remained a constant presence in Eliza's life for years after his arrival from North Carolina. He was an Episcopal minister, and he began work as the rector of St. Peter's Parish in nearby Columbia upon settling at Hamilton Place. He and his wife and their child moved into their own plantation estate in 1836, finally giving Eliza fewer people to serve. Meanwhile, he left St. Peter's Parish and began holding worship services for his extended family and their captives in his new mansion, which he dubbed Ashwood. Lucius Polk and his household attended services at Ashwood, and their close relationship exposed Eliza more directly to Christian clergy.[40]

Christianity and slavery became inextricably linked for them there. The house of worship had Greco-Roman columns and slave quarters. Leonidas largely avoided the topic of slavery in his sermons, and he never publicly condemned it during his ministerial career. He did not claim that slavery opposed Christianity or the Constitution, nor did he call the practice immoral. Then again, he did not have to verbally take a stance on the issue, because holding services on his plantation suggested that slavery was Christian. Moreover, he enslaved people during his ministerial career. As the 1830s ended, he held over one hundred people in captivity in Maury County. He stopped leading the services in 1839, when he became a missionary bishop for Episcopal churches in the Deep South and subsequently left for Louisiana.[41]

The services at Ashwood were the spiritual roots of St. John's Church, which the Polk brothers erected on the family land from 1839 to 1842. It lay next to Ashwood and across the street from Hamilton Place. The lands of all four Polk brothers intersected at the spot where they built the church. Eliza had experienced three years of quiet respite from the sounds of construction after Ashwood's completion, but the building of St. John's brought three more years of such noise to her ears. Moreover, enslaved people performed the labor for constructing the church. They cleared the land, and they formed bricks from clay on land from the family plantations. They made the pulpit, the desk, and the indoor woodwork from the cherry trees they had chopped.[42]

The closest Episcopal church to the Polks was St. Peter's Church in Columbia, and a nationally famous minister took the helm there from 1840 to 1841. George W. Freeman of North Carolina had delivered two sermons on slavery's compatibility with Christianity in November 1836, and parishioners responded favorably to them. Newspapers reprinted his messages, and a publishing company printed his two sermons together as a book in 1837. The Polks were likely heartened by their new local minister's views: "[Slavery] is as agreeable to the order of God's Providence that some men should be the bond-slaves of others, as it is that there should be different conditions and grades in society, and that among these, there should be 'hewers of wood and drawers of water.'"[43]

The hammering for the new church's construction finally stopped in the summer of 1842, and on September 4 Leonidas returned to Maury County to consecrate the newly completed building. The facility was "capable of seating five hundred persons," noted Polk's son William Mecklenburg Polk. The Polk brothers had planned the construction with the intent of providing enough separate spaces for the enslavers and the enslaved. The balcony was the "slave gallery," and Eliza and her fellow captives had to find space elsewhere in the building if the seats there filled. "By the time the white congregation were seated in the body of the church, the door, the vestibule, the gallery, and staircase were crowded with blacks, even the vestry-room was filled with them, one old man sitting within the doorway almost at the very feet of the clergy," said the junior Polk. In order to accommodate attendees who could not read lyrics in the hymnals, "the psalms and hymns were given out in the old-fashioned way—two lines at a time."[44]

Lucius Polk had dreams larger than Hamilton Place, and they involved Eliza's possible relocation out of Tennessee. He aspired to run a plantation in the Deep South, and as early as January 1839 he began traveling alone to Louisiana to pursue his goal. A relative wrote, "Tell cousin Lucius we heard from him while he was in Orleans through old Mr. Jackson, who sends his respects." Eliza's years as a domestic worker did not bode well for her potential transition into field labor in the Cotton Belt. Its plantations hosted diseases and demanded grueling physical labor from their captives, and consequently lowered the life expectancy for the laborers. Enslaved people in states to the north dreaded sales to the Deep South and went to great lengths to avoid that fate. Fortunately for Eliza, Polk decided not to move there with his family and captives.[45]

While Polk visited Leonidas in Louisiana in the spring of 1841, Mary Ann gave birth to a fifth child at Hamilton Place. By then, at age twenty-four, Eliza had helped care for over a dozen children from her enslavers. She was still young, but she was old enough for one of those babies born over the last twenty years to enter adulthood and become an enslaver. Moreover, that person would enslave Eliza herself.[46]

⚞ 3

The Young Mistress

Eliza's days at Hamilton Place were numbered in the fall of 1842, when John McLemore's daughter Kate became eligible to claim ownership of her. Unlike the previous women who had enslaved Eliza, Kate learned very little about managing enslaved laborers. She was only twelve years old during the sale of 1834, when her family lost all their captives. Her mother died exactly two years afterward, and fourteen-year-old Kate inherited the role of household matriarch. She was the only female family member left at home.[1]

Kate assumed control of a household mired in poverty. Her father lamented to Jackson's private secretary Andrew Jackson Donelson in 1836, "When in my troubles and when the whole of my personal effects had been sold under execution to pay the debts of others, my credit went down so low that I had not credit to purchase *bread* for my family." McLemore gave power of attorney of the family's land in Davidson County to Sheriff Williams. Robertson Topp, who personally knew Andrew Jackson's friend H. R. W. Hill, assumed control of McLemore's holdings in Memphis in 1837, as the family relocated to that city. In 1841 McLemore lost his real estate in Mississippi.[2]

Probably through McLemore's relationship with Topp, the McLemore family met Topp's local acquaintance Thomas Yates Gholson. In early 1841 Gholson moved to Memphis after having achieved some prominence as a lawyer in Columbus, Mississippi. Then, after a brief trip to his hometown of Raleigh, North Carolina, in July 1841, he returned to Memphis and married Kate there two months later. Like her, he had lost a parent when he was a child. Gholson's father—lawyer and US congressman Thomas Gholson of Virginia—died in 1816, when the junior Thomas was six years old. Two years later, in Raleigh, the congressman's widow married the proslavery Episcopal minister George W. Freeman, who would briefly be the minister at St. Peter's Church in Columbia, near Hamilton Place. Freeman prohibited his followers from dancing, attending the theater and the circus, and wearing modern fashion.[3]

Eliza's transfer to Kate brought the servant to enslavement by newlyweds for the first time. In Catherine Donelson McLemore Gholson, Eliza gained an enslaver with a strong independent streak. Kate spent her adolescence away from the trappings of Donelson wealth in Nashville, and her father had less reason to travel there from Memphis to visit General Jackson at the Hermitage after her mother's death. Her estrangement from both the Hermitage and the Jackson White House left her with a minimal relationship with her granduncle. Moreover, her father's financial collapse spanned the presidencies of Jackson and Van Buren, and she saw little relief during those twelve years of Democratic rule.

These factors may have influenced her decision to marry a member of her granduncle's political opposition. As part of the Whig Party, Thomas Gholson belonged to an organization that sought to end Jacksonian democracy and keep Jackson's acolytes from winning public office. The party opposed Jackson's disregard for the separation of powers and his scorn for the rule of law. In Mississippi Gholson had supported the Harrison–Tyler ticket, and he attended Whig meetings in town to help the campaign on a local level. As a result, his political fortunes rose with that pair's ascension to the White House. A periodical from his hometown in North Carolina noted, "Mr. Gholson is a very warm Whig." Jackson was still smarting from Van Buren's 1840 electoral loss when Kate wed a Whig less than one year later.[4]

As of 1842 only three of the original five enslaved servants from the 1834 auction remained with the Polks. Jackson transferred the furniture and the enslaved people Malinda, now age eighteen, and Julius, age sixteen, to Mary McLemore Walker. By then, the Walkers owned a home just outside of Memphis, and as of 1840 they enslaved a woman, four girls, and one boy. They had experience as a couple and as enslavers together. Unfortunately for Malinda and Julius, they experienced this transition without the continued guidance of their older sister-figure Eliza.[5]

Kate and her new husband may have initially resided with her father and brothers in Memphis. Shelby County did not record any real estate purchases by the Gholsons during the first three years of the marriage. Also, Gholson began operating a law office with Kate's brother A. J. McLemore in Memphis shortly after the wedding. Gholson's political affiliation apparently did not prevent A. J. from socializing with him and going into business with him.[6]

Eliza had previously navigated the dynamics of the McLemore family, but Kate had to train other new workers how to cater to her. Months before marrying Kate, Gholson owned nine people between the ages of five and sixty in Mississippi. In 1841 he was charged a tax in that state of $7.87, and the captives and a watch were his only taxable properties that year. However, within five years he lost all but one of his enslaved people. Gholson purchased land in Memphis in the early 1840s, and he likely had to sell his laborers in order to afford the real estate.[7]

To ensure that Kate kept her birthright, her granduncle stipulated that she alone owned Eliza. Polk's deed specified: "the negro woman Eliza to Catherine McLemore now Catherine Gholson for her separate use." Whatever debts her husband incurred were his responsibility, and he could not resolve them by selling Kate's enslaved servant. Jackson was not alone in making such a stipulation; many antebellum planters willed or gave captives to their daughters alone.[8]

Kate stood to earn a significant amount of money by enslaving Eliza during her peak years of fertility. The captive was twenty-five years old in 1842 and capable of reproducing laborers as soon as Kate and her husband wanted them. Jackson's arrangement with Polk required that any children born to Eliza belonged to Kate alone. As Polk put it, "I do by these powers . . . transfer, convey, and deliver . . . to the said Catherine Gholson the said Negro woman Eliza with her increase."[9]

Regardless of how many new people Kate exclusively acquired, her husband did not seem to mind the arrangement. "We have no objection to married women having their rights, nor to their having full control over their property," Thomas Gholson wrote years later in a local newspaper, "but what is wanted is to have it all on record, so that no one will be deceived. Then they can appoint the worse half [the husband] their overseer and credit will be given according to the circumstances of each case." The deed that transferred Eliza to Kate sufficiently documented the new bride's exclusive possession of her.[10]

In September 1842 Eliza departed Hamilton Place to serve her new enslaver. Polk brought her two hundred miles westward to Shelby County. They traveled in mild September heat, unlike the heat of July on the trip from Nashville to Hamilton Place eight years earlier. When they reached Memphis, Eliza returned to a bustling urban environment. On the other hand, Memphis was a city different in character from Nashville. She lived near the Mississippi River—a much busier waterway than the Cumberland. In Memphis, horses pulled carriages taking people to steamboats. The boats whistled frequently and loudly, and slave traders constantly loaded captives resembling Eliza into the vessels. Memphis was the largest slave-trading city of the Mid-South.[11]

The bustling levee at Memphis, Tennessee, in 1862. *Alex Simpliot
sketch from* Harper's Weekly, *July 5, 1862, Library of Congress*

Eliza finally arrived at John McLemore's home in Memphis,
where the Gholsons had settled after their wedding. She once
again became an urban domestic captive, and the transition
returned her to service for the "young mistress," as Eliza called
Kate. Perhaps both Kate and Eliza were surprised by the weariness on each other's face after the eight years of hardships they
had suffered. Still, they were the same people, and the familiarity
of their personality traits may have eventually counterbalanced
the newness of their physical changes.[12]

With the surviving McLemores in Shelby County, Kate's
extended family had close access once again to Eliza. There
was old "Mr. Macklemo"—still handsome but grayer and more
wrinkled in the years since Eliza's sale to Hamilton Place. John
Jr. and A. J. were adults, and the youngest boys were in or near
adolescence. A. J. and Gholson ran a law practice together, and
A. J.'s sizable collection of books about the laws of Tennessee

likely helped them in their work. Mary and her husband James Walker lived outside the city on their plantation Villa Rose, where they raised their three children. Polk delivered to them Eliza's adolescent sibling-figures Malinda and Julius, who reacquainted themselves with Mary McLemore Walker's laconic nature, and they acquainted themselves with the plantation's other enslaved laborers.[13]

Within Eliza's first year away from Hamilton Place, Malinda gave birth to her first child, a son, in 1843. She named him Thomas—a name that connected the newborn to his mother's roots, for Molly and Judah had been enslaved by Thomas Hopkins. The baby must have felt like a nephew to Eliza. Malinda had barely a year to nurse her own baby before having to divert her attention—if not her milk also—to her enslaver Mary's newborn son Melville. He arrived in August 1844, and Mary likely directed Malinda to cater more to him than to little Thomas.[14]

On January 1, 1843, Eliza spent her first New Year's Day with the Gholsons. It was without suspense for her because of the losses she had suffered in transit from Hamilton Place to Memphis. She did not have to worry about how her new enslavers would separate her from her siblings for the year, because Polk and Jackson had already permanently separated them. Also, she was the enslaver's most valuable enslaved person. Kate did not incur debt and therefore did not have to entertain the thought of selling Eliza or hiring her out.

Eliza's reunion with the surviving McLemores ended after barely half a year. During the last week of March 1843, John McLemore, A. J., and the Gholsons prepared to depart permanently from Memphis. "I expect to be at Nashville in about eight to ten days from this, with my father," A. J. wrote to a cousin on March 30, "and intend settling up all my affairs, both of a *private* and *public* nature." Eliza served a chaotic household that week. "I write in a great hurry and in the midst of noise and confusion," A. J. noted to his cousin.[15]

Father and son indeed went east to Nashville, but the elder eventually returned to Memphis. "Mr. Macklemo" still had real estate to sell in Memphis and Fort Pickering. Moreover, he had visited Nashville as a fallen figure among his peers who still resided there—including Andrew Jackson. The city had nothing to offer to McLemore, and he lacked the means to restore his financial reputation.

Meanwhile, according to A. J., Thomas Gholson had "determined on moving to Louisiana immediately." The Gholsons planned to board the steamboat *Talleyrand* and travel to St. Martinville, where Gholson intended to establish a law practice and a "small plantation." After A. J. completed his business in Nashville, he intended to reunite with the Gholsons in St. Martinville and resume practicing law with Gholson. At the time that city, which lay next to Bayou Teche, was on the rise; it became incorporated that spring. "We have all been busily engaged for the last week *packing up* and getting ready to leave," A. J. revealed to his cousin.[16]

St. Martin Parish would certainly be a much different environment for Kate and Eliza than the life they had known in Tennessee. As people accustomed to urban settings in the Mid-South, the two women had no experience with the swamps, marshes, mosquitoes, and alligators of Louisiana's bayous. In Tennessee they had encountered few if any Creoles and French-speaking people, who comprised a prominent portion of St. Martin's population. However, the plans fell through. Instead, by late May, A. J. remained in Nashville, started his own law practice there, and attended school at Nashville University, where he earned his second degree that fall. The Gholsons never purchased any land in St. Martin Parish, nor did they establish a plantation there.[17]

With the Gholsons' abandonment of Louisiana, Eliza once again avoided the grim fate of becoming an enslaved plantation laborer in the Deep South. Her continued domestic service to Kate was one of the more consistent aspects of the Gholson household.

Although Gholson struggled to cultivate multiple sources of income over the next few months, the financial upheaval did not affect Kate's legal possession of Eliza. While practicing law in Memphis, Gholson bought one lot of real estate in the city on November 9 for $150 but sold it away the next day at the same price. He co-owned a grocery store throughout 1844, but the main partner's death at the end of the year precipitated the immediate collapse of the business.[18]

Eliza's sibling-figures Malinda and Julius experienced a more financially stable enslavement than she did. Kate's older sister Mary possessed her own real estate. On April 9, 1844, she paid over two thousand dollars for land near Memphis and Fort Pickering from her father's friend—Davidson County sheriff Willoughby Williams. He took on Andrew Jackson's role of looking after the McLemore children's wealth and welfare. Like Mary's family furniture and enslaved people received from the Polks, her new real estate from Williams was "for her separate use," as the deed put it. Her financial comfort ensured that Julius and Malinda would stay enslaved at Villa Rose for the duration. Moreover, according to the deed, Mary McLemore Walker acquired some of the plantation's land in her own name.[19]

When the Gholsons were ready to relocate, they did not move far from Memphis. On April 10, 1844, the Gholsons invested in a new city with some of the wealthiest yeomen in Shelby County. Robertson Topp, Nathaniel Anderson, and William Vance ran a law firm, and they were trustees of the neighboring town of South Memphis. The law partners sold one lot of land at the corner of Union and Linden Streets to Gholson for eight hundred dollars, and he subsequently moved the family and Eliza there. They were just two streets east of the Mississippi River.[20]

The Gholsons permitted Eliza to regularly socialize outside of their household, and they did not accompany her for those occasions. On Sunday morning, February 25, 1844, she left her quarters and went to the corner of Poplar Avenue and Third

Street. She made sure to carry her pass from the Gholsons, so the slave patrols would not arrest her on her journey. She entered a building full of people—some who looked like her enslavers and some who looked like her. She went to the area reserved for African Americans, and she began worshiping with the others in the building. The service at the First Presbyterian Church of Memphis started, and she became a member of the church before the meeting ended.[21]

Her enslavers did not join First Presbyterian. Instead, they gave Eliza a significant amount of agency by permitting her to attend church without them. Such leniency on Sunday mornings was common among urban enslavers; many of them fully expected their captives to return home immediately after the worship service concluded. Still—within the confines of the church walls, for one morning per week—her time was her own. Eliza could worship during the service and mingle with fellow members before and after service, all without the eyes of her enslavers upon her. None of the McLemores in Memphis were members either. Her life in that church, therefore, was quite a change from her experiences worshiping with her enslavers' family on the family plantation in services led by the enslaver's brother.[22]

In addition, Eliza's freedom of choice concerning church attendance partially reflected the religious influence of Thomas Gholson's stepfather on him. George W. Freeman said of enslavers, "If we are in any measure responsible, as we are taught to believe we are, for the souls of our children, we must be, in at least an equal degree, responsible for the souls of our slaves." The Gholsons applied that notion to their holding of Eliza to a less strict degree than the Polks had. Her new captors did not force her to worship where they did, but she had to attend church *somewhere*. After all, if she committed an immoral act in town, her sin supposedly reflected badly on them as the enslavers.[23]

First Presbyterian was one of many congregations of the Presbyterian Church in the United States of America denomination, which grappled with the issue of slavery at the time Eliza joined. Moreover, its struggle with slavery spanned almost her entire life. In 1818, when she was one year old, the denomination's general assembly officially declared that slavery opposed human rights, God's law, and the Christian gospel. The assembly proclaimed, "[It is] manifestly the duty of all Christians to use their honest, earnest, and unwearied endeavors to efface this blot on our holy religion, and to obtain the complete abolition of slavery throughout Christendom, and if possible throughout the world." However, slavery persisted, and nearly a quarter century later, a committee of the 1842 general assembly unanimously declared, "It is inexpedient for the General Assembly to take any action on the subject of slavery." Thus, Eliza's new church had recognized the wrongness of slavery but had done nothing as a collective to work to stop it.[24]

On the other hand, the denomination charged its enslaving membership with providing the best quality of life for their captives. This high quality resulted not from money but rather from education. Enslavers were to educate their unfree laborers in order for them to receive Christian instruction and exercise peaceable citizenship. By distancing themselves from Eliza's practice of faith, the Gholsons allowed her to fraternize among people with the means to bestow the gift of literacy on her.[25]

Eliza's attendance of worship services exposed her to people who shared the skin color of all her enslavers but not their views on slavery. The church had about ninety-three European American members and about twenty-six African American members from across the city. She was able to meet European Americans who had no interest in enslaving her. While most of the European American members enslaved fewer than one dozen people, one member did not hold any captives at all. Thus, the church directly showed to her that European Americans did not have to enslave people.[26]

Moreover, at least two of First Presbyterian's African American members were free people. The church listed each enslaved member by their first name and, in parentheses, the surname of the enslaver; Eliza appeared as "Eliza (Gholson)." However, the church identified the free African Americans Eliza Chub and Jefferson Brown by both their first and last names, not unlike the listings of European Americans, without parentheses. Chub's husband John, who joined the following year, worked as a black-smith, and he and his wife lived in an apartment. Eliza worshiped with a couple who modeled how to live as free African Americans in Memphis and how to attain and maintain self-employment.[27]

A few of the African American members of First Presbyterian were enslaved when Eliza joined but became liberated within a few years. The couple William and Rachel originally appeared with only their first names and "(Armour)" for their enslaver when they joined the church in 1842, as did Adaline (Yeats) the following year. However, by 1850 the federal census listed all three people as free people, and their respective full names changed to William Armour, Rachel Armour, and Adaline Yeats. Eliza witnessed these transitions, and she recognized the possibility of living in Memphis as a free woman.[28]

African Americans comprised one-fifth of First Presbyterian's membership in February 1844. As more people joined the church in the twenty months after Eliza became a member, the percentage of African American members remained the same as of November 1845. The church was only slightly less diverse than the city at large, in which African Americans comprised about one-fifth of the population. Eliza therefore experienced a demographic microcosm of Memphis at First Presbyterian.

Eliza's choice of the Presbyterian Church may have resulted from a sense of familiarity with the denomination. Betsy Donelson McLemore's mother had raised her and her siblings in that faith, and it influenced how she conducted her own household. At the time the denomination disapproved of dancing and theater. Kate, for her part, grew up to marry a man who, although not raised Presbyterian, received a similar upbringing. Consequently,

Eliza's choice to join First Presbyterian required her to abstain from performing and viewing the arts.[29]

The instability of the Gholson household awaited Eliza after each Sunday worship service ended. When Gholson's brother William moved to Cincinnati in 1844, he renounced slavery and manumitted all his captives. Eliza was at that moment at her closest proximity to manumission, because she had never belonged to a family that voluntarily freed its enslaved people. Unlike Thomas Gholson, however, the older brother's career continued to rise, and he formed a new law practice in the North. He did not need the wealth from slavery to reestablish himself as an anti-slavery attorney. Meanwhile, the Memphis Gholsons soldiered on, and Kate—who finally had her own captive after so many years without one—held on tightly to her human inheritance.[30]

Eliza joined First Presbyterian as Kate became pregnant, and she attended the church while guiding the new mother through her first pregnancy. The "young mistress" gave birth to a new Donelson—Josephine Gholson—on October 9, 1844, and for Eliza the new arrival was no ordinary baby. Although the Polks had added multiple children to their family during Eliza's time at Hamilton Place, those babies were mere children of the trustees caring for her. Josephine's birth was different, because Eliza, with any children she might give birth to, was suddenly destined to transfer permanently to Josephine after her parents' deaths. When Eliza looked at the infant, she saw the face of her future enslaver—a third generation of Donelson captivity.

Andrew Jackson's ownership of Eliza ended when Kate claimed her in September 1842, and he stopped subsidizing her enslavement. As his health deteriorated in his final years, he increasingly called on his captives at the Hermitage to perform tasks for him. His support of slavery did not waver. On his deathbed, he offered a rare acknowledgment of the humanity of his unfree laborers by promising to meet them in Heaven. On the other hand, he did not liberate any of them in his will.[31]

With Eliza out west in Memphis, Jackson became a largely irrelevant figure, if not a nonperson, in her life. The Gholsons were urban Whigs and did not hold parties for the major planters who ruled Tennessee's Democratic Party. Jackson did not socialize with the couple at their home or the Hermitage, whether because of old age, long distance, or political differences. Meanwhile, after Jackson's beloved Democrats lost the White House in 1840, people no longer called on him at the Hermitage for counsel on national matters. As a result, the Hermitage faded as a major location in national politics in the early 1840s.[32]

Lucius Polk's cousin James K. Polk ran for the US presidency as a Democrat in 1844, and he defeated his Whig opponent. Months later, on March 4, 1845, he took the oath of office. Jackson was in ill health at the Hermitage, but he lived to witness the return of the Democratic Party to power and the vanquishing of his political foes. The new White House occupant was yet another US president with whom Eliza had been personally acquainted. She had served him as early as 1833, when he and his wife brought Mary McLemore from the East Coast to the McLemore house.

Andrew Jackson died at the Hermitage three months and four days after President Polk's inauguration. His passing ensured that he no longer held any control over Eliza. However, he remained politically influential from beyond the grave. A devout disciple of Jacksonian democracy, President Polk adopted the policies of his late personal friend. The new president supported the continuation of slavery in the United States, and he retained the policy of Indian removal. He reappointed Jackson's protégé Henry Dodge to the position of governor of Wisconsin Territory shortly after his inauguration.[33]

The new commander in chief also followed Jackson in establishing a relationship between the White House and John McLemore. In 1845 President Polk appointed McLemore to a federal position—superintendent of mineral lands. The appointment required McLemore to leave Memphis—and the South overall—and to work at a military post that lay six hundred miles away to the northwest. He would have to live without his entire family and his daughter's enslaved servants for years instead of weeks or months. McLemore accepted the offer, and he moved to Fort Crawford in Wisconsin Territory. His jurisdiction extended two hundred miles from that fort to the northwest at the Falls of St. Anthony.[34]

Eliza faced another separation from the enslaver who had "raised" her. After only three years in Memphis, most of the McLemores she had served in childhood were out of her life. At least this time they left the home where she was enslaved instead of selling her away from them. Nevertheless, Kate was now the only original McLemore left in town, and she too had to cope with the absence of her family. She was already raising Josephine without the benefit of her late mother's wisdom, and her father's new appointment removed his counsel from her too. Only Eliza remained as an elder from Kate's childhood home to assist her with the baby.

Meanwhile, Gholson's search for work took him out of Tennessee and beyond legal work. He and lawyer W. F. Davis opened a firm in Louisville, Kentucky, in late 1846. At the same time, Gholson acclimated himself to the community, joining the local branch of the Independent Order of Odd Fellows. By 1847 Kate, little Josephine, and their enslaved servants also left Memphis to join Gholson in Louisville. The relocation forced Eliza to say goodbye to the circle of friends and acquaintances she had developed at First Presbyterian over the preceding three years.[35]

The Gholson party gathered at the dock at Memphis and boarded a steamboat bound for Louisville. The trip took Eliza farther north than she had ever traveled. The vessel reached the southernmost tip of the state of Illinois, where the Ohio River entered the Mississippi. Superficially, the land did not look different from what she had seen in southeastern Missouri or southwestern Kentucky moments earlier. The same plants that grew along the river in those states also appeared by Illinois. Nevertheless, Eliza had just entered the waters of a free state.

The vessel then turned east from southern Illinois into the Ohio River and continued on. For the rest of Eliza's journey, the river functioned as a boundary line between freedom and slavery. The free states Illinois and Indiana lay to the north of her, and the slave state Kentucky lay to the south. African Americans on the docks to the south of her boarded steamboats while in chains, bracing themselves for sale downriver, but African Americans at points north of her did not. In addition, more people who looked like her were on the southern bank than on the northern bank.

The steamboat finally entered Jefferson County, Kentucky, and then stopped at Louisville. With each step off the vessel, Eliza walked farther away from the free city of Clarksville, Indiana, behind her. She had never lived outside of Tennessee, and her confinement to that state had kept her in a location heavily shaped by both John McLemore and General Jackson. Both men had invested in Memphis's early development, and Jackson's electoral success made Tennessee a major state in national politics. In contrast, neither McLemore nor Jackson had established major political or financial inroads in Louisville, and Eliza's relocation there allowed her to live away from the influence of those men for the first time.

By the summer of 1847, Gholson and Davis shifted their professional work from law to technology. Their firm launched a service for forwarding letters by telegraph, and it financially supported the development of a Cincinnati–Louisville telegraph line by a competitor of Samuel F. B. Morse. The partners also worked as agents for a life insurance company. Gholson traveled constantly to solicit sales of stock for the telegraph, because he personally knew potential investors in the North (New York and Philadelphia), the Midwest (Cincinnati), the Upper South (Baltimore, Louisville, Memphis, and St. Louis), and the Deep South (New Orleans). His travels left Eliza's enslavement at Kate's discretion, but the captive's previous labor for Betsy and Mary Ann during their husbands' absences made her quite experienced in serving the women of President Jackson's family.[36]

As of 1847 the Gholson household in Kentucky consisted of Thomas and Kate Gholson, Josephine, and three enslaved people. (The tax records did not record the names, ages, or genders of the enslaved.) The captive who belonged to Gholson was worth five hundred dollars, and thus was either an adolescent or a middle-aged person. That year's tax assessment for Jefferson County listed Kate as the owner of two enslaved people, but she had not bought any people in either Memphis or Louisville while enslaving Eliza. Therefore, Kate's only other captive besides Eliza was almost certainly Eliza's son or daughter. Kate's two enslaved people were collectively assessed at eight hundred dollars; the combined monetary value was standard for mother-child pairs at the time.[37]

Gholson and his partners W. F. Davis and T. P. Shaffner became swept up in controversy surrounding the telegraph project. While Shaffner was working on the telegraph in Frankfort, Kentucky, a report from that city's newspaper announced in early October that the partners had ended their contract with Morse's competitor to work with Morse himself. A newspaper in Louisville charitably said of the partners, "Gholson, Davis, and Shaffner are entitled to credit for the promptitude with which they have relinquished all enterprizes [sic] which could only detract from the just fame of Prof. Morse and the reward due to him for his wonderful invitation." Shaffner claimed the competitor's machine simply did not work, but the press in Louisville wondered whether it stood to make less money than Morse's telegraph.[38]

Meanwhile, Gholson went into debt, and he took drastic measures to address his expenses. Although he could not legally sell Eliza to pay his debtors, his fundraising efforts disrupted her enslavement again. He mortgaged the family's lot in Memphis and then traveled back to Louisville on October 27. Two days later Gholson and Davis announced the termination of their partnership, and shortly thereafter Gholson and his family and captives returned to Tennessee.[39]

The Gholsons recovered from their hardships in Louisville by playing to their strengths. They started by generating some income through the sale of their old lot in South Memphis at the corner of Union and Linden. Then they traveled to Nashville, where they established a new residence by mid-November. Gholson severed ties to his interests outside of Nashville such as the telegraph project, but he had only his legal skills to try to peddle in his new location. Meanwhile, Kate regrouped in a familiar environment. She and Eliza had grown up there, and A. J. still resided there. On the other hand, just as Kate's mother had struggled with the household in Nashville during her husband's financial woes, the "young mistress" experienced similar problems with her own husband as she came back to that city.[40]

Eliza had not lived in Nashville since her sale away from the McLemore household thirteen years earlier. The Gholsons forced her return to the county whose sheriff had separated her from her siblings, but she at least did not have to stay in that same residence. In addition, the return to Nashville signified how intensely Eliza's enslavement restricted her physical movements and her personal development. She was enslaved in her thirties in Nashville by a Donelson, just as she had been when she was a child. Kate kept her there as if the interludes at Hamilton Place and Memphis had never happened.

Nashville was Eliza's third relocation with the Gholsons after only five years of enslavement by them. The frequent resettlements marked a different kind of instability in her enslavement. In addition, the move away from Louisville severed any new social networks Eliza had developed there, just as the move *to* Louisville had done. She returned to Nashville in extreme social isolation. Despite whatever grief she felt, she still had to perform her duties to her enslavers, but her long-standing role would soon confront significant challenges.

≋4

Marriage and Property

As soon as Eliza and her enslavers settled in Nashville in November 1847, Thomas Gholson announced to a Louisville newspaper, "I will be in Louisville in the course of two or three weeks, or sooner, if the health of my family will permit, to attend to the settlement of my old business." He included the qualifier because his wife Kate had become ill with consumption— now known as tuberculosis. Eliza had never cared for a dying enslaver, but Kate's rapidly deteriorating health forced her into that role. As she continued serving little Josephine and performing household duties, she learned how to give palliative care to her ailing captor.[1]

On July 2, 1848, the "young mistress" died at the age of twenty-six. None of the papers documenting Kate's ownership of Eliza stipulated an immediate transfer to Josephine in the event of Kate's demise. As a result, for the first time in over a quarter century, a Donelson did not enslave Eliza. Gholson kept her unfree, holding her in the same household and sparing her the humiliation of being inspected at a sale. The Donelson family gradually played less of a role in Eliza's life. In 1849 A. J. started work as the deputy clerk and master of chancery in Shelby County, and he took Gholson, Josephine, and Eliza back to Memphis to live with him in his office building. His father was in Memphis too, having recently ended his government service in the Northwest. However, financial troubles continued to plague "Mr. Macklemo," and by the early 1850s, he relocated to San Francisco, California, to search for gold.[2]

Gholson sent four-year-old Josephine to Holly Springs, Mississippi, to live with his half-brother George Freeman, who had a wife, children, and enslaved laborers. As a result, the only child Eliza was caring for was her own, if indeed that child still lived. Gholson accumulated property in Memphis for Josephine to claim upon reaching adulthood. After he received all the money due from the buyer of the old family lot at Union and Linden Streets in January 1849, he acquired three lots over the next two years in trust for his daughter. The county recorded the little girl as the sole owner of each lot.[3]

Eliza was closer to loved ones in Memphis, and she returned there just in time for her family to grow. Unlike her, they remained tied to the Donelson family, and they had stayed in Memphis during her relocations to Louisville and Nashville. They had not enjoyed her level of autonomy in enslavement, but her unstable captivity with the urban Gholsons contrasted sharply with the monotony of the large plantation. Mary McLemore Walker still enslaved Eliza's younger sibling-figures Malinda and Julius at Villa Rose. In 1848 Malinda gave birth to her second son, Horace. Three years later Eliza's nephew-figure Lewis arrived.[4]

Eliza ventured away from her enslaver's household enough times for one of the few free African American men in Memphis to court her. The city's First Presbyterian Church, which she had attended before her brief enslavement in Louisville, had just launched the Memphis Colonization Society in June 1848. Her new suitor—whose name does not appear in any records— was a staunch supporter of the organization's mission "to aid in colonizing to Liberia the free colored population of the United

States." He did not wish to permanently relocate to Liberia, but he reportedly wanted to help freed people who were willing to sail there and start their new lives.[5]

The couple married, but because of the bride's legal status as an enslaved person, Shelby County did not officially recognize the union. Marriage did not prevent enslavers from selling enslaved women and any of their children away from their husbands.[6]

Either Eliza or her husband, or the two together, asked Gholson about the possibility of manumitting her. With that request the couple risked Gholson's wrath and the physical means by which he could legally inflict it on them. Fortunately for them, they found a receptive audience in the enslaver, and his willingness to entertain the petition suggested that he gravitated toward his stepfather's more lenient portion of religious instruction on slavery. George W. Freeman told enslavers, "Ensure the exercise of a mild and merciful discipline over your slaves, as well as an abundant provision for their wants." They were also to "do every thing in their power to make [captives'] situation comfortable, and put forth all reasonable efforts to render them contented and happy." Moreover, Freeman saw captives as not social equals but at least biological equals to captors. "You should never forget that, low as they are in the scale of humanity, they are yet human beings and have the feelings of human beings," he declared, "feelings too, with many of them, as delicate and sensitive as your own, and which demand to be respected, and carefully preserved from outrage."[7]

On the other hand, Gholson's stepfather had taught him that slavery did not contradict Christianity. Freeman noted that in the Bible, "The relation of Master and Slave is frequently spoken of, but never with one word of disapprobation." Gholson set a price for Eliza's manumission, and, until she paid it, he also charged her husband for the time she spent away from him. "I married a free man of color, who hired my time of my master, who promised me my freedom upon the payment of $1,000," she later explained. Her memory of the price showed her awareness of her own financial worth—and the magnitude of the funds she and her husband would have to raise. It also suggests that her son or daughter was no longer living, as there is no record of Gholson selling a child between 1840 and 1848. Or perhaps the price Gholson set was for Eliza and the child but the subsequent death of the child was too painful a memory for Eliza to include in her affidavit.[8]

Sometime between July 1852 and March 1853, she and her spouse bought one lot of land and a house with their savings. "My husband and myself worked hard, and he invested our savings in a house and lot in Memphis, which was held for us in Mr. Gholson's name," she recalled years later. Gholson's handling of this purchase demonstrated both trust and necessity. Tennessee law prohibited African Americans from making real estate transactions. The couple then leased out the property for eight dollars per month, and Gholson collected the money from whomever rented it. Eliza recalled years later that the property was "held for us in Mr. Gholson's name," but she considered marital acquisitions as joint ones in practice; full manumission promised to make them de jure joint acquisitions too. Indeed, city tax records over the next two years recorded Gholson as owning real estate in Memphis's Sixth Ward—South Memphis—at a value of one thousand dollars; it was the only land he held in his own name after moving back to Memphis.[9]

Eliza probably worked in others' homes as either a babysitter or a caretaker for someone sick or infirm. She knew how much money employers paid for that work in the city; she recalled years later that in Memphis women performing such labor—working as a "nurse girl," as she put it—usually earned ten to fifteen dollars per month. She had plenty of experience for the position, having served multiple babies of enslavers and having provided palliative care for Kate. Eliza's hired-out employment for funding her manumission was common among antebellum African American women. They did not define freedom as the absence of work but rather as their ability to control the nature of their labor.

Semi-freedom allowed Eliza to work to earn the manumission fee instead of merely performing tasks at the enslaver's whim.[10]

State officials in Tennessee had soured on adding freed African Americans to the state's population. In 1851 the state enacted a new law, which required all newly manumitted people to immigrate to Liberia within two years of their manumission. The law did not apply to Eliza's husband, who was already free. "We are in favor of a law compelling every free negro to leave the State," explained a supportive local newspaper, "for we consider every free negro a common nuisance, to be summarily dealt with as such, in a slave-holding community." Any person failing to comply with the law faced possible re-enslavement. In preceding years Memphis residents relocating to Liberia had needed to travel to Georgia in the spring and board a steamboat that sailed from the Gulf Coast and across the Atlantic Ocean to their destination.[11]

At some point in 1852 or 1853, Eliza's husband made this trip with other freed people but with the intent to return to her in two years. "He went out with them because he was used to travelling, and it was necessary to have some one to assist and take care of them," she explained. The couple planned to finish paying off the cost of her manumission and claim their house upon his return. Their plan, however, assumed that Gholson had intended for the real estate in his name to go to them and that he would transfer it to them. Unfortunately, Eliza's husband died while abroad. She lost her husband and their plans for a future together; she also lost his help in paying for her freedom.[12]

As Gholson accepted Eliza's manumission payments, he invested in more unfree people. In addition to his recent real estate purchases for his daughter, he acquired people in trust for Josephine—perhaps to replace Eliza. In March 1849 he bought Genina, a "mulato slave for life about thirty-six years old . . . sound in body and mind." However, he did not enslave her for very long, and by 1851 Eliza resumed her role as the sole enslaved woman at his home.[13]

In April 1850 Gholson purchased a man named Peter, age twenty-two, for $950. Over the next two years, Eliza and Peter comprised the entire enslaved population of Gholson's household. Local tax records recorded him as enslaving two people in Memphis's Fourth Ward from 1850 to 1852. He hired Peter out for labor; in the 1850 census, Peter appeared as a resident of a city ward other than the one where Gholson lived. The tax records' listing of Gholson with two enslaved people also meant that he could no longer have enslaved any of Eliza's children as of 1851. Eliza may have been mourning the loss of her child while also grieving the demise of her husband.[14]

In November 1852 the staff at the *Memphis Eagle and Enquirer* invited Gholson to relocate to New Orleans for the coming winter season and work as the periodical's correspondent there; he was also to generate sales of the periodical in New Orleans. He accepted the invitation, which meant leaving his two enslaved people in Memphis for an extended period without his supervision. On Wednesday, November 10, Gholson left Memphis by steamboat and arrived in New Orleans within five days. During his first week there, he saw the Verandah Hotel and a slave pen near it. New Orleans was the country's largest market for the slave trade, and dozens of local slave brokers made the business omnipresent there.[15]

After writing a report on November 20, Gholson took a hiatus from writing for the next ten days. He likely returned to Memphis during that period to retrieve Peter and then bring him to Louisiana to sell him there. The captive's departure from Memphis did not bode well for Eliza. After all, Gholson had acquired Peter in trust for Josephine. Moreover, after Kate's death, Gholson claimed Eliza for himself. If he chose to sell his daughter's valuable property in order to alleviate his own financial problems, what prevented him from selling his own enslaved woman of lesser monetary worth?[16]

On the other hand, the selling of Peter also reflected the captive's status on Gholson's taxes. Although the county listed Josephine as owner in the deed, the city recognized only her father's ownership. In the three years the enslaver held both Eliza and Peter, he maintained ownership of them for tax purposes, which gave him the authority to sell them. In contrast, all the land that Gholson had bought for his daughter remained in her name, and he never sold any of it to meet his financial needs. Only the enslaved people were his monetary security in case of emergency.[17]

Gholson registered at the Arcade Hotel in New Orleans on December 6. Businessmen and reporters gathered there, and the venue hosted auctions of enslaved people. Two streets to the east lay a slave pen run by brokers Bernard Kendig and James W. Boazman. On December 8 Kendig bought Peter for his aunt, who owned many captives in her nephew's pen. Peter had been at the Arcade Hotel for no more than forty-eight hours. If Gholson regretted selling part of his daughter's inheritance, he placed those feelings into his work. He gloomily announced about cotton that day, "The market to-day is drooping—to use a broker's phrase, 'sick.'"[18]

On February 15, 1853, the post office at Memphis held a letter for "Eliza Gholson." She was one of only three African Americans among the hundreds of people having mail there that day; a local newspaper identified her as "Gholson, Eliza colored." This strongly suggests that Eliza knew how to read. Considering her semi-freedom from the Gholsons, her access to free African Americans, and her diverse church community, she probably acquired her literacy during her enslavement in Memphis. Many newspapers reprinted the names of recipients for three to seven consecutive days if their letters remained unclaimed. She may have immediately retrieved her letter, because the newspaper dropped her name from the recipients' list after only one announcement.[19]

The reference to "Eliza Gholson" was telling. The deeds documenting her sales provided only her first name, but the writer's addition of a surname for the addressee associated her identity with her enslaver. Gholson himself likely sent the letter from Louisiana. Although Eliza had already married and become widowed by 1853, his use of his own surname revealed a focus on her as his captive. The name "Eliza Gholson," like Tennessee itself, did not recognize her marriage. Because Gholson did not write any newspaper reports from New Orleans between February 16 and March 7, he may have informed Eliza by letter that he intended to take her to New Orleans. The two-week break from the newspaper allowed enough time for him to return to Memphis and bring her to New Orleans by steamboat. At the time, African American women—enslaved or free—rarely traveled alone, especially across state lines. Many of them were turned away from coaches, trains, and boats, because European Americans did not want them to travel unaccompanied and with the same amenities.[20]

By removing Eliza again from Memphis, Gholson ended her second phase of partial autonomy there and assumed more control

The Mississippi River below Baton Rouge, Louisiana, in 1858.
The Illustrated London News, *April 10, 1858, Library of Congress*

over her daily life. He arranged for her to take all her clothes with her, because many buyers of enslaved people wanted their new captives to already have their own wardrobe. The steamboat took her down the Mississippi River into the Deep South. Captives of other passengers walked aboard the boat and entered the "servants' quarters." Some likely boarded the vessel at other cities, like Vicksburg, but others left farms and plantations with their enslavers for the trip. Enslaved people with passes boarded alone, because their captors had hired them out for labor either on the boat or at another destination. When the vessel stopped at bustling New Orleans and Eliza stepped into the city, she heard, perhaps for the first time, the French language and French-accented English among its occupants. Her enslavement in Tennessee and Kentucky had not exposed her to the Creoles of Louisiana.[21]

Among other recent newcomers to the area were Colonel Richard Christmas and his wife, Mary Christmas, of Tallula, Mississippi. They arrived in New Orleans on February 15, 1853, registering as guests of the St. Charles Hotel. Their marriage was four months old, and Mary was five months away from giving birth to her first child. Richard was a first cousin once removed of John Christmas McLemore, and Gholson may have known him through Kate—Richard's first cousin twice removed. The newlyweds may have felt fortunate to have survived the trip, for that same day a steamboat floated in flames down the Mississippi River. Three of the two dozen passengers died, and one of them was a "colored cabin boy" who fell overboard and drowned. More good fortune was to come for the Christmases in New Orleans—at Eliza's expense.[22]

Slavery was on Gholson's mind in the context of the cotton market. He wrote for the *Memphis Eagle* on February 12: "The great staple cotton has thus far commanded a fair ruminating price to the producers. . . . As a tolerably good sign that planters think good times will continue, negroes sold for $2,200 to $2,300 [payable] on one, two, and three years time, at a large sale in

St. Mary's Parish the other day." He revealed that he was no abolitionist, because he considered the high prices for the captives a
boon. "We all hope for the present high times to continue, and
we act on this hope," he cheered. Then again, he had a personal
interest in the high value of enslaved people, because he was preparing to accept an offer on Eliza in Louisiana. As she later put it,
"Mr. Gholson got badly broken up in money matters."[23]

Gholson met with the Christmases during the first month of
their stay in New Orleans. On March 7 he wrote a report about
a "grand soiree" that he had attended that day at the hotel where
the Christmases lodged, and the couple may have also partic-
ipated in the event. At some point that month, the newlyweds
agreed to pay him eight hundred dollars for Eliza—a fair if not
generous price for a woman of thirty-six years. The Christmases
then removed her from his custody and became her new captors.[24]

The ever-observant Eliza kept the transaction and its date
seared in her memory. She remembered vividly in August 1860:
"I became the slave of Mr. Christmas 7 years ago last March."
She was also aware of the details concerning her exchange, recalling that Gholson "pawned me to Col. Christmas for $800." She
knew that although at that moment the Christmases held her, she
still belonged to Gholson. More importantly, the arrangement
for her manumission remained intact, but Gholson could not
free her until he fully repaid the Christmases. He lost his claim
to her, not unlike Thomas Hopkins and the McLemores during
her childhood, but he at least retained the possibility of regaining
that claim.[25]

By the end of spring 1853, Eliza and the Christmases took their
first trip by steamboat together. They sailed from New Orleans to
Louisville, where Mary Christmas was raised. Born Mary Phillips in 1834 in Kentucky, she came from a long line of planters.
She was orphaned before age ten and then raised by her aunt
and uncle. The couple owned real estate valued at $90,000, and
they enslaved twenty people. Phillips's grandfather had kept

thirty-two people captive shortly before his death in 1841. Eliza had previously experienced enslavement in Louisville by the financially struggling Gholsons, but the Christmases exposed her to the city's wealthy planter class.[26]

Phillips's guardians had raised her to accumulate and nurture her own wealth, and she applied those lessons to her own life as an adult. Before marrying, she and Richard Christmas had signed a contract that specified her sole ownership of all property she brought into the union. She also retained exclusive possession of the items she inherited from others after marrying him. In the late summer of 1853, for example, she officially claimed ownership of her late grandfather's land.[27]

The new bride soon began the process of passing down her life lessons to a child of her own. While in Louisville, Eliza served a newborn baby for the first time since Josephine Gholson's arrival nine years earlier. Mary Christmas gave birth to her first child—daughter Norma—in her mother's home on July 6. Eliza later claimed, "I have nursed and taken care of the child from her birth." She also disclosed that her enslaver "has always been feeble," and this physical weakness may have led Mary to direct Eliza to nurse the infant. Eliza herself made a point of saying that she had both "nursed" and "taken care" of Norma, suggesting that she had both breastfed and raised the child. The unfree nurse thus taught the newborn one of her first lessons: the enslaved lived to serve her.[28]

Many slaveholding women of ill health assigned their captive women as wet nurses for newborns. Some of the nurses cared for all the babies of a plantation, but other nurses were directed specifically to either the enslaved children or the slaveholder's children. Considering Eliza's complaint that the Christmases kept her "closely confined," as she put it, she likely nursed only little Norma.[29]

As soon as the baby latched onto Eliza's breast, the Christmases' enslavement added a biological element to their financial arrangement with Thomas Gholson. Norma became dependent on Eliza's body for survival. This new dynamic of Eliza's captivity affected her too. "I am so attached to the child," she later admitted. Nevertheless, she still waited for Gholson to repay his loan.[30]

In early October, the Christmases and Eliza left Louisville. Their boat drifted westward down the Ohio River. For two brief days, free states surrounded Eliza to the north once again. But on the third day, the vessel turned southward onto the Mississippi, and the free states faded from view. When it reached the small town of Tallula, Mississippi, the vessel docked at a location called Shiloh Landing. Above the landing rested a vast, stately mansion. Eliza had arrived at her new home—the plantation Shiloh.[31]

She walked onto the dock and for the first time entered a rural plantation by the Mississippi River. The riverside cities Memphis, Louisville, and New Orleans had been centers of endless urban busyness—the traffic of steamboats on the water and coaches on the ground, the crowds of people in the streets and at the docks. In contrast, the only endless busyness at Shiloh was the labor performed by the plantation's dozens of enslaved people. The sloshing of steamboats sailing either northbound or southbound to Shiloh Landing periodically disturbed the river, but far fewer steamboats stopped at Shiloh than in the cities. The stillness of the riverside swamps bred mosquitos, and they carried diseases that threatened to take the lives of those who lived there.

At Shiloh Eliza became one of about one million enslaved African Americans whose captors transferred them from the Upper South to the Lower South between 1800 and 1860. Fifty-one percent of Mississippi's residents lived in captivity as of the year 1850. In addition, Shiloh lay in Issaquena County, in which the practice of slavery smothered the environment even more intensely than statewide. The county's 4,105 enslaved people comprised 92 percent of the population; only 373 of the 4,478 residents were free, and just seven of those free people shared Eliza's African heritage.[32]

Issaquena County was still new, and its newness showed that Mississippi was as much a part of the recently expanded West as it was a part of the South. Enough elite planters had relocated to the area for the state to establish Issaquena County in 1844. However, most of them were content to just build massive plantations there and reside somewhere else, leaving their scores of captives to toil year-round on the land. As a result of the planters' rampant absenteeism, the county did not develop the churches and other social organizations that existed in other counties. The Christmases' acquaintance Albert Triplett (A. T.) Burnley lived in New Orleans, but he bought eleven hundred acres in Issaquena County for $1,795. Other absentee planters included William C. Smedes and Thomas Kershaw.[33]

As Norma's personal nurse, Eliza enjoyed some privileges that most of Shiloh's enslaved people did not. She avoided the sunburns and heatstrokes that plagued the plantation's field laborers in the scorching Delta heat in the subtropical, moist clay fields. The mosquitos did not annoy her as much as they bothered the captives toiling in Issaquena County's steamy swamps. Within Shiloh's walls, she did not have to worry about encountering the bears, wolves, and wildcats that roamed the county.[34]

Nevertheless, Eliza still suffered. Mary was a sickly mother and requested the enslaved servant's constant attention. She benefited from Eliza's experience in having nursed a terminally ill slaveholder, but the new enslaver restricted Eliza more heavily than Kate did. Although the Christmases held over one hundred people at Shiloh, Mary relied exclusively on her new captive. Eliza later complained, "I . . . have had scarcely any time to myself, or to see the other slaves." She missed out on the activities that emotionally and spiritually connected the other enslaved people on the plantation. The absence of a public gathering place kept her either uninformed or slowly informed about the events involving Shiloh's captives.[35]

Eliza's diet may not have drastically changed with her transition from a semi-free woman in the Mid-South to enslavement by a planter in the Deep South. The Gholsons' constant financial struggles would have made the purchase of separate foods for Eliza a luxury, and she probably ate the couple's leftovers. The Christmases likely made similar provisions for Eliza because of her close proximity to them and her constant presence in the family's house. In contrast, slaveholders in rural Mississippi generally rationed pork, cornmeal, sweet potatoes, grits, and rice to their captives, thus restricting them to fatty and starchy foods. Some captors allowed field hands and their enslaved children to raise their own chickens and corn, but Eliza was too busy serving the female Christmases to devote any time to maintaining a coop and small cornfield.[36]

Despite Mary Christmas's illness, she cultivated a circle of wealthy acquaintances in Tallula after settling in Shiloh. In June 1854, acting independently of her husband, she purchased sections of land from state legislator and fellow Kentuckian Fielding Davis. He owned at least two plantations in Mississippi. The massive local plantation Dunbarton lay in Issaquena, and he enslaved over seven dozen people there. Eliza likely encountered and briefly served Davis because of his interactions with her captor. Also, Mary's transactions with Davis marked the closest proximity that Eliza had come to White House politics in years, because President Zachary Taylor had appointed his friend Davis to the position of US marshal. The relationship between Mary Christmas and the marshal was the first that Eliza saw in which the connections to the presidency were voluntary and not through blood relations or marriage.[37]

If Eliza ever thought about running away from Shiloh, the county sheriff's track record of catching fugitives was likely to have dissuaded her. Throughout 1854 alone, the sheriff caught and jailed eleven runaways. Most of them were from Mississippi, but some had enslavers from Arkansas and Louisiana. In October the sheriff arrested seven fugitive men at once, and they sat in the jail while awaiting retrieval by their enslaver. Moreover, he was not averse to jailing women, as when he incarcerated a runaway woman from Holland's Landing months later.[38]

The county, however, did not have a perfect run of fugitive arrests. In February 1855 Issaquena County experienced a rare but significant breach in security. Four enslaved people—two men, a woman, and her three-year-old daughter—ran away from the plantation of Frank W. Moore. "They are thought to be in a Flat Boat somewhere on the river," reported the *Vicksburg Whig*. In the newspaper Moore announced a reward of two hundred dollars for the return of his laborers. Therefore, Issaquena's residents learned that successful escapes from the county were possible, and news about the fugitives likely reached Shiloh. Moore was an acquaintance and close neighbor of the Christmases.[39]

That same year nature wreaked havoc on Issaquena, and Eliza and the Christmases survived a county-wide drought. It underscored how little relief Eliza received from the weather in the Deep South. The sun was unrelenting, and the spring and summer seasons brought sweltering humidity. Eliza had spent her entire enslavement in the Upper South and had not previously experienced such hot and hazy summers as in riverside Mississippi. Norma latched onto her only for feeding times, but the humidity clung to Eliza's skin and clothes all day long. Indeed, at Shiloh, slavery seemed to have taken the form of air.[40]

Even in the winter months, the weather in Tallula was warm. Snowstorms happened rarely in Mississippi, usually only in January. Tennessee, as a Mid-South state, had more seasonal variation, which symbolized the diversity of Eliza's enslavement there—rural plantations and urban homes, constant labor and Sundays off. In contrast, the sameness of the tropical weather in Mississippi reflected the enslaved woman's unyielding routine of confinement.

Mary spent the spring of 1855 buying real estate in Issaquena. She purchased three different areas of county land from the state of Mississippi itself. The state's government acquired property from people who had defaulted on property taxes, and it then held public auctions of the land. In April she bought real estate from James Dick Hill—the son of Andrew Jackson's friend H. R. W. Hill. The junior Hill lived in New Orleans, but he sold his land in Issaquena through a local attorney-in-fact. Eliza likely went with Mary to each sale and thus probably saw the son of the man who had arranged her sale to Jackson over two decades earlier.[41]

The Christmases and Eliza left Shiloh and traveled once again to spend the season in Louisville in the summer of 1855. This trip was at least her third to that city, and the itinerary remained the same. She suffered another stop at Memphis, where she hoped someday to permanently reside. After the boat left Memphis, the free states Illinois, Indiana, and Ohio beckoned her along the Ohio River before she reached the slave state Kentucky.

As much as Mary Christmas enjoyed buying her own property, she needed her husband to help her to manage it in her illness. On August 30 she placed in trust to him all the property she had independently purchased after her wedding and all the land, enslaved people, and other items she had inherited from her paternal grandfather. Those possessions were still for her "sole, separate, and exclusive use," according to the corresponding deed, and the arrangement kept "full power to her at all times to dispose of the same or any part thereof at her discretion . . . as if she were unmarried." Upon her death, only her "issue" and "blood relations" could inherit her property. The couple delivered their agreement to Jefferson County's clerk on September 8— with Eliza and little Norma likely in tow to witness another exposition of Mary's independence and financial agency.[42]

Gholson remained in debt to the Christmases, consequently delaying Eliza's manumission arrangement with him. Moreover, her freedom became less of a priority for him. Shortly after transferring her to the Christmases, he stopped reporting in New

Orleans and retreated to Memphis. Upon his return, he paid the rest of the money he owed for one lot of land, and he received the warranty deed for the real estate. Without the cash he had received from pawning Eliza, he would not have been able to secure the inheritance of that lot for his daughter. He had sold the property he held for Eliza and her husband sometime in 1854; the city's tax records from July 1854 to July 1855 listed him without any land to his name.[43]

He grew sick from consumption almost immediately after leaving New Orleans, inheriting his late wife's repeated coughs and debilitating pain. He still claimed Eliza in his taxes for the period of July 1854 to July 1855, valuing her at the lease's price of eight hundred dollars. However, he eventually accepted his inability to care for himself, and he decided to resettle permanently in Holly Springs, Mississippi, in his half-brother's household. In his illness there, he reunited with his ten-year-old daughter Josephine.[44]

On December 1, 1855, Gholson died in debt to the Christmases, and the couple became Eliza's new owners. Her ties to the Donelson family were permanently severed; Josephine no longer stood to inherit her—or any enslaved people—from her father. Mary Christmas remained sickly, but she no longer had to worry about losing Eliza's care. Norma's enslaved nurse was at Shiloh permanently.[45]

Eliza's losses were catastrophic. Gholson's demise nullified his promise of manumission, and she lost any money she had paid him for it. She was severed from her younger virtual siblings, her church community, and the semi-autonomy she had enjoyed in Memphis. She lost the property she and her husband had purchased, although she did not know that. And she realized the worst fear of so many former fellow captives of the Upper South: she had been taken downriver into permanent slavery in the Deep South. She was officially an enslaved person of the Mississippi Delta.

Fifteen months later events in Washington, DC, changed Eliza's prospects, should she ever achieve freedom, and confirmed the

Christmases' hold on her. In March 1857 James Buchanan, a Democrat, was inaugurated as US president, and he hinted that the US Supreme Court would soon permanently settle the issue of slavery. Days later the justices announced their verdict on whether enslaved Missourian Dred Scott had become free when he was taken to free territory in the North. The court ruled, "[Persons of African descent] are not included, and were not intended to be included, under the word 'citizens' in the Constitution, and can therefore claim none of the rights and privileges which that instrument provides for and secures to citizens of the United States." The opinion noted, "That unfortunate race . . . had for more than a century . . . been regarded as beings of an inferior order . . . so far inferior, that they had no rights which the white man was bound to respect." If Dred Scott was not a citizen, he did not have the right to sue. In addition, their ruling in *Dred Scott v. Sandford* extended slavery's legality beyond the slave states and into all federal territories, granting enslavers the freedom to bring their captives from a slave state to any territory without having to free them.

Roger B. Taney—the court's chief justice—rose to that office in 1836, when Congress approved of his appointment by President Jackson. The president had owned Eliza for over one year when he nominated Taney. Both men committed acts that preserved Eliza's enslavement but in different ways. Jackson had purchased her in 1834 to keep ownership of her in his late wife's family, and Taney in *Dred Scott* twenty-three years later declared that the Christmases could enslave her in any territory they chose. The case's outcome marked the peak of the slavery dynamic of Jacksonian democracy, because it allowed enslavers to continue to push westward with their captives until they reached the Pacific Ocean. It was also an underlying cause of the Panic of 1857, as speculators in the East who were heavily invested in western railroad stocks and lands in the territories realized that struggles over slavery would threaten their holdings.[46]

As the Christmases' hold on Eliza tightened, more people assumed authority over her. On August 20, 1859, Mary gave birth to her son Richard Jr.—a new heir-apparent as Eliza's enslaver. Whenever Mary's husband went away from Shiloh, an overseer named Byrd Douthit took full control over the supervision of the plantation's laborers. Douthit was thirty years old in 1859. Eliza's previous enslavement by the Gholsons and her current service to Mary Christmas had long acclimated her to being older than her enslavers.[47]

Ever since Eliza's transfer to the Christmases' home in Tallula seven years earlier, life had barely evolved on and beyond the plantation. Mississippi's population rose by almost 200,000 people throughout the 1850s, but 55 percent of the state's 800,000 residents were enslaved in 1860—just four points above the percentage from ten years earlier. Meanwhile, Issaquena County's population nearly doubled, but that increase did not lessen slavery's grip on the county. In 1860, 587 of the county's 7,831 people were free. Even more foreboding for Eliza and her fellow captors, none of the county's free people that year were African Americans. Skin color designated who was free and who was enslaved in Issaquena—a sharp clarity that Eliza had previously experienced in the McLemore household but not in an entire county.[48]

On the other hand, within a year something unexpected happened to significantly break the monotony at Shiloh. The Christmases themselves caused the break, thinking the change would bring good fortune to them. However, it also had the potential to greatly benefit Eliza.

≈5

Manumission Promised and Denied

On January 1, 1860, Eliza spent her seventh consecutive New Year's Day in the Deep South, and the Christmases decided for the seventh time to keep her with them. She had served at Mary's side constantly since March 1853. An enslaved woman caring for her sickly enslaver typically slept on the bedroom floor, allowing her to learn the rhythm of her captor's snores over the years. Eliza's care kept the enslaver alive during that time, but that attention did not produce any significant improvement in her enslaver's health.

Mary was temporarily in New Orleans in early 1860 to settle some of her husband's affairs in real estate. She remained sick and likely brought Eliza with her to the city where the Christmases had first acquired her. In New Orleans the captive had no legal opportunity to become free, because the State of Louisiana had prohibited the emancipation of enslaved people three years earlier. However, she was once again in a city full of free and semi-free African Americans, coming and going as they pleased and controlling their own labor.[1]

The color of Eliza's skin especially branded her as an enslaved person in New Orleans. Ten years earlier in Memphis, the seventy free African Americans who identified as "black" outnumbered the fifty-two who identified as "mulatto." However, in New Orleans in 1860, three-fourths of the free African Americans were "mulatto," and a similar percentage of the enslaved were "black." Eliza had seen very little variation in color in the households of her captors. She and her family were "negro" in various sales receipts, and the enslaved populations of the McLemores and the Christmases contained far more "blacks" than "mulattoes." Even when she saw more "mulattoes" at First Presbyterian Church in Memphis, she and other "blacks" still worshiped alongside them. In contrast, the distinctions in status in New Orleans by gradation of color would have made the concepts of slavery and freedom more complex for her.[2]

By May Eliza and Mary were back at Shiloh, and the enslaved servant returned to the grind of isolated labor on a large rural plantation. Issaquena was the second-wealthiest county in the nation as the 1860s began, and the bulk of that wealth came from slavery's phenomenal profitability. In 1860 18 percent of slaveholders in Issaquena County and three other Mississippi counties enslaved at least 50 people, and the Delta's largest enslaver resided in the county, with over 800 captives—five times the size of Shiloh's slave community. The average value of a farm in Issaquena was over $30,000. Richard Christmas's real estate value of $150,000 and his wife's own $40,000 in land well exceeded that average. Also, in that year and the previous year, enslavers earned $350 per captive between the ages of ten and seventy—a demographic to which Eliza belonged. Mary enslaved 10 people in Mississippi, and her husband kept captive 156 people.[3]

Mary's health became so precarious that the family hoped a summer in the North would heal her. They arranged to travel for two weeks by steamboat to St. Anthony, Minnesota, where they would stay for even more weeks. The state's climate was "unsurpassed by any within the limits of the entire Union," said a New Yorker writing about Minnesota ("and becoming more and more daily sought after by invalids from the Southern and Eastern states, especially from the sunny South"). The writer reasoned, "A dry, bracing climate is greatly preferable, for consumptives in particular, to a moist, variable and debilitating atmosphere." St. Anthony also attracted tourists because of the Falls of St. Anthony, the only major waterfall on the Mississippi, and many visitors boasted about the beauty and healing powers of the falls. Of course, Minnesotans themselves supported that assessment. "Almost every boat comes [to Minnesota] laden with travelers, to see the country and indulge in summer recreation," a St. Paul newspaper reported in July 1860. "The largest portion of these are from the South, and they all speak of the invigorating effects of the climate upon them."[4]

Some southerners brought one or two enslaved people with them on their vacations in Minnesota, and the Christmases decided to do likewise. The trip meant leaving the slave South and entering the free North, and the decision came with risk. An enslaved person legally became free upon setting foot in a free state, especially if the enslavers voluntarily brought the captive there. But the Christmases were desperate for Mary to heal, and in the two years since Minnesota became a free state, no enslavers vacationing there had complained about their captives abandoning them and settling in the North. Eliza's enslavers had no reason to suspect they would suffer that fate.

Nevertheless, the Christmases were not alone in their caution, and Minnesotans themselves knew of southerners' reluctance. The fear of northern locals telling the enslaved about their new legal freedom in a free state—or "interference," as many Minnesotans put it that year—pervaded in the South, and that fear kept many prospective visitors from traveling north that summer. Tourists had "an apprehension that they might be interfered with," according to a St. Paul resident. Therefore, Minnesota's proslavery press fervently promised the opposite to southerners. "The most fanatical meddler in the affairs of others has never yet been bold enough here to practically illustrate his doctrines by interfering with travelers in pursuit of health," boasted one periodical, "whatever may be his ideas of the abstract right to do so."[5]

Newspaper accounts were explicit about the dynamics that year. The *Minnesotian and Times* of February 29, 1860, promised, "We assure our Southern friends that they are always welcome to visit us, and to bring their servants with them. No one will ever molest them. They will find that all politeness, goodbreeding and courtesy does not live South of Mason and Dixon line." A Minnesota correspondent of the *New Orleans Times-Picayune* observed drily on August 26, 1860, "Gentlemen, with their families, are here from Louisiana, Mississippi, Kentucky, and other Southern States: spending their money with livery stables, boatmen, shops and hotels, much to the delight of the grateful recipients, who, whatever they may think of us as men and women from slave territory, have a great respect for our purses, if not our persons."[6]

The summer of 1860 was an awkward time for enslavers to visit any free states. It was a presidential election year, and the future of slavery in the country overshadowed all other campaign issues. At its national convention, the proslavery Democratic Party divided over the issue of territorial slavery. One faction called for slavery's legality in all territories, but another faction preferred that each territory's residents vote on whether to legalize the practice. In contrast, the Republican Party, which opposed slavery's expansion beyond slave states, easily chose former congressman Abraham Lincoln of Illinois as its nominee. As the Democrats struggled over the summer to nominate a unifying candidate, Republicans expressed giddy optimism in Lincoln's chances of winning the presidential election that fall.[7]

In this climate, the Christmases dared to illegally extend their practice of enslavement into the North for the summer. Moreover,

Minnesotans had elected a Republican governor the previous fall. Multiple southerners in federal offices in the state resigned from their positions in protest and returned to the South, preferring to lose their livelihoods instead of sharing the state with a Republican. However, for the Christmases, medicine had no political affiliation. They were going to a Republican free state solely to bring Mary to the celebrated healing power of the falls, and she wanted her trusted unfree servant by her side.[8]

Eliza may have had high personal value to Mary because of the wisdom and experience that came from serving the same household for seven years, but Eliza's monetary value was falling because of her advancing age. By selecting her for the trip to Minnesota, the Christmases did not risk losing any of their highest-value young adult captives. At forty-three years old in 1860, Eliza's prospects of childbearing were faint and growing dimmer. The absence of "mulatto" children born at Shiloh during the previous seven years suggested that neither Christmas nor any overseer habitually forced himself on any of the estate's enslaved women. However, Eliza refused to marry a fellow captive or start a family with one, and the absence of evidence of her fertility in recent years also contributed to her decline in monetary value. "Col. Christmas would not let me marry any one but one of his plantation hands," she recalled. Having previously wed a free African American person, Eliza knew: "It would be worse for me if I married a slave."[9]

Minnesota was potentially just another place for Eliza to serve the family without enjoying much contact from others. She may have recognized the name of the falls because of John McLemore's federal appointment on the Upper Mississippi, but he had vacated that position over ten years earlier. At first glance the Christmases' trip did not appear to benefit her.

Eliza's enslavers, however, gave her the incentive she had long awaited. Norma's seventh birthday fell on July 6, during their planned time away from Shiloh, and they vowed to free Eliza upon that milestone. It is easy to imagine the joy Eliza must have felt after having worked for her own freedom for so many years.

It was also an unusual vow for the Christmases to make, because Mississippians rarely freed their captives in 1860. The market for unfree labor remained high, and there was too much money to be made by selling people off a plantation instead of freeing them from it. Also, enslavers had to remove their laborers from Mississippi before freeing them, because the state banned manumission in the 1850s. Therefore, Eliza could not become manumitted unless she left Mississippi with them.[10]

When Eliza packed for the trip, her friends helped to prepare her for freedom. They bought or made many articles of clothing and gifted them to her. She had also received clothing from her late husband's friends when she was in Memphis. In the antebellum era, free African Americans in cities across the country purchased clothes in stores, and some enslavers permitted their captives to do so. By building a new wardrobe, Eliza gained yet another aspect of autonomy: she was choosing how she wanted to look in her potential freedom.[11]

She treasured the clothing she received. Years later she recalled, "My colored friends gave me some good clothing." The "good" quality of the clothes implied that they were among the best articles the friends had owned. The clothing was probably significantly different in appearance and quality from her usual wardrobe. Free African Americans used their clothes as a political statement, distancing themselves from slavery by dressing as dissimilarly from enslaved people as possible. They chose formal and genteel attire to symbolize that they deserved to be as free as the European Americans who typically wore such clothing. Such apparel contrasted with the clothes enslavers annually allotted to their laborers strictly for the purposes of performing labor.[12]

The clothes were also a source of wealth, given as gifts and thus her own. Many enslaved people took clothes from their enslavers when constructing their liberation through their wardrobe, but they had to be far from anyone who would recognize who had first worn those clothes. In contrast, Eliza's new clothes symbolized her independence.[13]

Eliza would have been proud to pack a wardrobe that did not include any clothes from the Christmases. She planned a clean break from slavery—and from European Americans in general—through her clothing; as a free woman, she would possess only what came from herself. She later claimed that she herself purchased clothes for the trip. Her choosing of clothes for the voyage constituted one of the few acts the Christmases did not influence while enslaving her. She estimated that her trunk contained enough clothes to last through the first two years of her freedom. According to one report, she packed "bandanna handkerchiefs, cotton petticoats, calico gowns, [and a] straw bonnet."[14]

The day of departure from Shiloh for Minnesota arrived, probably at the end of June. Henry Christmas—the colonel's young adult son from his first marriage—did not go, and Eliza's later recollections of caring for only Mary and Norma suggest that the junior Richard stayed behind with another nursing enslaved woman. Because of Shiloh Landing's location by the Mississippi River, Colonel Christmas, Mrs. Christmas, Norma, and Eliza did not have to travel far to board a passenger steamboat However, the vessel they boarded did not carry them all the way to Minnesota. Northbound boats from the Deep South sailed no farther than St. Louis, because that was the last stop in a slave state. Slaveholders had rented out many of the captives to work as deckhands and cabin servants, and those laborers remained enslaved as long as the boats sailed along slave states. In St. Louis, Eliza and the other passengers were to leave the boat and board a northbound vessel destined for Minnesota.[15]

The first northbound boat offered few surprises for Eliza, who by 1860 had taken multiple steamboat trips within the Deep South. She was accustomed to following her captors up past the enslaved deckhands to the cabin level, where free and enslaved

African Americans tended to wait on passengers. After 11:00 PM European American passengers retired to their beds. African American captives of passengers slept on the floor of either the servants' quarters or a parlor room, the cabin servants brought their cots onto the cabin floors, and deckhands slept on the deck among the cargo.[16]

On the boat Eliza was part of a temporary collection of African Americans, but her work as Mary's personal attendant kept her from much interaction with them. Then again, on steamboats all the slaveholding passengers kept their captives close to them. Isolation prevented the enslaved from commiserating with others who shared their predicament. The absence of community shaped antebellum African American steamboat travel.

There was an exception: musical performances. As with the performative nature of labor at Hamilton Place, the employees at the cabin level usually provided nightly entertainment. Each evening, from eight to ten, some of the "cabin boys" retrieved their violins, broke into song, and danced to the music. But these interactions were fleeting. Musicians at Hamilton Place worked together for years with little turnover, because the Polks rarely sold people. The plantation's laborers familiarized themselves with each other's musical capabilities, and they catered to their enslavers' musical tastes. In contrast, however well the cabin servants fraternized aboard the steamboat, they were together only for the weeklong duration of the trip.

European American female travelers in a family shared a room and allowed accompanying servants, enslaved or free, to sleep there on the floor, and Mary and Norma likely did the same for Eliza every night of the trip. Mary's illness aboard the boat made Eliza's presence at her side especially important. However, at forty-three years old, the enslaved woman had passed her peak in physical health. Although she was used to sleeping on floors, she had not slept for longer than one week above a river that jostled her body from side to side across the vessel floor. This trip demanded such discomfort from her and for twice the length of time. Still, she endured the disrupted nights for the sake of becoming free.[17]

Boats at that time took about three days to sail from Tallula to Memphis. The first two days were the most monotonous. They began and ended with Eliza attending to the Christmas ladies in their room, located on the side of the boat for women passengers. Meanwhile, the boat passed by plantation after plantation and their endless cotton fields and magnolias. During the daily dining hours, Eliza and the other African Americans aboard waited until all the European Americans finished their meals in the dining room. Then, when the room was empty, the African Americans ate the food that remained. Despite the demeaning treatment, the segregation allowed Eliza to enjoy a rare moment away from her enslavers during her waking hours.[18]

On the third day of the trip, the boat sailed completely out of Mississippi, out of the Deep South, and that evening the vessel stopped at Memphis. Eliza was too far from the plantation Villa Rose to see it from the boat. She could only have imagined how her virtual siblings Malinda and Julius looked as adults in their mid-thirties, how her nephews had grown into adolescence, and how many more nieces and nephews had been born after the Christmases acquired her. First Presbyterian Church, however, lay only a couple of streets away from the riverfront. She was within walking distance of the place where she had first experienced a limited amount of freedom. Nevertheless, the gravely ill Mary needed her, and Eliza stayed with her in order to be manumitted by her.

The boat left Memphis and sailed for three more days, passing the free city of Cairo, Illinois, where the Ohio River flowed into the Mississippi from the east. Eliza had previously sailed up the Ohio from here to Louisville. This time, however, Eliza stayed on the Mississippi and sailed farther north.[19]

On the morning of July 6, Eliza woke up enslaved. Although

two days had passed since the Fourth of July, Eliza's true Independence Day was to be July 6, the day her captors had promised to manumit her. She merely needed to wait for them to do so, and the vessel's destination at St. Louis was the first opportunity for them to fulfill their vow. The boat was either approaching St. Louis or already there on Norma's birthday.[20]

Ultimately July 6 turned out to be just another full day of forced labor instead of freedom for Eliza. She remained enslaved by the Christmases as Norma's seventh birthday ended. The captive consoled herself after the fact by recalling how little faith she had put in her captors' word. "I had not much confidence that they would keep their promise," she said years later, "for my mistress has always been feeble and she would not be willing to let me go." However, Eliza's actions in preparation for the trip showed she had enough faith to invest her meager finances in clothing for her to wear after manumission. Moreover, she had believed her enslavers enough to pack a trunk with her liberation in mind. The Christmases' broken promise instead left her with a two-year wardrobe but no occasion to wear it—nor any evident possibility of needing it within the next two years.[21]

Did the Christmases intentionally lie to Eliza? Or did they change their minds in the moment, seeing how badly Mary needed her work? Did they dangle another promise of eventual freedom? Whatever happened, it is also easy to imagine Eliza's fury and disappointment.

Panoramic view of St. Louis, 1855. *Leopold Gast and Brother, Library of Congress*

The boat reached its final stop at St. Louis in the slave state of Missouri, placing Eliza in a major slave market. As she and her enslavers exited a vessel from the Deep South, slave traders on the dock directed their enslaved people aboard steamboats destined for that region. As in New Orleans, St. Louis's streets hosted slave pens and auction blocks, and slave coffles marched on the docks and in the streets. Although Eliza expected her manumission in St. Louis, she had to make sure not to agitate her enslavers on the matter. After all, they could easily sell her to a trader and buy another person, just as they had bought her in New Orleans. She was legally vulnerable to ending up in a coffle or a pen and on a block, with brokers oiling her skin and plucking out the body hairs they considered excessive or unsightly.[22]

Missouri was one of the few slave states that permitted manumission in 1860, but it did not allow people freed within its borders to remain in the state. They did not have to immigrate across the Atlantic Ocean to Liberia after acquiring freedom, as in Tennessee, but they had to move to a state where their presence was legal. Then again, Eliza did not want to reside in Missouri. She mistakenly believed she still owned real estate in Memphis, and she wanted to return there. But first her enslavers had to free her.[23]

Instead of taking her to the local courthouse to free her, the Christmases brought her aboard another boat so they could continue sailing northwest to Minnesota. St. Louis's "Daily Packet of

Northern Line Steamers" offered "increased facilities." To apply
to board from St. Louis, people went to either the wharf-boat at
the foot of Locust Street or the Northern Line Packet Office at
67 Commercial Street. Boats sailing for St. Paul left St. Louis
each day in the late afternoon—at either 4:00 PM or 5:00 PM,
depending on the vessel. The Christmases and Eliza entered one
such vessel in time for the evening departure, and the sun began
to set—not only on that day but also on Eliza's hope to have been
freed in St. Louis.[24]

This steamboat was different from the others on which Eliza
had traveled. Enslavers filled this boat as with the previous one,
and some of them were sickly. Not all the slaveholding passengers
hailed from slave states along the Mississippi River. Some of the
passengers had reached St. Louis earlier on boats from points
eastward, especially along the Ohio River. Thus, Eliza sailed with
captors and captives from Kentucky and as far away as the Car-
olinas. The twangs of the Upper South, the drawls of the Deep
South, and the French influence of New Orleans all rang out
aboard the vessel.

Nearly all the employees aboard vessels on northern waters
were European Americans—from the officers down to the waiters
and crewmen. When boarding the Minnesota-bound boat, the
deckhands Eliza passed on her way to her captors' cabin looked
like her enslavers. On the cabin level, she crossed paths with
European Americans at the ready to serve the Christmases.
When the Gholsons had given her agency to move about Memphis on her own, she likely encountered working-class European
Americans while passing through the city streets. However, this
second northbound boat placed her in a closed setting in very
close proximity to poor and working-class European Americans,
especially those who performed domestic labor similar to hers.
This was a source of conflict and competition: the poor whites
competed with free African Americans for jobs, while looking
down on them.

The few free African American employees on Upper Mississippi steamboats worked as stewards, cooks, cabin boys, and chambermaids. Only twenty-seven of 221 African American ship employees residing in St. Louis were deck firemen. No African Americans were on thirty-seven of the city's ninety-three boats in 1850.[25]

Northern steamboats separated people in ways besides skin color. On northern vessels, the passengers and the officers ate together. After they left the dining room, African American enslaved people ate with the ship's waiters and crew. Moreover, the ship's employees ate the same foods that Eliza and the other captives did. Therefore, the boat's social hierarchy placed her low because of color but equitable to some European Americans because of their employment.[26]

The quartering of the enslaved remained consistent between southern and northern vessels. Eliza probably slept on the floor of her enslavers' room each night on the Minnesota-bound boat. The refusal of her captors to manumit her in St. Louis must have lodged deep in her memory, and the sting of the broken vow tainted the remainder of her enslavement to them. But, at least for the time being, she restrained herself from raising the issue so as not to jeopardize another possible opportunity for them to keep their word.[27]

Meanwhile, the vessel took Eliza farther north than she had ever been. The boat sailed past Missouri on the west, and free states lay on both sides of the vessel from that moment onward. Illinois soon greeted Eliza to the east of the river, and Iowa sat to the west. No matter how much farther north the vessel carried her, each stop for the rest of the journey gave her de jure freedom. She ceased to be a legal captive, because her enslavers voluntarily brought her to states that prohibited slavery.

The Mississippi River itself was different. In the South, Eliza passed by sweeping riverside plantations growing cotton, sugarcane, and rice. Enslaved African Americans there rowed small rafts beside the steamboat, delivering materials to neighboring homes. In the North, greenery and forests still bordered the river, but they did not emerge from red, clay-like soil like that of the Cotton Belt.

Two days after leaving St. Louis, the boat stopped at Dubuque, Iowa. It was a city of thirteen thousand people, but only about four dozen of them were African Americans. European Americans poured into the vessel, but no new enslaved people walked aboard. As a result, the steamboat's percentage of people resembling Eliza's enslavers grew, and the proportion of African Americans shrank. Those demographic trends continued for the rest of the trip northward.

After departing Dubuque, the boat traveled for over 250 miles—usually a three-day journey. For the remainder of the trip, small villages lay along the river's margins. At least one threshing machine and other farming equipment were in evidence at each subsequent stop past Dubuque. Eliza felt the vessel maneuver around the multiple little islands in the Upper Mississippi. One fellow passenger complained that, because of those islands, "at no place can both shores be seen at one time until Lake Pepin is reached." They cleared the islands when reaching the lake. "The river is very low now," wrote the passenger, "and the boat was continually getting aground as we proceeded up."[28]

The boat's occupants ate whatever foods the crew members could acquire while sailing upriver. Much of their diet consisted of creatures of the water—but not the catfish that swam in abundance down South. Instead, Eliza ate local fish like walleye and crappie. At the northern stops, the crewmen also acquired multiple lambs and roaster pigs to prepare and serve to the passengers.[29]

During the third day beyond Dubuque, the vessel sailed past Iowa, reaching Minnesota. While traversing the 140 miles from La Crosse, Wisconsin, to St. Paul, Minnesota, the steamboat steered around more islands, and the river expanded beyond its

The front entrance to the Winslow House, 1860. *William H. Jacoby, MNHS*

usual width. When the vessel reached the town of Hastings, the state of Minnesota lay on both sides of the river. At that point Eliza was just twenty miles away from St. Paul.[30]

Eliza was used to river cities like Memphis and Louisville, but St. Paul must have seemed very crude to her as a much newer and smaller city. She disembarked with her enslavers, finally in a free state for an extended period. Her captors merely needed to find a local government building and inform an official of their wish to manumit her. As the capital of Minnesota, St. Paul had the most government facilities in the state. Buildings for the legislature, the governor, and judges were at the couple's disposal.

But the Christmases did not free Eliza. Instead, they took her with them to a stage line that three times daily traveled the eleven miles between St. Paul, the head of practical navigation on the Mississippi, and St. Anthony, the new city on the east bank of the river at the Falls of St. Anthony. Eliza and her enslavers rode together in the coach for an hour, following a road cut into the prairie by the military. The vehicle finally approached a six-story hotel—the Winslow House. The palace of blue hewn limestone was only four years old; its builders had quarried the stone from the neighboring bluffs. The building's riverfront lay on Prince Street, the rear on Bank Street, and the sides on Second and Cross Streets.[31]

The passengers exited the coach and entered the building. Richard Christmas registered his party on July 12, 1860, noting himself by name but identifying the others as "wife, child and nurse." Male heads of families at that hotel and others commonly listed family members by relationship and captives by their labor skills. The anonymous identification of Eliza as "nurse" was not unlike her listing by age, gender, and color in the previous month's US census.[32]

For the next few weeks, Eliza and the other enslaved people at the Winslow labored in selective anonymity. The locals and guests may not have known Eliza's name, but they knew who enslaved her: she was the Christmases' servant girl or the Christmases' nurse. Because she was the only captive the Christmases brought, her status as their possession sufficed for her identification. Before the end of the summer, however, she would meet someone who wanted to know her beyond her labor, become acquainted with her, and learn about her feelings and thoughts.

The Winslow House, 1860. *MNHS*

≋ 6

The Hotel and
the Seamstress

A tourist in St. Anthony in the summer of 1860 remarked, "There is more wealth congregated at the Winslow at this time than at any other house in the country. Many families from the South make this their home for the Summer, and several of these families have been pointed out to me as *millionaires*." The six-story Winslow House was probably Minnesota's most elite hotel. At the time, the average charge for a night at a hotel in Minnesota was fifty cents. The Winslow charged guests four times that—but it offered much more splendor and comfort than its competitors.[1]

Because its staff protected enslavers from antislavery laws, the Winslow House also became an extralegal haven for wealthy southern tourists like the Christmases. After the Dred Scot decision in 1857, slavery was briefly legal in Minnesota Territory—but when Minnesota became a state in May 1858, it was not. The Panic of 1857 increased the economic struggles in the territory, making its people even more dependent on income from tourism. But the failure of two state bills that would have legalized slavery for tourists in March 1860 reflected the population's general opposition to the practice.

Nonetheless, hotel proprietor Christopher Woodbridge McLean attracted southerners to the hotel by advertising his business in southern newspapers. Having resided in St. Louis from 1853 to 1854, he knew firsthand about the South's slaveholding culture. Also, he was a Democrat, and he agreed with his party's support of slavery's expansion throughout the country. As a tourist from South Carolina bluntly put it, "McLean is no Black Republican."[2]

McLean's hotel greatly resembled the Virginia Hotel, where he had resided in St. Louis. Located on Main Street, the Virginia stood six stories high, and it measured 120 feet by 320 feet. It housed up to four hundred guests, and about 130 enslaved people were usually on hand to meet the visitors' needs. The Winslow contained and employed fewer people, but St. Anthony as a free city did not attract as many enslavers as St. Louis did.[3]

The hotel was palatial. It had "200 elegantly furnished rooms, with pipes of cold and hot water for the comfort of guests." Gentlemen and ladies mingled away from each other in gender-specific parlors. Guests entertained themselves in rooms for reading, billiards, and balls. The guest bedrooms, water closets, and bathrooms were on only the upper four floors. European American guests ate in the main floor's dining room, which contained two room-length tables seating one hundred people altogether. A musical band performed in the dining room during the meal.[4]

Many of the Winslow's southern guests were mixing business with pleasure. In 1851 territorial leaders had forced the Dakota people to sign treaties ceding the southern half of the state, and European Americans flooded into the territory to speculate in land and make investments. The town of St. Anthony was incorporated in 1855; the town of Minneapolis, across the river, was incorporated a year later. (They merged in 1872.) For over a decade, southerners had come to the Northwest for temporary stays without having to worry about freeing their captives, because the federal government welcomed their investments in the land. Some of the permanent settlers who began arriving in the 1850s developed business partnerships with the enslavers. The settlers physically altered the environment with funding from enslavers but without the permanent physical presence of the slaveholders' captives.[5]

St. Anthony constantly had something under construction, and each new structure made the area less rural and less untouched. It was slowly but surely becoming a *city*, and tourists opposed the changes. A visitor from Louisiana considered the environment "ruined by Yankee enterprise." He complained, "Mills, foundries, dams and lumber rafts have spoilt all of nature's romantic loveliness by their innovations, and you would be astonished to see the hundreds of houses recently erected here." And then he bitterly chided the typical new Minnesotan: "If he could, he would convert the Garden of Eden into a barley field or indigo farm, and saw up the 'tree of life' to make clapboards."[6]

The opulence of the Winslow House had hardly any relevance to Eliza's new life in the North. While the Christmases and other enslavers basked in the hotel's extravagance, their captives were too busy to appreciate the beauty of the building. The Winslow, for its enslaved people, was little more than an elite prison. Eliza's isolation aboard the steamboats continued at the hotel, where she spent most of each day in her enslavers' room, caring for Mary and Norma.

Except for the indoor plumbing, Eliza did not receive the same amenities as the European American guests because of her skin color. When free African Americans first arrived in St. Anthony in the late 1850s, they could not immediately secure shelter in the city. The Winslow quartered them in the basement until they found homes for themselves in town. Because the hotel did not

The Winslow House towers over other buildings in St. Anthony in this view taken from Minneapolis in 1860. Logs escaping the lumber mills damaged the limestone cap that forms the falls, furthering erosion and clogging the riverbed. *MNHS*

provide separate rooms for the enslaved, they slept either in the basement or with their captors. Eliza likely slept in the Christmas ladies' room.[7]

The Winslow's enslaved guests probably spent much of their downtime during the summer of 1860 in the basement. During the daytime, under its ten-foot ceilings, the hotel's physical plant bustled. A local African American operated a barbershop, and another part of the basement functioned as the St. Anthony post office. Along the front and sides of the hotel were a stage office, an office for arranging travel by boat or train, a grocery store, a saloon, and a storage room. A steam engine of fifteen horsepower heated the entire hotel and distributed water to all the floors. The bakery, the kitchen, and separate rooms for washing, drying, and ironing clothes all lay in the rear of the hotel. The cooks prepared the food there, and Eliza and others laundered clothes for their enslavers in that space.[8]

The rooms in the basement's rear were especially important for Eliza and the other African Americans. A door to each of those rooms opened from the back of the hotel on Bank Street. The employees working in those rooms entered and exited the hotel from them instead of via the front entrance, and African Americans staying in the basement probably did the same. Unless Mary Christmas insisted on her enslaved servant's constant presence near her, Eliza did not enter and leave the Winslow from the front door with her. Rather, the captive exited through the rear basement to meet the enslaver at the front for departures together; and, upon their returns to the hotel, the servant left her out front, retreated to the rear basement door, and climbed the steps to reunite with her in their room.[9]

Each time that servants and African Americans entered and exited the rear of the Winslow's basement, they waded through a steamy haze of combined odors. The emissions from the boiler, the soap from the laundry, and the foods from the kitchen and bakery wove into each other as they rose to the ceiling of the basement, never to reach beyond the hotel's subterranean depths to the wealthy patrons above. Of all the hotel occupants, the servants and African Americans spent the most time at the basement rear and consequently suffered the most exposure to the haze. The combined aroma of soap, baked bread, and cooked meat was the smell of urban service at the hotel.

There were some reminders at the Winslow that the enslavers were not in the South anymore. The Winslow, like the northern steamboats, employed European Americans; moreover, they were the *only* employees at the hotel. Irish immigrants comprised most of the live-in staff, and they worked in the kitchen, served the meals, cleaned the facility, and waited on guests. Service labor was largely the only kind of work offered to them in St. Anthony at the time. Indeed, most of the Irish immigrants in the city in 1860 listed their occupation as either "labourer" or "servant."[10]

The hotel also mirrored the northern steamboats in distinguishing occupants by class. All servants at the Winslow, regardless of their color, dined in the hotel kitchen in the basement, but they ate the same food as that of the European American guests. The restriction of dining accommodations to the kitchen for enslaved people and servants was a common practice among hotels in the antebellum North. When in the company of European Americans, Eliza had known no other arrangement.[11]

The Winslow probably provided healthier meals for Eliza than the fats and starches on plantations in Mississippi. Turkeys and deer roaming nearby one moment appeared soon afterward on dinner plates throughout Minnesota. Many of the state's hotels offered stews to patrons, and plum pudding was a common dessert. Guests of the Winslow ate such dishes as baked pike, roast veal, roast lamb, and boiled corned beef. The hotel's cooks were British, German, Irish, and Swedish, and they applied European ingredients to the meals they prepared.[12]

With European Americans cooking the food at the Winslow, Eliza's time at the hotel was the longest extended period in which African Americans played no role in preparing her food. She was accustomed to whatever flavors, spices, and other culinary touches she and her fellow captives had placed in the meals in Tennessee and Mississippi. In the latter state, especially, enslaved people made cornbread and other delicacies via cornmeal batter, and they added fried pig skin to bread. In Minnesota Eliza's palate must have experienced significant culture shock.[13]

Some European American servants took offense to the hotel's placement of them among African Americans, because the arrangement suggested social equity. Nevertheless, they needed the work and had to tolerate the company of the enslaved. The hotel kitchen marked perhaps the first time Eliza closely encountered European Americans who resented her presence among them *because of* her enslavement.[14]

Meanwhile, guests continued to arrive. The Prince family of

Mississippi registered at the Winslow, trying to escape from some recent local infamy. Martha Prince, her three children, and her three enslaved servants had arrived in Minnesota one month earlier, and they initially stayed at the International Hotel in St. Paul. Henry Sparks—one of her captives—escaped from the family, with the intention of marrying a local free African American woman employee of the International Hotel, but European Americans found him and sent him on a riverboat back to the South. The Princes' troubles gained statewide attention when the governor angrily demanded to know who sent Sparks away from Minnesota into slavery. To salvage the rest of the vacation, the Princes took the remaining two captives with them out of St. Paul and up to St. Anthony. "We learned that the fugitive from the International Hotel was found at a public house a short distance out of St. Paul," a local newspaper reported. "He was arrested by the Deputy US Marshall."[15]

The ways in which Prince exercised her power over her enslaved servants differed from how Eliza's past and present enslavers treated her. Prince brought only her male captives with her to Minnesota; unlike Mrs. Christmas, Prince did not need to have the constant company of enslaved women. Also, Prince had brought three captives with her to Minnesota. Most of the other enslavers who came to the Northwest for vacations did not register more than two enslaved people with them on the steamboats and at the hotels, and Eliza was used to traveling as her captors' sole enslaved person. Moreover, the Christmases chose to isolate Eliza in Minnesota by taking only her from among Shiloh's enslaved people.

After Sparks's return to the South, Prince's two remaining enslaved servants brought to the Winslow their perspectives on the failed escape of their fellow captive. They likely shared their stories with Eliza and other African Americans in the hotel basement or directly outside the hotel at the rear. Those two areas were important places for communication among the facility's

African Americans—part of St. Anthony's grapevine. In the antebellum South, enslaved people communicated information to
each other through complex networks from plantation to plantation, without their captors' knowledge. Any important news the
Winslow's enslaved visitors learned from having overheard conversations among enslavers, locals, and fellow captives probably
found its way to the ears of the enslaved attendees of the twice-
daily meals in the basement kitchen.[16]

The grapevine also distributed ideas about liberation to people who may have been unaccustomed to conversations about
escapes. Any information Eliza heard about Sparks allowed
her to learn about someone who shared her desire to seek freedom in Minnesota. She may have heard details that showed her
what steps to avoid when developing her own plan for freedom.
Sparks's actions demonstrated that making such an attempt was
at least possible. No one at the Winslow told Eliza how to successfully become free in the state, because no enslaved person
had yet accomplished that feat.

There were other probable topics for discussion among the
hotel's enslaved guests besides ideas for liberation. They likely
told stories to each other about the homes they had left behind,
the loved ones they missed, and the overseers they did not miss.
Perhaps they shared common feelings of surprise over the coolness of the local summer climate. Socializing in or near the hotel
kitchen may have sparked a conversation about that day's supper
and how different it tasted from the spicy foods they enjoyed in
their slave communities down south. Eliza and the Sparks men
may have compared their experiences about life in Mississippi.

The hotel's mandated times and places for skin-color segregation guaranteed that the enslaved received some respite from their
enslavers. The Winslow offered breakfast and an afternoon dinner
for guests; Eliza separated from the Christmases whenever they
ate with other European American guests in the hotel's dining
room. The hotel had gathering rooms like parlors and saloons for

the European American guests but not their enslaved servants. Thus, the captives had to relax in the basement, or tend to laundry, whenever their captors ate and socialized with one another.[17]

One day during her first week in St. Anthony, Eliza received another opportunity for solitude, and Mary Christmas herself initiated the separation. Her frock required mending, and she told Eliza to go into town with it and have a seamstress repair it. Eliza complied. Traveling without her captors, she probably walked to the basement floor and waded through the soap- and food-scented rooms to leave through the rear door.[18]

She likely overheard European immigrants conversing in various tongues during her passage through St. Anthony. Having spent much of her enslaved life in cities, she was accustomed to hearing a cacophony of European languages in public urban areas. On the other hand, the European ethnic demographics differed in St. Anthony. Four hundred people from Germany and an equal number from Ireland, about one-fourth of the local population, resided in the city that year. Nearly all the city's remaining residents were people of European descent but born in the United States. As a result, the English language overwhelmed other languages in St. Anthony more than in New Orleans, where French remained prominent.

Despite the similar numbers of German and Irish people in St. Anthony, more of the former than the latter owned and operated businesses there and in Hennepin County at large. Some German immigrants catered to local tourism outside of the hotels. In 1860 seven people in the county worked as "saloon keepers," offering such liquor as Hermitage and Old Crow to weary southern travelers. Of those seven barkeepers, only one was Irish; the rest had come from Germany.[19]

Moreover, Eliza was surrounded by southerners only when inside the Winslow. Among all the city's permanent residents as of that summer, about sixty were born in the South. Most of the southern-born residents were children, born either to midwestern migrants or European immigrants. The only Louisiana-born resident was a six-year-old daughter of German immigrants. Only one citizen—a European American woman in her early twenties—came from Andrew Jackson's home state of Tennessee. In addition, none of the townspeople were born in Florida, Georgia, Kentucky, or Mississippi.[20]

As a result, barely any of St. Anthony's citizens knew first-hand about the region whose oppressive culture and lifestyle they enabled and appropriated at the expense of people like Eliza. The residents passively took their cues from the tourists who fed them. If southerners said that interfering in the enslaver–enslaved relationships they brought to St. Anthony was untoward, who were the locals to argue? After all, the townspeople did not own anyone and could not speak authoritatively to their financially powerful guests on the matter. Eliza was in one of the worst free places to be illegally enslaved—a community that needed the patronage of its violators.

The open, public presence of enslaved people in St. Anthony was also part of the culture of southern cities Eliza had seen. Enslavers walked the streets with their captives. Years later a local journalist identified the typical antebellum tourists in town as "stately, moneyed Southerners, in many cases with their colored retinues."[21]

On the other hand, a closer look at slavery in St. Anthony revealed differences from southern urban slavery. No slave patrols walked the city streets to check for enslaved fugitives, and there were no slave pens or auctions or coffles. The city did not provide whipping posts for enslavers to publicly lash their captives. The absence of these items reflected Minnesota's legal status as a free state, and it supported the viewpoint of local supporters of slavery that the practice in Minnesota was solely a private matter between captor and captive. Moreover, none of the people who enslaved anyone in St. Anthony resided there, nor did any of the enslaved.

The local free African Americans and the visiting enslaved African Americans barely fraternized in St. Anthony. Unlike Memphis and Louisville, St. Anthony did not have a town square in which the enslaved socialized with European Americans and free African Americans. The tourists kept their captives near them and tended to go only to businesses in town that served them without confrontation. They exposed their practice of slavery only to the local elites who hosted them at the Winslow or to the immigrants who fed them or made their drinks. Consequently, enslaved African Americans had limited if any exposure to local African Americans and abolitionists—anyone who could tell them about living in freedom in St. Anthony.

Likewise, the eight African American families living in St. Anthony at the time had little in common with the enslaved visitors. The African American adult residents were freeborn, and they came from either New England or the Midwest. They had never experienced slavery and therefore could not relate to how captives like Eliza suffered from the control of their captors. Local African Americans avoided confronting European Americans, especially those enslaving African Americans. Moreover, their freedom in Minnesota did not totally protect them from possible enslavement, for during this time European Americans frequently kidnapped African Americans in free states (usually border states) and then sent them down the Mississippi into slavery.[22]

Very few of St. Anthony's European American visitors and residents bothered to distinguish the free African American residents from the enslaved visitors. Such thinking was not unique to the city, for Democrats throughout Minnesota tended to think that every African American within the state's borders had escaped from slavery in the South. Because of tourism, St. Anthony's captives well outnumbered the city's free African American residents for at least six months out of each year. European Americans walking the streets were more likely to see an enslaved guest than a free African American. As a result, as far as most European

Americans there were concerned, every African American they saw was enslaved—even the free ones.[23]

As Eliza descended from the Winslow's plateau to reach the seamstress's facility, she had every reason to assume that every African American along the way shared her situation of captivity. She was in a free northern city, but there were fewer free African Americans out in public in St. Anthony than in Memphis or New Orleans. It was as if the Christmases had brought rural Issaquena County with them to urban Hennepin County.

However, Eliza had a surprise when she entered the seamstress's shop. The proprietor was a tall African American woman. She had light skin, blue eyes, and freckles on her nose. Emily Goodridge Grey stood in her shop without any European Americans surrounding her or commanding her. Born in 1834, she was as old as Mary Christmas, young enough to be Eliza's daughter. The free African American woman took the dress and began working on it.

Both women were Christians, and they had worshiped in the Presbyterian denomination. In addition, Grey received her education in a Presbyterian school. She was the kind of free African American woman Eliza had encountered during her years at First Presbyterian Church in Memphis. They both may have agreed with the church's stance against dancing and disagreed with its refusal to condemn slavery.[24]

Grey was only one generation removed from slavery. Her father, William Goodridge, was born enslaved in Baltimore in 1806. His mother was enslaved, and his father was a European American man. At age five Goodridge became a minister's apprentice in York, Pennsylvania. The minister taught him to read and, in 1822, freed him. He lived there in the first four decades after his manumission, and he raised Grey and her six siblings there. Still, without firsthand experience of slavery, Grey herself could only empathize with Eliza's enslavement, drawing from whatever memories her father had shared about his own captivity.[25]

On the other hand, Eliza had little frame of reference for the wealth Grey enjoyed as a second-generation free person. By 1824 Grey's father owned and operated a barbershop in York. He also possessed thousands of dollars in real estate. Eliza knew of her parents only as enslaved, and they owned nothing to pass down to her. Grey was twenty-six years old in 1860 and running her own business, whereas Eliza at that age had just become the property of Kate McLemore Gholson in Memphis. Eliza had tried to own real estate in Memphis but lost it because of her captivity. In addition, she certainly did not know about being self-employed or running a business.[26]

At the plantation Shiloh, Eliza was isolated from anyone who might have had connections to the Underground Railroad or any abolitionists in Tallula, Mississippi. In contrast, Grey's parents raised her in the abolition movement. Goodridge helped enslaved fugitives through the local stops of the Underground Railroad. During Grey's early childhood, the Goodridges had once quartered a fugitive in their house. By 1850, when Grey was a teenager, her father began openly calling for abolition.[27]

As an adult Grey familiarized herself with her parents' cause. She became acquainted with local people who felt as she did about abolition. However, such people were few and far between, especially in St. Anthony. She complained that people were "never aroused except when the sinfulness of slavery was exposed, its patrons characterized as moral lepers, or their livelihood in any way placed in jeopardy by awakening the conscience of the nation." She had a point, because so many of her fellow townspeople needed money from tourists for survival. Her own home was directly behind a hotel.[28]

Despite her skin color, Grey enjoyed some of what Mary Christmas did and what Eliza wanted: a husband, children, and a home. Grey had married her husband Ralph in the early 1850s, and their first child arrived in 1855. Ralph's barbershop was in the nearby Jarrett (later Tremont) House. Grey kept chickens in her own coop; she and her husband worked together in their garden each morning, tending beans, carrots, potatoes, and tomatoes. She also looked forward to enjoying apples from their own apple tree. In addition, Grey received an education and knew how to read and write. She had lived in St. Anthony for only three years when she met Eliza. Although Eliza became literate in Tennessee, she could not further educate herself in Mississippi without breaking the law.[29]

There was a slight difference in how the two women looked, because Grey was a "mulatto" according to that year's census. Her light skin color resembled the color of the free African Americans Eliza had just seen in New Orleans the previous winter. Moreover, because Grey was the first free African American

The Winslow House, at left, in 1858. The Upton Block, which housed a store selling hardware and groceries, is at center, and the Jarrett House, where Ralph Grey had a barbering business, is at right. The Jarrett became the Tremont House in 1859. *Benjamin Franklin Upton, MNHS*

whom Eliza had seen in town, St. Anthony appeared to have the same stratification according to color that characterized New Orleans. St. Anthony had an even more rigid hierarchy than New Orleans, because in 1860 the *only* African American residents of St. Anthony appeared in the census as "mulatto." Therefore, if any African Americans in town were "black" like Eliza, then they were captives of tourists.[30]

For all of Grey's success, she was not completely divorced from discrimination because of her skin color. One of the few experiences she shared with Eliza was steamboat travel to the Northwest as an African American woman. Grey later recalled that when she sailed to Minnesota in 1857 for the first time, she came with her firstborn child, her cousin, and her cousin's new wife. Because of her cousin's acquaintance with a steward of the boat, the group stayed in a stateroom. She noted that not everyone was so lucky. "There were some ladies compelled to occupy beds made upon the floor of the ladies' salon," she lamented.[31]

Grey and her husband established permanent residence in Minnesota. In September 1857 Ralph Grey purchased real estate in St. Anthony for one thousand dollars from a European American couple originally from Maine. In the process the Greys became some of the first African American landowners in Hennepin County—and in Minnesota, in general. At the time most cities and towns in the state had no African American residents at all, and the only African Americans living in other places in Minnesota were enslaved people. Two years later Emily bought land in her own name elsewhere in the county. Thus, the Greys' distinction as free African Americans with financial means set them apart from the state's African American population at large.[32]

Meeting Eliza was part of how Grey adjusted to living permanently in St. Anthony. She did her best to foster a sense of community among the city's African Americans. "Very soon after my arrival [to St. Anthony in 1857]," Grey wrote in a memoir, "I became acquainted with all the persons of color living in

St. Anthony." After three years in town, more free African Americans joined her in the city or across the Mississippi River in the city of Minneapolis. As time progressed, they became models for African American newcomers on how to adapt to and survive in St. Anthony.[33]

While at Grey's store, Eliza decided to confide in her. This was a rare opportunity for Eliza to meet with a local free African American without her enslavers, and she could not afford to assume that she would have another chance. She introduced herself to Grey as Eliza Winston. With that introduction, she claimed separation from the Christmases. Winston was the surname she chose for herself, and she divulged it to someone who understood the value of last names among African Americans.

The enslaved woman then revealed another significant secret to the seamstress, confessing, as Grey recalled, "that she wanted to be free and was held against her will." With those words she accused her enslaver of conducting criminal behavior. However, she merely wanted freedom—not revenge nor even full justice for herself.[34]

Grey likely did not need for Eliza to mention her enslavement. She knew her neighbors. The summer had begun, and new African Americans in town during that season tended to be captives of tourists. Also, Eliza did not look like St. Anthony's African American residents because of her darker skin. After Grey's lifetime of freedom and three years of getting to know the city's African American locals, she was familiar with how free people carried themselves.

The seamstress understood, based on Eliza's remarks, that her new acquaintance considered herself legally enslaved in the Northwest. At the very least, Grey knew that setting foot in a free state constituted freedom, because she had always been free in both Pennsylvania and Minnesota. Grey announced to Eliza, "You are free now, if I could persuade you to think so." With that declaration the seamstress simultaneously informed Eliza Winston of her legal status and tried to convince her to act on it by at least acknowledging it.[35]

Eliza probably did not need much convincing, as her friends in the South had already told her, and she had initiated the conversation about her enslavement. Rather, she needed to know how to become liberated on her own if she could not persuade her enslavers to acknowledge her legal freedom. The Christmases gave no signs that they were exploring the possibility of manumitting her in Minnesota.

Eliza mentioned wanting to return to Memphis and claim her estate there, and she asked Grey if any European American men in St. Anthony would help her acquire her freedom. She had known of only European American men having the power to buy, sell, or manumit enslaved African Americans. Despite her desire to declare her freedom on Minnesota soil, she knew that such a declaration had to be validated by European Americans. In the most practical sense, they were the only ones who could legally write her free papers. In addition, they were the lawyers and the judges who would participate in any case she brought to court.[36]

The failed escape attempt of Henry Sparks also provided context for Eliza's request for European American assistance. If European Americans were to assist Eliza, then no one could explain her quest for liberation as mere skin-color solidarity. Instead, her desire for freedom would carry some significance among local residents, because some of their own neighbors would support her cause—even if it meant the mass defections of wealthy clientele and a financial loss for St. Anthony.

Grey vowed to explore options for finding European Americans to help free Eliza. The conversation wound down shortly thereafter, and they parted. As Eliza ascended to the plateau where the Winslow lay, she literally and figuratively had an uphill climb ahead of her. It was certainly physically easier for her to travel down and talk to a free African American than to return up to the hotel and slavery. Also, although Eliza was brave in talking to a local about her enslavement, the hard work of planning and carrying out her freedom still awaited her.

> Eliza reached the plateau, reentered the Winslow, walked up the winding stairs, and went to Mary's room. Another day of serving her captors eventually ended, and Eliza slept among the enslavers' snores for yet another night. The Christmases had no reason to suspect that anything significant had happened to their faithful captive.
>
> However, Eliza *had* changed. For the first time in years, she had met a free African American person—and a woman, just like her. As Eliza processed the revelations of her conversation with her new acquaintance, she shifted her pursuit of freedom away from manumission and toward emancipation. She no longer depended on the Christmases to liberate her. Rather, she learned that she had indeed freed herself the moment she stepped with her enslavers onto the soil of a free state, and she had a new friend to help her fully realize her new legal liberation.

7

The Abolitionists

Eliza spent each day of the second half of July settling into her new routine of service at the hotel, while simultaneously awaiting the chance to disrupt that routine with her escape. But July transitioned into August without any additional correspondence from Emily Grey. Mary rarely sent Eliza on further errands outside of the hotel. Instead, the captive stayed with her and with Norma in the hotel room. On the trip to Minnesota, Eliza had been able to look forward to a specific day: July 6. Without additional communication with Grey, Eliza had no way of knowing which day at the Winslow would be her last day in captivity.

At the start of August, Richard Christmas had more to do in Minnesota in his spare time. The state's fishing season officially began, and the enslaver enjoyed the pastime. Locals and tourists flocked to the lakes near St. Anthony, trying their luck in the sport. Some tourists were not content with visiting the lakes for just the day. A periodical in St. Anthony noted, "Several parties have taken quarter at Lakes Harriet and Calhoun [now Bde Maka Ska] and are delighted with the entertainment which the waters and the prairie afford." Both lakes were about an hour's carriage ride from the hotel.[1]

Tourists in Minnesota visited multiple locations that lay minutes or hours away from each other, and they often stayed hours or days at a time in places away from their hotels. Guests in St. Paul might take a day trip to see St. Anthony Falls and Minnehaha Falls. Lodgers in St. Paul, St. Anthony, and Minneapolis went fishing in lakes away from the urban areas. Although some enslavers took their captives with them, others did not. It was a common practice for an enslaving tourist visiting a free state to lock the enslaved in the hotel room there, take a brief trip to another destination, and then retrieve the captives after returning to the hotel. If Eliza ever noticed during mealtimes that some enslaved servants did not appear for that day or for days at a time, they may have been incarcerated in their captors' hotel rooms.[2]

A few of Richard Christmas's acquaintances from Issaquena County, Mississippi, joined him in Minnesota at the Winslow House. William C. Smedes, Thomas Kershaw, and A. T. Burnley checked in at the hotel while the Christmases and Eliza were there. As people who formerly belonged to the Whig Party, Christmas and Burnley were the most likely enslavers to visit a free state. Unlike slaveholding Democrats, who refused to enter a northern state with a Republican governor, Whig enslavers were willing to believe northerners who promised to leave the captives alone. Like Christmas, Burnley had previously toured the Northwest. He had tuberculosis, and he traveled for his health's sake.[3]

Some chronically ill people traveled to St. Anthony with the intent to die while partaking of the beauty of the environment. Marmaduke Shannon, who published the *Vicksburg Whig* newspaper in Mississippi, brought his two daughters with him to the Winslow, because one of the girls—Mary Shannon—was severely ill. She succumbed there on July 29, and her survivors returned home to Vicksburg. Her demise was a reminder that Mary's survival was Eliza's best hope for freedom. If widowed, Richard would likely become even more reliant on Eliza to care for his children and thus be less likely to free her.[4]

When Mary was not isolating Eliza, the captive could have interacted with the enslaved people who accompanied the tourists from Issaquena County. Burnley, for example, brought one enslaved servant with him to St. Anthony. Burnley's captive offered Eliza a reminder of the enslaved population of Tallula. Such conversations may have been bittersweet, because a successful pursuit of freedom meant that she would never see her acquaintances from her home of the past seven years. Nevertheless, for the time being, she was in close proximity to someone who had a sense of how she felt as an Issaquena resident displaced in enslavement in the free North.[5]

Eliza and the others probably talked about how one of their own became entangled in the criminal justice system in ways that reinforced his legal freedom. Winslow guest John Matherson arranged for the arrest of his captive James E. Cochrane on August 8, because Cochrane had allegedly stolen some clothing from his captor. Cochrane faced arraignment that day, and the judge convicted him and sentenced him to pay twenty dollars and Matherson's court costs. He faced three months of incarceration if he defaulted on his payment. His conviction in St. Anthony showed the Winslow's captives that their captors enjoyed access to justice from St. Anthony's courts. On the other hand, the possibility for an African American to begin a three-month sentence in August meant the defendant would remain in Minnesota until November, two months after the year's tourism season was to end. The local courts appeared to treat African Americans as free people and ignore the enslaver–enslaved relationship to the point of extending a sentence past the duration of the enslaver's vacation.[6]

In another example of possible good fortune for Eliza, her captors took their vacation in a free state that had a dedicated abolitionist population. From the time Minnesota Territory was organized in 1849, a core group of people had made clear their beliefs that slavery was wrong. Ministers preached against it in missionary churches, and more people heard that message as they moved from the East Coast to the Northwest throughout the 1850s. Writers wrote antislavery essays, and editors established newspapers that publicized the atrocities associated with slavery and the efforts to end the practice.

Abolitionism took hold among some elite Minnesotans, because they had the financial means to promote it. Before they migrated to the state from the East Coast, they had lived in well-to-do families. They had moved to the West to add to their wealth in a new land. In that regard, they were no different than Eliza's first enslaver, Thomas Hopkins, who had migrated west from Virginia to Tennessee a half century earlier. Also, their wealth allowed them to afford to risk offending the Democrats and non-abolitionist Republicans who resided in Minnesota.[7]

On the other hand, none of the abolitionists served Eliza well during the first five weeks of her enslavement in Minnesota. To be sure, the activists were aware that enslaved people lodged with their captors in town. Abolitionists had gone multiple times to St. Paul to boo and hiss at southerners disembarking from the steamboats with their enslaved servants. They entered the lobbies of hotels the tourists patronized and monitored their activities from there. But whatever annoyance the behavior may have caused, it did not compel any of the guests to manumit their laborers.[8]

Moreover, despite the presence of abolitionists in St. Anthony for over a decade, they had only recently organized to actively oppose slavery. The Hennepin County Antislavery Society was just seven months old when Eliza arrived in July 1860. The society's pleas to Republican local officials to take harder antislavery stances fell on deaf ears. The party was content in saying that slavery should not extend into territories, but its officials were reluctant to discourage southern tourism by calling for stronger enforcement of the law.[9]

Ironically, even local Democrats considered Eliza legally free within Minnesota's borders. Defenders of the vacationing enslavers said the enslaved did not have to stay with their captors while in the state. However, the enslaved had no money to buy their own food or rent a place to live; they were dependent on their captors. Freed African American women would compete with European immigrant women for scant job openings as domestic laborers, and freed men would similarly compete for work. Still, to locals, the hesitancy of enslaved visitors to escape came either from ignorance or from a lack of motivation to free themselves. Moreover, if they did not seek freedom in a free state, perhaps they did not deserve it. As a local bluntly told one visitor, "if slaves were so stupid that they did not desire liberty, it would not do much good if they had it."[10]

The abolitionists believed that only the enslavers and government officials had the power to liberate enslaved people, and they advocated on behalf of the captives without having spoken to any of them. As a result, the dismissiveness of the enslavers and the negligence of the officials had created an impasse for the abolitionists. Emily Grey, however, was not part of the local abolitionist movement. Her initial contact with Eliza broke from the movement's top-down approach, and it rekindled her experience as a child of an Underground Railroad conductor. By helping Eliza to free herself, Grey empowered the enslaved instead of looking first to the enslavers and officials as keepers of the power. As an African American woman, she knew the importance of finding one's own voice and advocating for oneself. She also knew the significance of meeting with women who encouraged each other to find their own voices.[11]

Eliza's statement to Grey disproved the local notion that the enslaved were too "stupid" to become free, and it gave the abolitionists firsthand evidence that the enslaved in Minnesota wanted freedom but did not know how to acquire it. If Eliza became free through the efforts Grey devised with activists, that method of liberation would become a blueprint for them to free any other enslaved visitors who expressed their desire for freedom. Grey's conversation with Eliza finally broke the movement's stalemate. Grey's next step was to approach the local abolitionists themselves.

Grey knew she needed to reach those activists, contact Eliza again, and have them all meet in the same space to develop a plan. She first connected with local minister Charles C. Secombe. She had known him for years, when he and his wife first invited Grey to attend their church shortly after her arrival in St. Anthony. Despite Minnesota's status as free, Secombe considered it important to constantly decry the practice of enslaving people. "His mouth was not muzzled in the pulpit when occasion required he should speak against the national crime of American slavery," Grey later recalled. She regularly attended his services.[12]

After conversing with Grey, Secombe talked to local abolitionists. Among them, William D. Babbitt had the most experience as an antislavery activist. He was born in New York and raised in Michigan. He had begun his abolitionist activism in his youth, because even then he felt intense concern for the plight of enslaved people. He had a professional and personal relationship with fellow abolitionist Gerrit Smith, and he grew acquainted with many other leaders of the antislavery movement. Smith was an abolitionist philanthropist, donating money to people devoted to freeing the enslaved. Babbitt and Smith both attended the National Liberty Convention in Buffalo in 1848, where the famed formerly enslaved abolitionist and orator Frederick Douglass spoke. After years of activism in New York, Babbitt briefly lived in Moline, Illinois. From there he moved upriver in 1854 to Minnesota, where he became an abolitionist pioneer.[13]

For Babbitt abolitionism was an ideological and spiritual cause. He believed, "The only effectual way of ridding our land of Slavery is by bringing the public mind to see and deplore the evil of it." The way to win over hearts and minds was through "a kind and courteous yet firm and fearless agitation of the subject by all proper means." In that regard he did not want free states to portray themselves as suggesting "in a sectional spirit the supremacy of the North over the South." Rather, he sought "the supremacy of Freedom over our whole Country."[14]

Babbitt's recollections about Eliza revealed that he first learned about her local enslavement eight days after her arrival in St. Anthony. However, the veteran activist needed more concrete information about her plight before committing himself to the cause. "On or about the 20th of July 1860, I was informed that certain persons in St. Anthony illegally held as slaves were desirous of obtaining their freedom, and wished to know if any one would aid them," he later noted. "I replied that if the parties really desired to obtain their freedom and should themselves make the effort, and any attempt was made to kidnap or restrain them, I would assist them, and protection should be afforded them." His caution with Eliza was consistent with his desire for himself and his colleagues not to appear as agitators imposing themselves and their politics onto their southern guests.[15]

Silas Bigelow expressed willingness to help Eliza when approached in the first week of August 1860. He echoed Babbitt's concern for the legitimacy of the issue. "I was applied to, in behalf of a colored woman, then stopping at the Winslow House, St. Anthony, to render such assistance as might be necessary to protect her in the enjoyment of her rights under our laws," he later recalled. He and his colleagues subsequently kept speaking with Grey "in order to satisfy [them]selves fully that the said colored woman had not been tampered with, but had expressed but her own earnest desire for her freedom."[16]

The men put the onus on Grey to find out if Eliza truly sought her own liberation. They told the seamstress what to say, and the messenger was to relay the captive's responses to them. By giving Grey such responsibility, they put significant trust in her communication with them. Her messages thus determined the direction of the local abolition movement's work, and she became a rare African American and female leader of a movement among European Americans in antebellum Minnesota—and in the antebellum United States.[17]

Meanwhile, a European American woman named E. F. Bates conducted surveillance on Eliza in the name of abolitionism. Bates, aged twenty-two, was a seamstress originally from Ohio. Although she had never lived in the South, her home was near the Greys by the Tremont House hotel, and every year she saw vacationing southerners bringing their enslaved servants. With her abolitionism, she could ultimately help to prevent slavery from coming into her neighborhood ever again.[18]

Despite Bates's antagonism toward enslavers, she managed to gain the trust of one of the Winslow's guests. She worked as a seamstress for Henry S. Dawson of Louisiana. He and an enslaver named E. W. Jack were largely responsible for the annual influx of southerners to Minnesota. They had spread word of the state's attractions to their fellow southerners since 1856, when they first spent the summer there. Moreover, both men were in Minnesota as of July 1860. Dawson was likely familiar with the locals who complained of the annual arrival of slavery in their communities. Fortunately for Bates, her newness to the area hid her abolitionism from her employer.[19]

Bates's work for Dawson at the Winslow placed her in close proximity to the Christmases and allowed her to witness their treatment of Eliza at the hotel. Bates then reported to her fellow activists. "Special inquiry was . . . made as to whether those persons had themselves proposed to escape or whether it had first been suggested to them by others," William Babbitt later remembered. "Conclusive proof was furnished us to show beyond question that the proposition came from the slaves themselves. No aid was asked by them in making their escape until they were betrayed by a person in whom they had confided." (It is not clear why he referred to more than one enslaved person.) Bates's espionage likely provided some of the "conclusive proof" that convinced Babbitt to help liberate Eliza. Bigelow learned from the intelligence that Eliza had "stated that she very much desired her freedom but was so closely watched and restrained from the enjoyments of her freedom that she could not get away without help. She also stated that she had for a long time been promised her freedom in July last."[20]

Meanwhile, Grey's communication with Eliza also yielded fruit for the abolition movement. Grey relayed Eliza's words to her abolitionist contacts. That information was enough to convince the activists to start working together to free Eliza. "Learning these facts, we have acted in accordance with them," Bigelow said.[21]

Eliza's complaint of being "restrained from the enjoyments of her freedom" was significant. She referred to herself not as enslaved but as free; therefore, she had taken Grey's declaration "You are free" to heart. The statement showed her understanding that she had already legally acquired her freedom in Minnesota by setting foot there, but her continued captivity demonstrated that the Christmases did not permit her to exercise it. The activists determined that, because the Christmases kept Eliza enslaved, her only means of becoming unrestrained was through permanently leaving the Christmases altogether.[22]

Grey planned a meeting with Eliza at her home, which lay behind the Tremont House hotel. The hostess assigned Bates to escort Eliza from the Winslow to behind the Tremont, and Bates complied. There is no record of how—or whether—Eliza gained permission to leave the hotel.[23]

Eliza and Bates arrived at their destination, and Grey welcomed them inside. At that moment the hostess became the first conductor of Hennepin County's Underground Railroad (UGRR). All conductors of the UGRR across the country provided various forms of assistance to people escaping from their enslavers, but no abolitionist in Hennepin County had received the opportunity to directly shelter them away from their captors before Grey opened her home.[24]

Moreover, St. Anthony's strong proslavery politics and its significant dependence on southern tourism made the city an unlikely location for effective railroad conductors. By temporarily sheltering and counseling Eliza, Grey violated the town's unofficial law demanding that locals leave the enslaver–captive relationships of southern visitors alone. She risked her neighbors' wrath and, by extension, the physical safety of her family. She also stood to lose local customers.

The hostess likely kept her two young sons at home with her while her husband worked in his barbershop. Her commitment to abolitionism showed through her sons, because she named them after people who worked to free the enslaved. Her firstborn William received the name of her father, who had aided enslaved fugitives in Pennsylvania. She named her second son after Toussaint L'Ouverture. Almost seventy years earlier, the enslaved namesake had led a successful revolution on the island Santo Domingo with his fellow captives against French, Spanish, and British forces colonizing it. The Goodridges may have learned about him when an article about him and Santo Domingo appeared in Grey's hometown newspaper *York Gazette* when she was nine years old. Toussaint Grey was also a source of pride for his mother, because she believed he was "the first colored child born in what was then the city of St. Anthony, Minnesota."[25]

The selection of Grey's home as the meeting place mattered for Eliza's sense of comfort. It dictated that her friend—the African American seamstress—was taking charge of the gathering. Grey had invited abolitionist European American women into her home for the meeting, and her presence among them may have validated their presence for Eliza. Also, the willingness of the women to listen to a captive gave Eliza the reassurance to tell her story to them. The European American women heading to Grey's house were rare among abolitionists nationwide, because they—like Bates—accepted the leadership of an African American.

Then again, the European American women were at Grey's home specifically to be with Eliza. The women were not Grey's friends or close acquaintances. As the spouses of gentlemen and lawyers, they did not share the same economic class or social circle as the African American seamstress and wife of a barber. Still, they all had a common interest in helping Eliza become free, and Grey was the one person in town whom Eliza knew and trusted. Therefore, the women had to go to Grey to get to the captive.[26]

At the time European American women involved in the abolition movement rarely included African Americans in activities. They attended speeches by women like Sojourner Truth, but European Americans invited such speakers to their organizations and events. They did not tend to participate in events African American women initiated or organized. But because Grey had been St. Anthony's only African American woman, and she was not politically active, local European American women were left to themselves by default.

In addition, ethnic identity determined how women saw the purpose of abolitionism. For many European American women, the movement allowed them to emerge as leaders in their own right, and it empowered them to engage in issues that did not involve domesticity. In contrast, African American women used the movement to liberate their own people from slavery, and the urgency they felt in that context meant they did not always wait for others to invite them to participate in activities. Thus, Grey's ability to bring the women into her home and direct them was no small miracle.[27]

Before the gathering at the Grey house, the European American guests had probably never met with two African American women at the same time. These particular women had come to Minnesota from free states in New England. Babbitt's wife Elizabeth was born and raised in Maine, whose African American population had comprised only 0.1 percent of the people statewide in 1850. Unless African American women worked as

domestic laborers for the European American women's households or those of their acquaintances, Grey's European American
houseguests likely did not encounter African American women at
all—in the Northeast or in Minnesota.

The gathering eventually began, and Grey's guest of honor
proceeded to discuss her enslavement. The women listened atten-
tively as she spoke. When she finished, the women responded
by telling her that she should be free. If Eliza needed validation
from European Americans about her freedom, she received it at
that moment. Moreover, they promised to remain with her in
her transition from slavery to freedom. They vowed not to simply
abandon her in Minnesota without a supportive community, nor
would they leave her without any protection from the southern
tourists and their local allies. According to Eliza, "[Bates] told me
there were those who would receive me and protect me."[28]

Their reassurances emotionally overwhelmed Eliza at that
moment. She had probably not felt such encouragement while
among European Americans since her days at First Presbyterian
Church in Memphis. According to the husband of one of the
abolitionists at Grey's house, "Eliza wept and trembled as [the
women] contrasted freedom with life-long bondage." The women
then revealed to Eliza their plan for her liberation. On the upcoming Sunday—August 19—Grey would take Eliza with her to the
First Congregational Church, ostensibly to attend Secombe's
worship service. A vehicle would be outside the church, and
beside it would be William Babbitt wearing a glove on his left
hand. Eliza would enter that vehicle, and then Babbitt would
drive her to a safe location—away from the tourists and their
local supporters.[29]

With this plan Secombe volunteered his church as another
destination on Hennepin County's UGRR. As an opponent of
slavery, he supported Eliza's attempt to become free, and he permitted Babbitt to meet her there and then take her out of the
city. A successful enactment of the plan had the potential for the

Charles C. Secombe's First Congregational Church is at center
in a photo taken looking north from the top of the Winslow House.
Benjamin Franklin Upton, MNHS

national UGRR to extend to St. Anthony. In recent years conductors in St. Paul had sent enslaved fugitives south to Illinois,
where the travelers could board a train to Canada. Secombe and
Babbitt had the chance to send Eliza south from St. Anthony to
St. Paul, where she could move on to Illinois and then Canada.[30]

Secombe's gesture offered to Eliza a new perspective on
Christianity. She had not previously met a minister who had an
abolitionist view of the religion. Abolitionism, as the active campaign to end the country's legal enslaving of African Americans,
had no place in the church, according to George W. Freeman—
the Polks' minister and Thomas Gholson's stepfather. Freeman's
book observed that Jesus preserved the status quo on slavery in
his day: "he habitually inclined to discountenance the dissevering
of those ties which he found binding society together." Jesus's
nineteenth-century followers should do the same, because slavery's existence kept the United States together. To Freeman,

abolitionism threatened those ties. Thus, both Freeman and Secombe spoke against national threats; but the former saw abolition as the threat, and the latter identified slavery as the threat.[31]

Local abolitionists made Eliza a *cause*. She was not the first enslaved person in Minnesota to attempt to escape from an enslaving tourist. However, no one in St. Anthony had ever fled from an enslaver, nor had any enslaved people reached out to the local antislavery community for help. The activists suddenly had their opportunity to make slavery less abstract to fellow residents of St. Anthony—and to Minnesotans at large. If the abolitionists failed with Eliza, they might not get another chance.[32]

Eliza left Grey's house and returned to the Winslow. She must have been thrilled, bursting with excitement about the freedom plan. Her news would certainly break the monotony of daily discussions in the Winslow's basement. She revealed her impending liberation, and its date, to one of the other enslaved African Americans. Unfortunately for Eliza, word about the escape plan soon reached Mary Christmas. Eliza later assumed that one of the other enslaved servants at the Winslow directly told the enslaver about the plan. After all, slaveholding women did not mingle among crowds of the enslaved, who kept to their own designated space. Mary and other enslavers were unlikely to have overheard revealing conversations. An enslaved servant may have told their captor, who passed on the word. In any case, someone who knew about the plan told the enslaver in a deliberate attempt to sabotage the impending liberation.[33]

Mary immediately responded by limiting Eliza's movement, just as she had done for seven years in Louisville and at Shiloh. In this instance she kept Eliza not only in the building with her but also in the same room. She locked Eliza with her and Norma in their bedroom at the Winslow. Of course, Eliza had spent most of her time in Minnesota in that room and with them, but the lock added a new element. The enslaver did not trust her faithful "servant."[34]

Mary had no other way to detain Eliza. In slave states, slave-holders who caught their enslaved people trying to escape could have them held in a county jail. Sheriffs in those states routinely locked up any enslaved fugitives they caught until their enslavers retrieved them. In contrast, Eliza's plans as a free African American woman to attend a church without her captors and then depart from there with a local person did not constitute crimes in a free state, and the local sheriff had no authority to incarcerate her on the Christmases' behalf.

The next day Mary, Norma, and Eliza met with Richard Christmas, and he learned what had transpired. The escape plan presented a logistical problem for the Christmases. While the Christmases did not have to surrender Eliza to the activists, the captive's allies could harass the couple at the Winslow as long as she remained enslaved. Their vacation was compromised.

On the other hand, the abolitionists could not help Eliza leave if they did not know where she was. Eliza's captors decided to flee the hotel with her at once. She helped her captors with their belongings, but they gave her only enough time to grab one dress for herself. They left her trunk full of new clothes behind. Nevertheless, she knew that "Col. Christmas and his family . . . were not coming back to the Winslow House to stay any more." As with her real estate back in Memphis, her new clothes were yet another significant financial investment she lost because of slavery.[35]

The Christmases had to decide where to go with Eliza. The best way to ensure that she would remain their property was by immediately hiring a coachman to take them back down to St. Paul, where they could board the first steamboat headed downriver. On the other hand, to retreat from a northerner's breach of etiquette was to let the abolitionists win, and Eliza's enslavers refused to allow the plans of a few women—especially an African American woman like Grey—intimidate them. The couple resolved to stay in Minnesota, to continue to defy state

law by enslaving Eliza, and to salvage what remained of their holiday. They chose to relocate to another destination in the state—
someplace where they did not think their enslaved servant's local
allies would find them.

Eliza exited the Winslow and approached her enslavers at the
front of the building. Unless any other slaveholders followed the
Christmases to wherever they were taking her, she would never
see their enslaved servants again. The grapevine had betrayed
her; she at least learned not to trust her fellow captives at the
Winslow. At new lodgings, she would have to familiarize herself with a new population of enslaved people and discern who
among them should earn her confidence. Worst of all, she had
lost another opportunity for freedom.

≋ 8

Enslaved at the Lake House

Eliza sat in the coach with the Christmases, heading to an uncertain future. The dress she wore and the one she was permitted to bring with her were her sole possessions. As she later recalled, one dress was "an old washing dress," and the other was "one calico dress." Her two options were standard for enslaved women throughout the antebellum era. Their enslavers forced them to wear clothes specifically for labor Monday through Saturday, but enslaved women received permission to wear clothing of finer but inexpensive materials—calico dresses, for example—on Sundays, especially for church.[1]

The enslavers' withholding of her wardrobe was their way of punishing her for planning her escape from them. The clothes from her friends and her late husband's friends were of significant monetary and sentimental value to her. The trunk would be waiting for her when she returned to the hotel—but only with them, as their unfree servant.

In the weeks after Henry Sparks's failed escape attempt, local supporters of enslavers reminded their fellow Minnesotans not to initiate any confrontations about slavery. A Democratic-leaning newspaper in Minnesota opted to give the tourists the benefit of the doubt. "They know as well as we do, that under our law no man can be a slave here," the editorial rationalized. The behavior of the Christmases toward Eliza laid bare the falseness of the claim, for they refused to recognize her legal freedom. In their search for new lodging, they needed to find another hotelier who cared as little for the claim as they did.[2]

The column also said of local enslavers, "They came with the knowledge that their slaves are free on our soil, if they choose to avail themselves of it." The message suggested that the onus was on the enslaved to have pursued their freedom before Minnesota granted it. It also implied that *only* the enslaved could request freedom for themselves and that Minnesotans were not to seek it on behalf of the captives. Ironically, Eliza became legally free the moment she disembarked from the steamboat onto Minnesota soil, and she had initiated her own quest for liberation via her conversations with Grey. She was still denied freedom. The experience taught her that adherence to others' rules did not guarantee that she would receive the rights or protections promised her. Then again, by August 1860 she was well accustomed to broken promises by authority figures.[3]

Eliza and her fellow captives were "free" in Minnesota not only in a legal sense but also in the context of capitalism. St. Anthony allowed the Christmases to retain possession of Eliza but did not permit them to sell her. In Minnesota she was worthless in the most monetary sense of the word; by having no price attached to her, she was *free*. However, her enslavers had to keep her with them in the Northwest for only one more summer month, and then they could make her worth hundreds of dollars again by taking her back to Mississippi.

Nearly four decades after Eliza left the Cumberland Plateau and headed west to the McLemores, she and the Christmases started their descent from the Winslow's plateau and rode to the southwest. Eliza had endured enslavement in Minnesota while hoping for freedom. Her enslavers sought relief from the heat of the South; Eliza suffered slavery's hardships as if she had never left the South. In that coach enslavers took her away from people who sought to help her, and they brought her to an unfamiliar destination for their own comfort.

They crossed the Mississippi River on the bridge upstream from the Falls of St. Anthony, then wove through the streets of Minneapolis. The new city was full of recent immigrants from Europe, not unlike St. Anthony and other cities Eliza had known. Two months earlier a fire had burned eighteen buildings to the ground. Minneapolis was far from a total loss, though, and the city's Nicollet Hotel remained standing. Weary travelers seeking accommodations headed there when the Winslow was full. The Christmases and Eliza may have passed some hotels as they rode, but Minneapolis was still too close to St. Anthony for the Christmases. They kept riding.[4]

The coach left Minneapolis and entered a rural part of Hennepin County before ascending a hill. After reaching the hilltop, the coach's wheels rolled over open prairie until the blue horizon of Lake Harriet appeared. The land began to gradually slope, and just below the carriage lay the lake, a regular destination for those who visited the small resorts of Richfield Township. The lake formed an oval that tilted slightly from northeast to southwest, but a pronounced, off-shape corner appeared at the southwestern edge of the lake. The vehicle made its way to the shore at that corner.[5]

The coach approached the body of pure water and stopped at a cream-colored brick boardinghouse. Eliza and the Christmases disembarked after seven miles of travel, and they walked toward the building. Because of Eliza's enslavement and skin color, she probably had to walk farther than her captors—to the rear of the lake house—unless they demanded her immediate attention by the front door.[6]

The Thornton House was hardly of the same luxurious caliber as any of the other places where enslavers held Eliza. Both

Lake Harriet, sketched in 1852 by Adolf Hoeffler. *MNHS*

The Thornton House at Lake Harriet. By 1900, when this photograph was taken, it had become the home of Charles Reeve. *MNHS*

the Winslow House and Shiloh had real estate values of about $150,000; the Thornton was worth only one-tenth of that amount. Eliza had always been enslaved by people who had money troubles, but they were skilled at putting on airs. With the Christmases' desperation came a decline in the opulence of the surroundings they chose.[7]

Instead of one dozen employees, there was only one—an Irish immigrant woman. The house had rooms, but none of the winding staircases or ballrooms of hotels and plantation mansions. Boardinghouses like the Thornton showed why promoters of tourism in St. Anthony talked only about the beauty of the nearby lakes and avoided discussing at length the small lodges at the shores. As one person put it that year, "The boarding houses are not generally very satisfactory." Fortunately for proprietor Frances Thornton, the Christmases at that moment prioritized a hidden lodge over a "very satisfactory" one, and they settled in at her place for the duration.[8]

In the confines of the Thornton House, Eliza was as surrounded by enslavers as she had ever been while in the South. The Christmases counted on the full-time occupants of the lake house to respect their enslaving of Eliza. The residents at the Thornton House were Thornton, four of her adult relatives, two English male laborers, and the Irish servant. Thornton herself was also English, and she became one of the elite in Richfield Township within three years of her arrival at Minnesota. Her boardinghouse stood on the 240 acres she owned on the southwest shore of the lake; her real estate was valued at $15,000 in 1871.[9]

The proprietor was one of very few wealthy people in Eliza's life who had not come from a slaveholding family. After immigrating in her twenties, Thornton had lived on the East Coast for three decades before coming to Minnesota. She raised her children in Massachusetts in the late 1820s and then in New York from the 1830s onward. In August 1857, while still a New Yorker, she purchased real estate by Lake Harriet for five thousand dollars.

Eighteen months later she had built the Thornton House, and she and her children became full-time residents of Minnesota.[10]

Thornton was more committed to slavery than many other newcomers to the Northwest. Even before she moved to Minnesota, she chose to gain riches by permitting slavery in her new shelter. When she had bought the land in Richfield Township, slavery was still legal in Minnesota Territory. She held no qualms about taking money from enslavers and watching people like Eliza work in captivity at the lake house. She had developed a business relationship with the Winslow House by opening her home specifically to guests of that hotel and entertaining them. She enjoyed the company of the Winslow's seasonal southern gentlemen. Moreover, she approved of slavery, and her reputation in that regard kept southerners coming to her establishment.[11]

The Freeman family, fellow guests at the Thornton House, had also come from Mississippi to Minnesota for respite. John D. Freeman, however, was no stranger to the North, because he had lived in New York before moving to the South. He began practicing law in Mississippi in 1838. He had spent almost half his time there in public life by 1860, serving as the state's attorney general in the 1840s and in Congress in the early 1850s.[12]

The former New Yorker acclimated himself to Mississippi's planter class by marrying into slavery and, by extension, immense wealth. As of 1860 he enslaved two dozen people; the number was the equivalent of his acquiring at least one slave per year while in Mississippi. Shortly after moving to Mississippi, he married the daughter of one of his new law partners. It was common for antebellum European American men in the South to consider the wealth of a potential bride when deciding whom to marry. Eliza was familiar with such men, having served three men who had married into the wealthy Donelson family of Tennessee.[13]

Throughout those years in Mississippi, Freeman openly and consistently approved slavery. He wrote in 1848, "Slavery is an institution coeval with the existence of the human race." Tying slavery to religion, he claimed, "By the law of all nations the right to hold African slaves in bondage pertains to the free men of all Christian nations." Twelve years later he professed that slavery was fundamentally American, and he saw no contradiction in the country's simultaneous quest for freedom and enslavement of people. "When the thirteen colonies declared their independence of Great Britain and assumed the position of free and sovereign States, slavery was a part of their domestic servitude," he noted. "When the Constitution of the United States was adopted in its place, slaves were expressly incorporated not only as a species of property, but also as a part of the federal community itself."[14]

The Thornton House's enslaved guests included the Freemans' enslaved servant. The family brought their seven-year-old girl Ann with them. If Eliza interacted with the child at the lake house, she likely felt maternal, just as Patsey had probably felt for Eliza many years earlier on the Cumberland Plateau. Ann was old enough to serve the adults in the family but young enough to play with the Freeman children. She was also the same age as Norma and may have played with her at the lodge.[15]

As of August 1860 Richfield Township was the farthest west Eliza had traveled, and slavery followed her there. No African Americans resided in the area—not even as live-in servants for European American households. Some of them may have arrived from the nearby cities Minneapolis, St. Anthony, or St. Paul; but many if not most African Americans at the lakeside that summer had been legally enslaved in the South before coming to Lake Harriet with their captors.

Visitors at the lakes engaged in various activities throughout each summer day. The random sounds of gunshots that reverberated from the lakeside's woods may have been most disconcerting to Eliza. "These people . . . pass away the time in gunning, fishing, and riding," reported a tourist from New Orleans. As an enslaved domestic who had spent most of her life working in cities for women and children, Eliza had little exposure to hunting.[16]

Despite the Thornton's remoteness, its basic provisions were on a par with those on the St. Louis–St. Paul steamboat and in the Winslow House. Pickerel, bass, and crappie swam in the water. At the lakeside wild strawberries grew and waterfowl roamed. The Thornton's servants prepared and served meals to the enslavers, and neither the lodge's domestics nor the tourists' captives dined with them. Lake-scented breezes mingled with the odors of roasting prairie chicken and crappie.[17]

That evening the locals returned to their homes and tourists retired to their rooms. Most likely Eliza slept on the floor of Mary's room. The weather was unseasonably cool; a tourist reported "a sharp frost" one night that week.[18]

> The boardinghouse did not have the sophisticated heating system of the Winslow House, and Eliza lamented that she had been forced to leave her year-round clothes at the Winslow. The unfamiliar calls of loons echoed across the lake as she fell asleep. When the sun rose, the crowing of roosters at nearby farms signaled the start of another day of serving Mary and Norma, and another day of tourism. The first of the coaches and their horses scraped the pebbles, and men bounded from the vehicles with their guns and fishing poles.

That morning ritual greeted Eliza on August 19 but with a significant difference. That was her first Sunday at the Thornton. While slaveholding Christian tourists across Hennepin County made plans for Christian worship attendance, their options were limited at Lake Harriet. A Methodist minister ran the only nearby church. Churches of other denominations existed in Minneapolis, St. Anthony, and St. Paul, but attendance would require the lodgers to rent a coach and ride for an hour. In addition, because they were in the North, they ran the risk of hearing an abolitionist sermon in a local church like Secombe's. The Christmases kept Eliza at the Thornton House that Sabbath morning, avoiding the abolitionists of St. Anthony.[19]

The Christmases' sabotage of Eliza's escape was an act of pride.

At that point the couple held on stubbornly to a sinking invest-ment: Eliza at age forty-three was well past her peak of mone-tary value. She had never produced children for them, and her advancing age diminished her ability to do so. Her financial value stood to only decrease as time passed. Some enslavers freed their captives when they reached Eliza's age, saving themselves the costs of support when their laborers were less productive. This also meant that the newly freed workers would have a harder time earning a living. On the other hand, Norma was young enough to still require some care by Eliza—and the Christmases found their captive especially useful on August 19, 1860, merely to discour-age and spite St. Anthony's abolitionists.

The exodus of the Christmases and Eliza from St. Anthony did not, of course, end the controversy over slavery there. Fel-low Mississippian vacationer Martha Prince continued to be concerned about keeping her captives at the Winslow. Just one month after Henry Sparks had attempted to escape, she had heard that local abolitionists would try to remove her remaining two enslaved servants. Southern tourists immediately formed a vigilante posse. Word soon spread to Lake Harriet about possible trouble with the two laborers, and the men residing and lodg-ing at the Thornton House unanimously decided to assist in the efforts to keep those African Americans with Prince.[20]

On August 20 the men left their families and enslaved servants behind and headed to St. Anthony. It was a Monday, and any local families enjoying time at the lake had returned to town; the departure of the men reduced attendance further still. The day promised to be less chaotic for Eliza, but she still had to serve Mary and Norma.[21]

Richard Christmas and John D. Freeman brought different experiences to the task of protecting enslavement. Christmas was accustomed to a rural setting, with a multitude of wooden shacks that housed enslaved people on plantations all over Issaquena County; Freeman was from Jackson, Mississippi, and had some familiarity with cities. But both men had witnessed slave patrols wandering through southern communities in search of enslaved fugitives. Some enslavers hired professional slave catchers to retrieve missing laborers. Searchers posted handbills in public spaces, hoping that the offer of a reward would lure people to help with the search. If Prince's captives tried to run away, Christmas and Freeman had southern models for the search.[22]

But St. Anthony did not have slave patrols, and no local sheriff or police officer possessed the legal authority to arrest African Americans simply for separating from their captors. Christmas and Freeman exhibited little concern for such legal details. By helping to form a vigilante group in St. Anthony to catch the two escapees, they unilaterally assumed the authority to capture and return Prince's enslaved servants (who had not, in fact, escaped). No local officials publicly discouraged the potential kidnappers from seeking the laborers, nor did officials tell the group to disperse.

Vacationers in St. Anthony brought their immense wealth with them to the city, and their independent, private search for their own runaways constituted part of the slave culture that came with them—the culture in which Minnesotans had promised not to interfere. Moreover, it was common in parts of the North for local officials to help catch enslaved fugitives. During the 1840s at least two different mayors of New York City directed the city's police officers to capture and return runaways. However, Sparks was not an enslaved fugitive, and the other two men were not enslaved, because Prince had voluntarily brought them to a free state. The southerners organizing to retrieve them did not constitute a slave patrol but rather a mob preparing to look for two free African Americans to kidnap.[23]

The local troubles of Prince's laborers put Eliza's own detention in Minnesota into context. The mob's sudden departure from the lodge was an expression of solidarity with Prince as a fellow enslaver in the Northwest. Southerners in Minnesota were prepared to mobilize anywhere to retrieve any enslaved African American fugitives within the state. Their organization showed that Eliza was strategic in developing a network of supporters with Emily Grey's help, for she as an individual was unable to fend off a mob alone. On the other hand, she did not know if her allies could gather to successfully free her at Lake Harriet.

When the men left the Thornton, the proprietor, Mary Christmas, Freeman's wife E. A. Freeman, and the two teenage Freeman daughters were on hand to assign tasks. E. A.'s presence at the lodge returned Eliza to the orbit of European Americans directly influenced by Andrew Jackson. From the White House in 1830, Jackson had appointed E. A.'s father to serve as Mississippi's US attorney. Six years later, while Jackson held Eliza captive, he assigned the lawyer to serve as a judge in Mississippi's Fourth District. Whether Eliza knew it or not, even in the far reaches of Lake Harriet, her former captor's legacy hovered over her.[24]

Meanwhile, abolitionists in St. Anthony had learned that the Christmases had taken Eliza to the Thornton. As when Grey informed them of Eliza's presence at the Winslow, the activists faced a challenge. Her allies somehow had to find her at Lake Harriet, conduct surveillance on her and her captors, and figure out how to help her escape. Rescuing her from the boarding-house presented an additional complication. Richfield Township did not have St. Anthony's network of abolitionists, and the small community had no church like Secombe's to serve as a secret meeting place for the activists. In addition, southerners and their supporters at the lakeshore were armed. The routine sounds of gunshots in the area gave southerners a perfect cover for shooting at the captive's rescuers if no one else saw them. By traveling one hour away from home to confront a mass of proslavery people on their own turf, the activists would be at their most vulnerable.

They began by organizing a party to investigate the lay of the land. At least two European American women volunteered for the trip, and one of them—probably the seamstress Bates—was acquainted with Eliza. Someone had to recognize her at the lake house, and Eliza did not personally know any antislavery men in St. Anthony. Although Elizabeth Babbitt was also an ally, she was seven months pregnant and thus not as likely to have made the journey.[25]

Emily Grey did not join the group. She was a free African American and a lifelong northerner, unlike the Thornton's enslaved African Americans. Freeborn and educated, she had no experience in feigning enslavement. Her presence would jeopardize the activists' ruse. Also, she was a wife and mother, and she may not have wanted to risk her life to help spy on Eliza.

The party boarded large lumber wagons and rode to the lake. They had likely made the trips to these popular nearby lakes in summers past and expected to encounter multiple enslavers, not just the Christmases. As Eliza's allies traveled to Lake Harriet, they may have coached each other on how to behave among those tourists.[26]

When they reached the Thornton House, the activists identified themselves as a fishing party and asked for refreshments. Thornton welcomed them inside, and the abolitionists fellowshipped with the southerners and their sympathizers. Regardless of how the activists felt about breaking bread with enslavers, they put politics aside for the sake of keeping Eliza safe and planning her freedom.[27]

While the enslavers and abolitionists dined together, the captives may have been in the kitchen with the cook or in the servants' quarters or outside of the house. The Thornton had much less room than the Winslow for captives of tourists to await their turn to eat. The abolitionists' time at the dinner table was time that kept them from searching for Eliza, but the meal was a necessity in order for the spies to gain the hosts' trust.

After the meal was finished, the diners rose from the table. Some of the masqueraders roamed throughout the boardinghouse and mingled with the occupants, secretly searching for

Eliza all the while. Other abolitionists went out of the house to explore the area around it while perhaps ostensibly enjoying the view of the lake. Neither faction of the group had any luck finding Eliza—at least, not at first.[28]

Fortunately for the spies, they realized that Thornton House was just like the Winslow House in how it provided space for African American laborers. Two of the women among the faux fishers outside noticed a door at the rear of the boardinghouse, just like the rear doors where African Americans entered and exited the Winslow. The women entered the Thornton through its back door and found Eliza in the room on the other side. She probably expressed surprise at seeing them, felt relieved that they had learned of her new location, and briefly spoke with them.[29]

If Eliza became excited upon seeing her acquaintances, she did not reveal her feelings to anyone. Like her former enslaver Mary Ann Eastin Polk at Hamilton Place, she was circumspect. Her experience at the Winslow had taught her not to disclose any information about possible liberation. Then again, there was hardly anyone to tell at the lake house. The Christmases and the Freemans wanted to enslave there, the Thorntons nurtured the enslavers' comfort, and little Ann was too young to appreciate the gravity of the situation at hand.

The abolitionists bade the hotel workers and guests goodbye, climbed into the wagons, and departed Lake Harriet for St. Anthony. Their excursion was a victory of sorts. The European American women of the lodge were none the wiser as to the espionage conducted by their friendly visitors, and the spies had confirmed Eliza's new location. In addition, the abolitionists had the information they needed to pass along to people who could help them rescue her. Eliza remained kidnapped, and the activists retreated to St. Anthony empty-handed. Their next task was to determine whom to ask for assistance.[30]

Legally speaking, Eliza as a free woman in a free state had every right to leave with the abolitionists that day, and they would not have broken any laws by inviting her to voluntarily go with them. However, the abolitionists lived in the same county as Frances Thornton, the employees of the Winslow House, and all the businesses in St. Anthony and Minneapolis that catered to tourism. The spies' departure reflected the strength of the tourist business in Hennepin County. If the activists openly took Eliza with them, they ran the risk of angering their neighbors. They stood to suffer repercussions such as boycotts, critical commentaries in newspapers, and violence from their fellow Hennepin County residents. They had tried a secret plan to free Eliza, but that plan's disclosure exposed them as abolitionists, willing to act. Their next plan to free her required assistance from someone outside their clique.

The abolitionists had not yet tried calling on local government officials to enforce the state constitution. They needed someone in law enforcement or criminal justice to confront the enslavers' appeasers, if not the enslavers themselves. Such a figure would have the authority to force the Christmases to free Eliza. Her emancipation would not only uphold the law but also validate the abolitionists' efforts. William D. Babbitt later recalled, "The next we heard from Eliza Winston was through her colored friends, who said she was closely confined and could not communicate with her friends. It was then determined that legal aid should be rendered her to escape from her oppressors. I never saw her and think no person on this side of the river saw her."[31]

After the departure of the abolitionists from the lakeside, Eliza returned her attention to the Christmases. Any disobedience on her part jeopardized whatever goodwill remained between them after her interactions with Grey and the abolitionist women. She already knew that her captors would not free her, and her only hope was that those surprising visitors would find a way to do so. By continuing to play the dutiful slave, she stood the best chance for her enslavers to stay at the Thornton long enough for her supporters to return and free her.

9

Rescue by Arrest

On the morning of August 21, 1860, Richard Christmas was still away from the Thornton, helping Martha Prince to prevent her enslaved servants from leaving St. Anthony. On the surface, nothing about Eliza's enslavement that morning was new. She had been serving absentee enslavers since her childhood. She put on her washing dress for yet another day's work serving the Christmas ladies at the Thornton.

But this new day was a vastly different one from Eliza's previous days at Lake Harriet.

It was a perfect day for an attempted rescue. Her allies faced a greatly reduced risk of being shot, because the vacationing men were still away at St. Anthony. The women and children remaining at the lake house were unlikely to resist. The abolitionists now knew exactly where to find her. They merely had to leave the St. Anthony–Minneapolis area without drawing too much attention to themselves from the Christmases' allies.

Outside the Thornton was another beautiful day at Lake Harriet, and some local supporters of enslavers arrived to spend time there. Among them was St. Paul resident Abram S. Elfelt. He and his wife had come to the state from Pennsylvania in 1851. He and his brother operated a dry goods store near St. Paul's upper levee, and he sold real estate. Many southerners, who formed a prominent part of the clientele for local real estate agents, lodged at the Thornton. Ironically, the brothers shared a distant connection with Emily Grey because of captive Africans. When the namesake of Grey's son—Toussaint L'Ouverture—led the enslaved people of Santo Domingo to a successful revolution in 1801, the Elfelt brothers' parents fled the island and settled in Pennsylvania.[1]

John Nininger of St. Paul, another real estate agent from Pennsylvania, was also at the lake that day. He was actively recruiting investors for a new town in Minnesota: a city named after himself. The town, like St. Paul, lay in Ramsey County. His prospective buyers did not have to travel far with him to see the land for sale. The Christmases and other rich southern vacationers at the lake were ideal investors for his venture. Just six months earlier, Nininger made $1,600 in one day in land sales to two different slaveholders. Lawyer C. D. Melton, who enslaved six people in South Carolina, bought $900 worth of real estate from him. Like visitor John Freeman, P. Lane came to Minnesota from Jackson, Mississippi, and his $700 purchase of land added to his wealth, which included two enslaved people. Nininger and Elfelt had a vested interest in helping Hennepin County keep southern tourists like the Christmases coming upriver each summer.[2]

Over an hour away from Lake Harriet, in Minneapolis, William Babbitt met with newspaper editor William S. King and lawyer F. R. E. Cornell. All three men shared the same Republican-leaning politics. They abhorred slavery. They conferred about how to make the local government intervene regarding Eliza's captivity. Babbitt had been in communication with Grey, who had told him about Eliza's "close confinement." This report convinced him to seek a legal outlet to liberate the enslaved woman, and he called his acquaintances in the legal profession for help.[3]

Eliza's allies decided to apply to a sympathetic judge for a writ of habeas corpus on her behalf. This legal procedure, guaranteed

Attorney F. R. E. Cornell. *MNHS*

in the US Constitution, uses the courts to protect against unlawful and indefinite imprisonment. A judge orders the person
holding someone in custody, or an officer of the court, to bring
that individual before the court to determine the legality of the
imprisonment. A writ from a judge would force the county sheriff to arrest Eliza and bring her to the judge's court. The judge
then had to convene a hearing and decide whether to emancipate
her or to rule her captivity as legal. And because Minnesota outlawed slavery, the abolitionists required merely a legalistic judge
to emancipate her. In the antebellum North, multiple abolitionists used the writ of habeas corpus to request that judges remove
enslaved people from their captors and bring them to courtrooms.
Babbitt likely was first exposed to the writ in New York, which
had passed a set of personal liberty laws—legislation enacted in
northern states to counter provisions of the fugitive slave acts.
Abolitionist lawyers and laypeople associated with the New York

State Vigilance Committee often relied on the writ to help free local captives. His friend Gerrit Smith, the longtime president of that organization, facilitated multiple writs for enslaved people in New York—some of whom went free. However, most of the public officials there supported enslavers, and some even helped captors kidnap free African Americans.[4]

The writ had been used in St. Paul just weeks earlier. On July 24, 1860, St. Anthony's *Falls Evening News* noted, "a *writ of habeas corpus* was served on Mrs. Prince by Chief Justice [Lafayette] Emmett, commanding her to bring before the Court her slave Henry whose escape we have noticed. The writ was issued upon the affidavit of a free black, alleging that the said Henry was illegally detained." Emmett never received the opportunity to decide about Sparks's status, because the enslaver forced Henry to return to Mississippi.[5]

St. Paul was an hour away, and the abolitionists decided to quickly find someone more local to take on Eliza's case. St. Anthony did not have prospects in their favor. The trial of James E. Cochrane had taken place there. Secombe's brother had defended him in court, and even the prosecuting attorney was a Republican. Nevertheless, the city's justice of the peace ruled against him, thus establishing a precedent in St. Anthony of a court siding with an enslaver and ruling against an enslaved African American. The abolitionists looked across the Mississippi to the city of Minneapolis for help.[6]

Cornell knew the perfect judge to approach in Minneapolis—his own former law partner Charles E. Vanderburgh. Vanderburgh presided over the Fourth Judicial District, which included St. Anthony and Minneapolis. The judge came from a Dutch family who had lived in the United States since the early eighteenth century, and was a Yale University graduate. After becoming a lawyer in 1855, he moved to St. Anthony and started practicing law with fellow New Yorker Cornell. Vanderburgh shared his partner's politics; one person described him as a "consistent Republican."

The partnership dissolved only when Vanderburgh was elected to the post in November 1859. Like Eliza, he was a Presbyterian. She had no choice but to accept the abolitionists' faith in the judge.[7]

Unfortunately for Eliza, neither Cornell nor Vanderburgh had expe-
rience in practicing law in the context of slavery. As lawyers in a free state, they had not represented enslaved people in free-
dom lawsuits during the years of their partnership. Moreover, her fate rested in the hands of a new judge in multiple respects. Van-
derburgh was the first resident of Minneapolis to serve as the judge of the Fourth Judicial District, which comprised Hennepin County. He had sat on that bench for only nine months as of August 1860, and during that time he did not deliberate on any freedom lawsuits. In addition, this was his first judicial post.[8]

Judge Charles E. Vanderburgh.
Charles H. Beal, MNHS

Babbitt and Bates put their legal strategy into motion, each giv-
ing an affidavit regarding Eliza's treatment in Minnesota. Their affidavits constituted part of the process in applying for a writ of habeas corpus for Eliza. The judge did not expect the application from them. To be sure, he knew that Hennepin County was, as he put it, "a summer resort for Southern people" and that those people "were accustomed to bringing their colored servants with them." However, no one had previously complained to him of the situation. Therefore, he was "unexpectedly applied to, to issue a writ," as he later remembered.[9]

Despite Vanderburgh's surprise, he accepted the applications and agreed to open his courtroom to hear Eliza's case. The Fourth District Court had been adjourned since August 16, and it was not to reopen until August 23. For Eliza's hearing to proceed on August 21, the judge also needed to bring her to court. Correspondingly, he issued a writ of habeas corpus for her.[10]

Vanderburgh's next step with the writ was to direct local law enforcement officials to implement it. The task of arresting Eliza fell to Hennepin County sheriff Richard Strout of Minneapolis. Born in Maine in 1819, Strout had spent his adulthood in the Midwest. He moved with his family to Ohio at age seventeen, and he relocated to the Falls of St. Anthony in 1856. As a local surveyor, he knew the layout of Hennepin County, and that knowledge became an asset for his new job in the late 1850s, when he became the sheriff.[11]

Hennepin County sheriff Richard Strout.
Hennepin History Museum

Although the lifelong northerner bore the responsibility for enforcing the laws of a free county, slavery tainted his local business transactions. He cofounded the town of Cold Spring, Minnesota, in 1857, with Joseph J. Gibson, S. W. Turner, and Sarah Jodon. Some of the money that funded the town's establishment came from slavery, because Jodon and her husband Benjamin Jodon had enslaved people in Virginia before the couple's permanent relocation to Minnesota in 1851. As of 1857 they lived in St. Anthony, and they kept an African American child under ten years old there. Gibson was the son of captors, but he did not enslave anyone as an adult.[12]

Strout himself was partly responsible for Richfield Township's permissiveness toward slavery. As one of the three town supervisors in office from May 1858 to April 1859, he witnessed Frances Thornton's first full tourism season as the proprietor of her boardinghouse. Strout's term as supervisor started on the same day that Minnesota became a free state, but Thornton's lake house became a popular haven for vacationing enslavers during his tenure in office. He had the power as both the county sheriff and a town supervisor to curb if not halt that development, but he made no such effort before leaving office. Instead, he and his fellow supervisors concerned themselves with determining the township's expenses and dividing it into districts.[13]

Judge Vanderburgh's writ forced a reckoning for Strout. In carrying out his task, the sheriff was essentially accusing his own acquaintances of breaking state law. Strout did not stand to financially benefit from apprehending Eliza, and he risked inciting the anger of the southern network he had worked hard to foster and the residents he had once governed. But his position as sheriff left him no choice.

To add insult to injury, at least two dozen abolitionists insisted on accompanying Strout to Richfield. By doing so they could see to it that the sheriff followed through on implementing Judge Vanderburgh's writ. Strout was a servant of their county, and he could not legally prohibit them from following him to the Thornton. The only women in the posse were likely Emily Grey and E. F. Bates. Babbitt later recalled, "As there was no person on this side of the river who could identify her, a lady from St. Anthony went along [to Lake Harriet] for that purpose, and asked another lady friend to accompany her."[14]

Deputy Sheriff Joseph H. Canney was also part of the group. Originally from New Hampshire, he had lived in St. Anthony for eight years as of 1860. He was a Quaker—a faith that opposed slavery. Canney, who did not have business ties to slaveholders, had no conflicts of interest in apprehending Eliza. He was matter-of-fact about his task. He remembered years later, "I was called upon to arrest and bring before Judge Vanderburgh, one Eliza Winston . . . and in company of Sheriff Strout and others, I proceeded to discharge my duty."[15]

Eliza's liberators were a diverse group of people, united solely in their mission to apprehend her and bring her to the courthouse in Minneapolis. The participants represented various economic classes—from the wage laborers like Grey and Bates to the wealthy gentleman Babbitt. Grey's and Bates's involvement kept the posse from being all-white and all-male. Strout was the sole person in the posse who fraternized with enslavers. Only he and Canney possessed the legal authority to arrest Eliza, and, between them, Strout probably was the only one who dreaded confronting the enslavers by the lake. Meanwhile, members of his posse relished the opportunity; otherwise, they would not have volunteered for duty.

It was unusual on any given day for Hennepin County's sheriff to organize a departure from St. Anthony and Minneapolis with local abolitionists surrounding him. Some of the bystanders watching them knew who they were, where they were heading, and why they were going there. The observers immediately rode off to the Thornton via shortcuts. They reached the lodge first, at about 10:00 AM, and they approached Mary Christmas to warn her of the incoming posse. Because the enslaving men of the lodge were still away in St. Paul, the people who came to warn the Christmas ladies were the only men on the premises. Medical doctor James J. Linn was one of those men. He and his wife were among Hennepin County's supporters of southern migration. US District Attorney Eugene M. Wilson—the son of an enslaver from Virginia—roomed at their home.[16]

After Linn informed Mary Christmas about the approaching posse, she had a significant choice to make—either to comply with Sheriff Strout and willingly lead him and the posse to Eliza, or to defy the law and refuse to help him find her. In all her twenty-six years on earth, she had not met with such a legal confrontation. Then again, no laws in Kentucky or Mississippi had ever forced her to face a significant loss of wealth and an unwelcome change to her lifestyle as a plantation lady. The law had always been in her favor.

She decided to challenge local authority by concealing Eliza. Whenever the enslaver saw someone suspicious approach the house, she instructed her captive to hide in the woods nearby. There were some false alarms that morning, and all of Eliza's moments in hiding distracted her from caring directly for the Christmas ladies. On the other hand, it was better for Mary to be overcautious and protect her property than to be lax and lose her to northern kidnappers.[17]

Moreover, Mary's decision showed initiative regarding a major investment, and it reflected her comfort in assuming total control of property that she and her husband shared. Her defiance revealed her recognition of her own power as a co-owner of the enslaved woman, and, like many enslaving women across the country, she refused to voluntarily cede that control to anyone. She hid her captive not only to protect her marital joint investment but also to preserve her increasingly fragile status and power in Minnesota as an enslaver.[18]

For Eliza, the absence of Richard Christmas from the boardinghouse did not mean the disappearance of any dominance over her. Whenever the patriarchs of certain households were gone, some enslaved people used those vacancies as their opportunities to test the boundaries of their enslavement. Some of them defied the orders given by female enslavers, and others simply ran away from the plantations. Eliza's obedience to Mary was a recognition of the enslaver's authority over her—an authority that had been cultivated by seven years of Eliza's exclusive service to Mary.[19]

Mary's directive was certainly unusual. Enslavers rarely instructed their captives to leave the premises if not directing them toward slave quarters or to another slaveholder. Nor did captors tell enslaved people to hide from law enforcement. Officers in slave states typically made sure that the enslaved were with their owners. But to keep her hold on Eliza, Mary had no other choice.

Ultimately, Eliza's deference showed that she saw Mary as just as much of an enslaver as Richard. To be sure, he had purchased Eliza, and she spoke of being "pawned . . . by Col. Christmas" or of someone's attempt to "buy me of Col. Christmas." However, she blamed Mary for reneging on the promise of manumission on Norma's birthday, saying "she would not be willing to let me go" because of the illness. Therefore, to Eliza, the enslaver's influence over her husband's property overshadowed which name was on the receipt or deed as the purchaser.[20]

Each time Mary ordered Eliza out of the lake house, the enslaved servant left through the rear door and hid in a hazel thicket. A multitude of wild hazel bushes grew by the Thornton. The captive chose a thicket close to the house in order to make herself more visible to people looking for her. Nevertheless, she obeyed her captor, because she also considered obedience to her enslavers as helpful to her goal of liberation. Whereas she had previously thought her compliance would help her captors find her worthy of freedom, she now thought it would make her a sympathetic figure for abolitionists and government officials working to free her.[21]

Eliza's retreats to the thicket for the mere sake of continued enslavement reflected Mary's sheer desperation to retain possession of her. The captive's crouch constituted her captor's last stand.

> Eliza's service suddenly shifted from nursing an invalid to crouching outside, amid hazel bushes, while squirrels and chickens scattered at her feet. Mosquitoes buzzed around her face, and birds flew above her head. Every sound took on a new meaning. Every clomp of a hoof and every rumble of a wheel might be a carriage carrying her allies. Crunching sticks and twigs might signal that abolitionists were walking toward her. Squirrels or rabbits racing past could be fleeing antislavery invaders. Every experience carried the possibility of freedom for her.

But possibility was not the same as reality, and uncertainty characterized Eliza's situation. In St. Anthony, Eliza's escape was specifically planned for August 19; in Richfield, she did not know when the abolitionists would return. The abolitionist seamstress E. F. Bates had spied on Eliza in the Winslow, but there were no allies secretly staying at Frances Thornton's boardinghouse that morning. There were no abolitionist safe spaces near the lodge in Richfield, unlike Secombe's church in St. Anthony near the Winslow. If Eliza's allies still planned to free her, she had no idea how they could possibly do so.

At midday the posse reached the Thornton from multiple directions, and again Eliza fled through the rear of the lodge for the hazel thicket. Strout, Canney, Grey, and Bates approached the front of the house, and Strout demanded to see Eliza. Standing from the front piazza, Mrs. Thornton made a dramatic gesture of solidarity with the enslavers by lying. She falsely informed the sheriff and Canney that Eliza was not at the house and had not been there all day.[22]

The worst fear of any enslaving vacationer in Minnesota had finally come to pass, for locals "interfered" with Mary Christmas's relationship with her "servant." The enslaver allowed them to look inside the house. Strout, Canney, Grey, and Bates entered the house and began to look for Eliza, while the rest of the posse stood outside.[23]

Some members of the posse carried firearms. They were willing to injure or kill anyone who interfered with the sheriff's apprehension of Eliza. On the other hand, they did not have to fire any shots that day, because they received a helpful tip. One of the lodgers at the boardinghouse told the posse outside that Eliza had just been sent into the hazel thicket. They immediately proceeded in that direction.[24]

With this latest retreat, Eliza exhibited a hint of disobedience. Babbitt later recalled, "I walked around behind the house and saw a woman about a rod distant, going slowly toward the bushes in rear of the house." Her deliberate slowness allowed the search party enough time to see where she headed. Such slowdowns of tasks were common among enslaved people. Eliza used it as a performance of sorts, feigning ineptitude or bewilderment while defiantly sabotaging the Christmases' control over her.[25]

Moments later the posse's two women spotted Eliza in the hazel thicket. She had hoped and expected her allies to find her, but when the women approached, she wept once again. The abolitionists' new plan was working, and she was closer than ever to finally becoming free. Grey's willingness to risk her life to participate in the rescue made her more than merely Eliza's benefactor; she became, as Eliza later put it, "my colored friend in St. Anthony."[26]

The ladies' cries aroused the attention of others in the posse, and they headed to the thicket. Babbitt approached Eliza. "I then stepped in the bushes and woods, and found Eliza a few rods from the house, standing in a path that led through the thicket," he later recalled. "I asked her if her name was Eliza Winston. She said, 'Yes.' Said I, 'Do you wish to be free, or return with your master?' She said, 'I wish for my freedom, but don't tell master or mistress that I said so.'"[27]

Inside the boardinghouse, Thornton continued to echo Christmas in feigning ignorance of Eliza's whereabouts. If the proprietor helped Strout confiscate the property of a guest, she would tarnish if not destroy her good reputation among southerners. In a sense, the cooperation of Thornton and Christmas can be seen as symbolic of the potential for the North and South to remain united—but at the cost of freedom for Eliza and other captives. Moreover, by aligning in order to keep Eliza kidnapped, the two women formed their own vigilante group, conducting an illegal activity.[28]

Sheriff Strout heard the commotion outside the lake house and found the posse with Eliza. The last time a sheriff had approached Eliza was at the McLemore home in Davidson County, Tennessee, where he had forced on her the humiliation of being sold and the trauma of her permanent removal from her home of twelve years. Strout, in arresting her and transferring her from the Christmases' custody to his own, was yet another man restricting her mobility. She had to put her fate in his hands and believe that he really would take her to court.[29]

On the other hand, she remembered what her friends and acquaintances told her: she was supposed to be free in the North. Sheriff Strout—representing law enforcement in a free state— had to uphold Minnesota's antislavery law. Whereas Davidson County's sheriff had conducted one of Eliza's worst moments in enslavement, Hennepin County's sheriff gave her the best one.[30]

Deputy Canney then reached Eliza among the hazel bushes. After the sheriff interrogated her, Canney did the same. By then Eliza was comfortable in divulging her desires for liberation to the posse at large. Their presence showed they knew of her longing for freedom, anyway. "I asked her name, and also asked her if she was restrained of her liberty," the deputy sheriff later recalled. "She gave me her name and said she wished to be free. I then asked her, if I took her before the judge, if she would then say before him and her master that she desired her freedom.

She said she would say so then and all the time if we would protect her."[31]

Even in those last moments of enslavement, Eliza exercised caution so as not to give her enslaver any impression of *wanting* to leave. She quietly told the posse, "I want to be free, but don't tell master I said so." But then she shouted, loudly enough for the occupants in the lake house to hear, that she did not want to go with them. The men told her she had to go, and she emerged from the woods to return to the Thornton one last time to prepare to leave the lake house—and the Christmases.[32]

Eliza reentered the boardinghouse from the rear door to retrieve her calico dress. She had no other clothing, no other possessions. She then took a few moments to change clothes, removing her washing dress and putting on the calico dress. That simple act was significant and symbolic. Enslavers controlled the labor of their captives, telling them when to begin and end their workdays. By taking off her washing dress of her own accord, Eliza demonstrated pointedly that she was stopping her work for the Christmases—not only for that day but also permanently.[33]

Her change of clothing also reflected the gravity of the new situation she would soon face. Her calico dress was her finest piece of clothing, worn to church or for formal occasions. Eliza was about to face a judge and request her emancipation. It was her lifelong dream and too important a moment for merely a washing dress.[34]

Mary confronted Eliza inside the house. The enslaver tried in vain to persuade Eliza to stay with her, pledging in desperation to bestow the long-promised free papers. But Mary was a diminished figure: Strout's arrest had removed her power to control Eliza's fate. Eliza had seen many other diminished people. The McLemores became a defeated family when Sheriff Williams took her away from them, and impoverishment and widowhood broke Gholson down to the point of pawning her. Of course, she and her enslaved acquaintances lived lives of constant defeats—exploitive labor conditions, forced family separations, and untimely deaths related to slavery. And suddenly, at the Thornton, something changed with Mary Christmas when Sheriff Strout and the posse arrived and saw Eliza there. The enslaver lost her power to enslave.[35]

Eliza no longer needed the false hope of her enslaver's promises. The sheriff had ordered the servant to leave with him. She had never broken the law up to that moment, and she did not start then. Also, she was about to go to court to ask for her freedom, and a violation of the law would not have put her in the best legal light before a judge.[36]

The enslaver's pleas stirred feelings of hurt and betrayal in the enslaved. The captor displayed a great degree of arrogance in expecting Eliza to violate the law. Mary also showed how gullible she thought Eliza was in thinking the captive would once again fall for the promise of liberation, especially after she had been abducted to the lake house to prevent exactly that. Eliza sharply reminded her enslaver of the broken vows. "She said she would give me free papers," Eliza later recalled. "I asked her why she did not in St. Louis." That question may have been the sharpest words Eliza had ever given to any enslaver.[37]

Mary did not address Eliza's retort. Instead, she continued trying to convince her to stay. "She said over and over again that I must not go in this way, but that they would give me my free papers," Eliza later remembered. Mary preferred controlling when to free Eliza instead of ceding that control to her or to some uncouth northerners. By losing the enslaved to the antislavery Minnesotans, the enslaver was losing face in front of her family, fellow southern tourists, and proslavery locals.[38]

Eliza rejected her captor's pleas. She finally told the enslaver, "I had rather go now," and spoke no further to her. Eliza turned her back on the Christmas ladies, and she walked out of the Thornton House for the last time. She boarded one of the posse's coaches, then rode away from the lake house with her allies and the officers. Soon afterward, lake visitors Alfred Elfelt and John Nininger rushed to St. Paul to tell the local Democratic newspaper what had just transpired at Thornton's place.[39]

With Eliza's departure, the women and children remaining in the boardinghouse must have been in shock. The Freemans' captive child Ann was still staying with her enslavers there when the entire exchange between Mary and Eliza took place. Ann's enslavers kept her with them at the lake house after the posse left, and the Freeman ladies awaited the return of the family patriarch to the lodge. Nevertheless, Eliza had just modeled for little Ann how to assert her own independence.

The Christmas ladies arranged to leave the Thornton House immediately. They returned to the Winslow and awaited Christmas's return—hopefully with Eliza. The trunk full of Eliza's clothes was a taunting reminder of the enslaved woman who had just escaped them and the freedom she was closer to achieving—a freedom that was completely out of their control.

While Mary waited, she began to care for herself in her illness and to see to her daughter's needs as best she could. She had no choice. Eliza had been her only enslaved servant for the past six weeks, and the enslaver could not legally purchase another person in Minnesota. Whether she became bitter at Eliza's defection or self-congratulatory toward her own ability to attend to herself, she was—for the first time in her entire life—without an enslaved person at her command. She could at least remind herself that her deprivation was temporary and that dozens of other enslaved people remained at Shiloh to serve her when she returned.[40]

When Sheriff Strout, Deputy Canney, and their posse led Eliza away from Lake Harriet and out of Richfield Township, the afternoon sun was at its brightest point, illuminating the path to the courthouse in Minneapolis. The seven-mile trip gave Eliza some time to think about how she would plead her case for freedom in court. Her long-awaited opportunity for liberation was moments away.

≋10

Freedom Trial in ᒧMinnesota

Eliza and her legal entourage rushed seven miles northeast to the courthouse, reversing the journey the Christmases had forced her to take. The horses trotted away from the pebbled lakeshore, across the prairie, down the hill and through the woods, and onto the grid of city streets. Urban environments like Memphis had always given Eliza more autonomy than rural ones like Shiloh and Richfield Township did, and her arrival in Minneapolis was bringing her closer to freedom.

Minneapolis had no town hall. However, to at least one writer, the city had an aesthetic advantage over St. Anthony on the other side of the Mississippi. "The Minneapolis side is perhaps the most beautiful," said the writer. This time Eliza's enslavers did not distract her from viewing it, but her rush to the courthouse and her anticipation of her hearing probably kept her attention from the city's beauty.[1]

The hearing provided an opportunity for Minneapolis to achieve some distinction after its first years in St. Anthony's shadow. Minneapolis would be incorporated in 1867, twelve years after St. Anthony. St. Anthony's city marshal John A. Armstrong kept law and order in Minneapolis, because the latter city did not have a police force. Minneapolis was also slightly smaller than St. Anthony. But the courtroom's location in Minneapolis made the city the host of the state's first hearing for an enslaved person's emancipation. Eliza and her allies also wanted Vanderburgh's court to be the state's first one to free a captive.[2]

Eliza had a political advantage in Minneapolis that did not exist across the river. "Minneapolis is a Republican town," declared the *Mantorville Express,* of Mantorville, Minnesota, and its politics differed from the proslavery tourist economy in St. Anthony. Also, Eliza's travel northeastward from Lake Harriet removed her from the westernmost part she had seen of the United States. Over nine hundred miles of westward travel—from the Cumberland Plateau in Tennessee to the Thornton House in Minnesota—characterized her lifelong enslavement, but her current movement in the opposite direction was a literal and figurative movement away from slavery.[3]

The carriage finally stopped at the corner of Fourth Street and Eighth Avenue, the location of the county courthouse. At the time courthouses had brought only misfortune to Eliza. Her former enslaver John McLemore's multiple defenses in courtrooms kept him from fully "raising" her, and one of his many losses in court resulted in her sale from his household. In Minneapolis, however, she was the defendant, and her freedom hinged on her ability to produce what had constantly evaded "Mr. Macklemo"—a courtroom victory.

It was the afternoon of August 21, 1860—Eliza's fortieth consecutive day in Hennepin County. She had spent those forty days in a legal wilderness, living as enslaved in a free state and with no other enslaved people from Shiloh to suffer with her. In addition, during the last week of her captivity, the Christmases kept her in what must have seemed to her an actual wilderness at the shore of Lake Harriet. Her arrest finally provided an opportunity for her suffering to end.

The sheriff escorted her up to the second floor of the court-house and into Judge Vanderburgh's courtroom. Reports agree that most of the spectators were supporters of the Christmases. A Democratic-leaning newspaper said that "seven-eights of those present" wanted Eliza to stay with the couple. The *St. Cloud Visiter*, published by abolitionist Republican Jane Grey Swisshelm, less charitably referred to "large crowds of Southerners and their lick-spittle toadies" in attendance. The attendees were primarily from St. Anthony and Minneapolis, able to reach the building on short notice.[4]

Richard Christmas and John D. Freeman entered the court-room. It was the first time in almost two days that Eliza was in the same room with them. Christmas approached her, handed her ten dollars, and then turned away from her. The gift was an expensive gesture, for she hoped to make that much in a month of work as a free woman. The gesture demonstrated the Christmases' massive wealth—part of which their enslavement of her had comprised. The colonel may also have paid her in order to coerce her to speak in court, either against emancipation or in favor of her continued enslavement.[5]

Eliza was not the only person he owed in the courtroom. Free-man agreed to be the Christmases' lawyer for the hearing. This position also gave the couple some leverage in the case. Although F. R. E. Cornell was a close friend of Vanderburgh's, the lawyer did not have the same prestige in Minnesota that Freeman had already achieved in both New York and Mississippi. As a district attorney in New York and then the attorney general of Mississippi, he had served in one of a state's highest legal offices. In addition, his election in 1850 to a single two-year term in the US House of Representatives demonstrated that he knew how to convince masses of people to support him—at least in Mississippi. His success in the North and the South meant he could win cases in both a free state and a slave state. The Christmases were fortunate that he just happened to have vacationed in Minnesota when they did, and that they were at the Thornton House at the same time.

Freeman had come to Minnesota to take a vacation, and he had only a matter of minutes to prepare for an unexpected, impromptu hearing. Because so many enslavers had entered and exited Minnesota with their captives for the past two years, despite its "free state" status, they and their supporters had no reason to expect a legal challenge.[6]

The slaveholding tourists and their local supporters looked to Freeman to preserve Eliza's enslavement—and slavery itself—in Minnesota. If he lost the case, southerners would effectively lose a northern state they had considered sympathetic to their slaveholding, and local tourism businesses faced the permanent loss of southern visitors' patronage. But the lawyer had the daunting task of convincing a judge from a free state to order a free African American's re-enslavement in a free state. Such an argument essentially asked Vanderburgh to violate Minnesota law.

Before the hearing started, Freeman approached Vanderburgh—one former New Yorker to another. The attorney requested that the judge forego the proceedings. In return, Freeman promised, his client would privately manumit the enslaved woman and therefore avoid the humiliation of a public emancipation beyond his control. The judge refused, the New Yorkers parted ways, and Freeman and his client resumed their preparation for the hearing.[7]

Other attendees came to support Eliza. Emily Grey and her husband Ralph Grey entered the courtroom, ready to witness how a judge in Minnesota would exercise justice for one of their own—and to see firsthand the results of their work. Although Eliza petitioned for her freedom, American justice itself was on trial. She was forcing the state's judicial branch to specifically determine whether Minnesota's constitution applied to African Americans.

The Greys joined the local European American abolitionists

in waiting for the judge to execute the state's laws concerning freedom. They stayed physically together through the hearing—a visible symbol of the solidarity between the enslaved and her allies. Eliza sat behind Emily Grey and between two European American women—Elizabeth Babbitt, who was two months from birthing a child, and E. F. Bates. Members of the integrated group deliberately placed themselves together in a public setting, and such an arrangement was a rare sight for Eliza. Although she had dined with European American servants on a steamboat and at the Winslow, those servants had merely followed the policies of their places of employment. And the resentment some of them felt at the imposition contrasted with the camaraderie exhibited by the abolitionists in the courthouse.[8]

Judge Vanderburgh entered the courtroom. No matter how he decided, the case's distinction as the state's first freedom hearing made the event a milestone. Still, he was taken aback by the large public attention to the hearing, as he understood it. "The issuance of the writ caused great excitement and interest in the community," he later remembered. "Upon the return of the writ, a great crowd gathered at the court house."[9]

Vanderburgh's court was the only legal mechanism through which Eliza could obtain free papers. Although Minnesota was organized as a free territory in 1849 and became a free state in 1858, the local government had not devised any means by which to effect an enslaved person's liberation within state borders. Unlike New York State, Minnesota did not pass a law to prohibit enslavers from traveling within its borders with enslaved people, nor did the state require anyone traveling with an African American to provide the African American's free papers. Instead, state officials governed by the honor system, simply trusting the enslavers to publicly regard the enslaved as free for the duration of their stay in Minnesota.[10]

Eliza's hearing marked the first time a government entity recognized her on her own terms. Before then, people documenting her existence in federal censuses and slave schedules listed her with anonymity—a mere hash mark beside the name of her enslaver. Deeds of sales to John McLemore, Lucius Polk, and Thomas Gholson in Tennessee courthouses identified Eliza solely by her first name. Her allies, however, had called her "Eliza Winston" in their request for the writ, and the court subsequently gave the hearing the official title *The Case of Eliza Winston, a Slave*. A few days after the hearing, William Babbitt and Deputy Canney gave affidavits to the local justice of the peace, and they both referred to her by that name. More importantly, in Eliza's post-hearing affidavit of August 24, she herself declared, "My name is Eliza Winston."[11]

In that one sentence of self-identification, Winston defined herself with a surname of her own choosing. She disregarded the surnames of all her enslavers. The court's recognition of her as Eliza Winston meant that it too would not identify her according to who enslaved her. She did not reveal the source of her surname, nor did the court request it.

The hearing title—*The Case of Eliza Winston, a Slave*—illustrated the paradox of enslavement in a free state. It suggested that Minnesota law considered Winston quasi-free. The reference to her as "*a Slave*" meant that the court still considered her enslavement as a legal fact despite the hearing's location in a free state, and it showed how deeply ingrained the association of African Americans with slavery was among Minnesotans and in the United States. On the other hand, the designation also showed that the court did not agree with the contention from local Democrats that she was not really enslaved, and the identification of her as enslaved had the potential to help her case.[12]

Winston filed an affidavit three days after the hearing, probably at the instruction of Judge Vanderburgh. Her imprisonment by the Christmases made it impossible for her attorney to submit her affidavit with his application for the writ of habeas corpus. The judge, realizing this case would be explosive, must have wanted the details on the record. Thus, her affidavit described events of the hearing, and it also gave details of her life that some newspapers printed in their reports on the case. She claimed she was thirty years old—an understatement by about twelve years. She did not discuss her family of origin at all. She mentioned her husband, their plans for her freedom, and the wealth they had acquired together, and she expressed her desire to marry again: "I might have married very happily with a free colored person, but Col. Christmas would not let me marry any one but one of his plantation hands, and I would not marry any one but a free person." She named each of her enslavers and summarized their treatment of her, including Gholson's ownership of the house she and her husband had purchased. Of the Christmases, she noted, "I have been closely confined, have had scarcely any time to myself or to see the other slaves, as most house servants can have, but I have never fretted or complained because I thought if I did my very best, they would perhaps give me my freedom." She described her trunk of clothing, left at the Winslow House. She mentioned wanting a job for pay as a "nurse girl" in Memphis. She noted that emancipation would keep her at work but in control of her own labor. By tying her liberation to employment, she showed that her petition was not sentimental. Like many other antebellum African Americans pursing liberation, she considered the United States her home, sought her place in it as a fellow citizen, and used legal resources to develop her relationship to the law as an African American. She had obeyed the nation's laws in her enslavement for forty-three years, but her presence in court exhibited her faith that the law could finally free her.[13]

Her references to her model behavior suggested an argument that meritocracy supplemented democracy. Her lifetime of good behavior without any enslavers having "found fault" with her, as she put it, entitled her to the protection of Minnesota's antislavery law. She falsely claimed "I was never sold," perhaps associating the sale of a person with an enslaver's disapproval of the person sold. Her own sale in 1834 had taught her that enslavers sometimes sold people because of mounting debts instead of an enslaved person's behavior. On the other hand, her character as a captive mattered more than the actions of the captors, because the writ and the hearing were both in *her* name. By mentioning her years of obedience and her wish to work in her freedom, she argued that she could be a productive member of society even with fewer restrictions on her life. She also showed her deep humanity: "I have nursed and taken care of the child of my mistress from her birth till the present, and I am so attached to the child that I would be willing to serve Col. Christmas, if I could be assured of my freedom eventually, but with all my attachment to the child, I prefer freedom in Minnesota to life long slavery in Mississippi."[14]

The hearing finally commenced at 5:00 PM, and Judge Vanderburgh arraigned Winston. He structured the hearing as an opportunity for the lawyers to argue for or against Winston's captivity, but he did not call for witnesses to testify during the proceedings. He allowed Freeman to provide a legal justification for Winston's present enslavement in Minnesota. Cornell was to follow Freeman and explain what legal basis allowed for the enslaved woman to be freed from the Christmases. After Freeman's remarks, Vanderburgh was to conclude the hearing with his judgment on the captive's fate.[15]

Christmas and his attorney approved of the judge's management of the hearing. They were disadvantaged by entering a courtroom in a state with a Republican governor and in a city whose majority supported that party. Nevertheless, as Vanderburgh remembered, "When the respondent and his counsel . . . discovered that it was to be a quiet and orderly judicial inquiry, in which they were to be heard and treated fairly, they appeared quite satisfied." For a judge committed to the fair exercise of the law, even an enslaver deserved his say in a free state's court.[16]

The judge called Freeman to speak, and the lawyer began his

remarks. He claimed that the US Supreme Court's decision in *Dred Scott v. Sandford* made Winston the property of the Christmases. To him, *Dred Scott* meant that enslavers could legally keep a person captive in any territory or state they chose, whether in the North or the South. As a result, the judge did not have the authority to tell US citizens to relinquish themselves of any humans they owned. Chief Justice Roger Taney had argued in *Dred Scott* that if a slaveholder took a captive into a free state and then back to a slave state, the laws of that slave state applied to the captive's legal status. Freeman ignored two facts: Winston had not yet returned to a slave state, and the *Dred Scott* decision legalized slavery only in *territories*—not in free states. Freeman argued, in effect, that Minnesota's laws mattered less than an enslaver's fundamental right to enslave. This was a risky position to take in a Minnesota courtroom.[17]

Freeman's interpretation of *Dred Scott* reflected his personal views about slavery as a national sovereign right, even in a country with some free states. "Some of the individual States have exercised the sovereign power residing in the people thereof to yield up the right of slavery within the limits of their State jurisdictions," he had noted in 1848. However, he claimed that if a small group of citizens wanted to enslave in free states, they had the right to do so. "This right, like all other sovereign rights of citizens of the Union, can only be yielded up by the common consent of the whole people," he argued. "Majorities cannot rule in such a case. The constitution protects the minority in the enjoyment of all liberties not yielded to the control of government." In addition, foreshadowing Winston's hearing twelve years before it took place, he specifically addressed free states in his comments: "We can safely say to our Northern brethren, these are our constitutional liberties. You have solemnly agreed as members of the federal union to grant us their enjoyment from any source, and much less by yourselves."[18]

Freeman did not help his case in Minneapolis by maligning

some of the citizens of Hennepin County. According to the article William King published on the events, the attorney, "in his
remarks at the Court House, took occasion to insult and slander
the ladies of this community in a most shameful and disgrace-
ful manner." The lawyer likely referred to Grey and Bates while
doing so, because they were the ladies who had worked the closest with Winston in giving her a day in court.[19]

As Winston listened to the lawyer, she heard an argument that
ran counter to her understanding of the law concerning slavery.
Before Freeman's remarks, no one had directly informed her that
she was legally enslaved in Minnesota. Her friends in both Memphis and St. Anthony had said otherwise. Even the Christmases
themselves knew that she was legally free, because they had hidden her from the abolitionists and the Hennepin County sheriff. Freeman's attempt to subvert Minnesota law in a Minnesota
court was as desperate an act as the Christmases' smuggling of
Winston to the lake house.

Freeman rested his case. Judge Vanderburgh then called his
old law partner to address the court. For the first time, Winston saw the man who chose to advocate for her in court, and
he was the first lawyer to ever represent her. Until that moment
the lawyers in her life—President Andrew Jackson and Thomas
Gholson—had enslaved her. It was deeply significant that this
lawyer would try to help her become liberated.

Freeman was attempting to legally extend *Dred Scott* to a free
state; Cornell took Minnesota's law at face value. He understood that *Dred Scott*'s legalization of slavery in Minnesota Territory had ended in 1858, when Minnesota became a free state.
Moreover, he kept his remarks extremely brief, reciting just one
sentence from that free state's constitution: Article 1, section 2.
"There shall be neither slavery nor involuntary servitude in the
state," he said.[20]

At last, Winston heard the local antislavery law for herself, in
the solemn, formal setting of a courtroom. Winston's friends and

her late husband's friends had mentioned she would receive freedom in the North. Emily Grey had told her, "You are free." The lawyer's words let Winston know that her belief in her friends' claims was not misplaced.

With no further reasoning, Cornell abruptly rested his case. Winston did not testify; Grey and Babbitt did not testify. By speaking so little, presenting the constitution's words as the prima facie evidence of unlawful imprisonment, Cornell displayed significant confidence in the strength of his argument. By focusing exclusively on the law and not on slavery as a moral issue, he avoided maligning enslavers—an important part of the economies of Minnesota's riverside communities—on a personal level. His brief argument was still a gamble, though, for he ran the risk of portraying overconfidence or arrogance. With Winston's emancipation on the line, he could not afford to be flippant.

Then again, what more was there for Cornell to say? He was in a courtroom, and to him the law—especially the Minnesota Constitution spoke for itself. His dramatic brevity and his restriction to mere recitation underscored that point. The state's exclusion of slavery had no clause of exception for seasonal tourists.

Besides freeing Winston, Cornell was attempting to establish a successful legal template. The state had multiple judicial districts, and African Americans enslaved outside of the Fourth Judicial District would not necessarily have the good fortune to petition in front of an antislavery, Republican judge like Vanderburgh. Cornell was crafting a legal argument that any counsel for a captive could use in any court throughout the state to convince a judge to emancipate an enslaved person. The lawyer's reference to Minnesota's Constitution sufficed, because its articles applied all over the state.

For Judge Vanderburgh, the decision was clear, and he offered his verdict after some brief remarks. He told Eliza Winston that she was free, effective immediately. Winston was emancipated at last.[21]

Through this verdict, Winston made one final break from Andrew Jackson's hold on her—and the state of Minnesota experienced some of the final throes of Jacksonian democracy. During his presidency the number of military officers enslaving people at Fort Snelling peaked, and private citizens first engaged in the practice there. Three decades later, the captivity of African Americans by southern visitors and temporary residents in Minnesota was still cheerfully embraced by Minnesotans engaging in business with southerners. This reflected two of the late president's major goals: westward expansion of the United States and protection of slaveholders. Jackson's appointee Roger Taney supported these goals with his opinion in *Dred Scott v. Sandford*, and that decision was a factor in causing the Panic of 1857, which in turn made Minnesotans more dependent on southern tourism. And just as Jackson ran roughshod over political norms through the spoils system, slaveholding tourists disregarded the laws of the free state of Minnesota. Winston's victory produced a compelling irony: a woman Jackson himself had enslaved defeated a part of his legacy in Minnesota.[22]

The judge then ordered the sheriff to remove Winston from his custody, and her allies immediately rejoiced. Elizabeth Babbitt and E. F. Bates hugged her. None of those women could vote or run for public office, but they had put their social networks to constructive use to help Winston. The victory validated their collective organizing and activity as women.[23]

Christmas's allies expressed their anger. The account published by abolitionist Jane Grey Swisshelm in her *St. Cloud Visiter* noted that a local clergyman immediately sprang from his seat and protested to Vanderburgh, complaining about the existence of the constitutional law that Cornell had cited. Swisshelm later claimed in her autobiography that Episcopal minister D. B. Knickerbocker had made the objection. The minister responded by calling her recollection "pure fiction," but he specifically refuted the accusation that he "openly criticised in court the decision"—rather than denying that he had criticized the verdict at all. If Knickerbocker indeed objected to the verdict because of the state's prohibition of slavery, then his rationale contradicted the notion of his southern proslavery Episcopal colleague George W. Freeman, who had said that it was not the church's role to challenge a society's status quo.[24]

More of Christmas's supporters tried to use the power of their voices to convince the judge to overturn his own decision on the spot. Christmas and his attorney were not among the rabble-rousers, and even Republican journalists made a point of noting that the southerners in the courthouse treated the proceedings with respect. "It is the universal testimony that the Southerners deported themselves as law abiding citizens and as courteous gentlemen," praised the *Falls Evening News*. Rather, the chaos came from Minnesotans themselves. The Christmases' local allies made their living by appeasing enslavers throughout each spring and summer, and they did not want their clientele to depart the state before the end of the tourism season because of the verdict. They also wanted the tourists to return the following year.[25]

Elizabeth Babbitt, Bates, Grey, and Winston moved through the unruly crowd, but Christmas caught up with the four women before they left the courtroom. Unlike the unhinged mob supporting him, he calmly and quietly approached his former property. He gave one last order to her: "Come, Eliza, your mistress is at the Winslow House and wants to see you." He appealed to whatever emotional attachment she still felt for his wife. And wherever Mary was, Norma, with whom Winston had especially bonded, would be too.[26]

The former captive did not fall for the sentimentality, and she wasted no time in exercising her legally validated agency. She answered his directive with just one word—no. Her reply was significant, because she refused a European American man's order for perhaps the first time in her entire life. She said a word that her mother Molly and grandmother Judah did not have the legal authority to say to their enslavers. In that moment she broke a multigenerational curse that had begun long before, when her African ancestors survived the grueling Middle Passage and arrived in the United States in chains.[27]

Winston initially tried to diminish her own assertiveness, adding to her emphatic no a cautious "not today." She then offered the possibility of going to the Winslow the next day to see Mary. But her allies would not allow her to surrender an inch to her former enslaver. They surrounded her and loudly protested. They had put in too much work for her emancipation to see her jeopardize it by returning to her former captor.[28]

Christmas was initially undeterred by Winston's agency and the abolitionists enveloping her. He told Winston "not to do wrong," suggesting that she *should* return to him. His reference to ethics was ironic. While antislavery activists uniformly wrote and spoke about slavery as wrong or immoral, Christmas applied ethics to Winston's decision about her submission to the practice.[29]

Winston dodged the enslaver's rhetorical trap. For her, "to do wrong" did not constitute parting from the Christmases. Moreover, Vanderburgh's verdict demonstrated that she was right to pursue emancipation. She stood her ground against Christmas. "I told him that I was not going to do wrong, but that I did not wish to go with him."[30]

At last, Christmas seemed to realize he no longer enslaved Eliza and could not dictate her activities. Instead of ordering her, he expressed curiosity for her immediate plans. He asked, "Well, Eliza, will you go with me or with these persons?" He held out hope that he still had a chance to bring her back to the family despite her multiple refusals to him, but his question tacitly acknowledged she had the agency to choose what to do next.[31]

Winston replied, "I will go with these ladies." Her decision to spend the first moments of her liberation specifically with women brought her full circle, because women had chosen to care for her throughout her enslaved life. Her mother and grandmother had raised her on the Cumberland Plateau and in Nashville. Free and enslaved African American women in the South had helped her pack for the North. Grey and Bates in St. Anthony led the effort toward freeing her. The company of women had given her encouragement, and her choice to be with them signaled that she still wanted if not needed that comfort from them in her freedom.[32]

All of Christmas's options closed at that moment, and his demeanor changed. He was a defeated man—not just in court but also in the eyes of his former property. He sighed in resignation, "Very well," and he made no further request for her return. As with Thomas Hopkins, the McLemores, and Thomas Gholson, the Christmases involuntarily lost their claim to Winston. However, unlike the previous dispossessions—all resulting from forces beyond her control—this time, she removed herself from the Christmases and from all enslavement. Winston, Grey, Bates, and Elizabeth Babbitt resumed moving toward the courtroom's exit.[33]

Judge Vanderburgh ordered Sheriff Strout to clear the courtroom, and Strout obliged. The sheriff had suffered a long and busy day, and the judge's two orders to him—to apprehend Winston and clear the room—bookended his hours in the whirlwind. His role in taking Winston from the Christmases put him at odds with the southern tourists and their local sympathizers, which included at least two of his business partners. He told the press that he "felt heartily ashamed of the whole transaction," thus trying to save face with his clientele.[34]

Christmas told his supporters in the courtroom that he accepted the judge's verdict. "Well, Colonel," a spectator told him, "You have lost your n——." Christmas responded, "Yes, I reckon so, but I have plenty more of them and it's all right." Indeed, more than 160 other captives still working at Shiloh awaited his return. In addition, Winston had personally served Mary and Norma—not him. As bad as he may have felt for his wife and daughter, he himself could afford to be philosophical about the hearing's outcome.[35]

His attitude did little to calm his supporters. Winston's liberation insulted the personal honor of the locals who sympathized with enslavers. Minnesotans had promoted their state as tolerant of enslaver–enslaved relationships that tourists brought with them. Many of them understood that Christmas had risked losing Winston by bringing her to a free state, and they did not fault Vanderburgh for his decision or Strout for following the judge's lawful order. Rather, they directed their anger largely at the abolitionists for forcing the issue and for creating a major public spectacle out of one guest's enslavement of one person. Minnesota's reputation as a state that respected southerners was on the line, and the mob formed to defend it.

In addition, Winston's emancipation meant that no one was taking care of her anymore. She was widowed, and she had no brother, father, or son to look after her. An unmarried woman's demand to be left alone and to take charge of her own life was as unusual as a petition for emancipation in Minnesota. The proslavery men's protests suggested a belief that, as both a woman and an African American, Winston needed to belong to *somebody*.

The crowd followed the new freedwoman and her supporters out of the courtroom and onto the steps outside the courthouse. There Christopher Woodbridge McLean, the Winslow House's manager, offered to have Winston kidnapped and brought to Christmas for enslavement, claiming that many were willing to abduct her ("plenty of us," he said). Christmas did not ask anyone to help him bring her back after the trial, nor did he publicly validate the manager's offer. Indeed, the proprietor spoke in a desperate move to save face after one of his customers had experienced the loss of a captive. By retrieving Winston, whether the Christmases wanted it or not, the manager would once again have a perfect record of satisfied customers. Not unlike Andrew Jackson's intervention to keep Eliza in the Donelson family,

McLean tried to keep the Christmas family from losing their valuable property. Thus, because of one man's pride, Winston's freedom remained vulnerable in a free state.[36]

The hotel proprietor's proposal to volunteer as a kidnapper for the Christmases was not a major deviation from his usual work. His job of lodging guests required him to cater to the desires and needs of wealthy enslavers. His meals had to satisfy enslavers' palates, and the carpets and artwork in the Winslow had to please the captors' eyes. On the other hand, such duties were for all the guests, and he did not distinguish meals and décor according to the number of captives his guests brought. Rather, his willingness to seize a human being and bring her to his customers was his attempt to appease the Christmases as enslavers.[37]

Sheriff Strout did not immediately respond to McLean's open call for illegal activity. No one in the mob tried to kidnap Winston in the courthouse, and McLean's request for her capture did not constitute an illegal act. On the other hand, Strout had the authority to intervene in a manner that would restore order. He did not receive a direct order from the judge about the outcry, so he did nothing.

Abolitionist William King followed Winston, Bates, Grey, the Babbitts, and the mob toward the courthouse steps. After the shout to kidnap Winston, King responded by reprimanding the crowd in his own booming voice. His loudness and the sharpness of his words distracted the crowd. He called them "a gang of slave-driving kidnappers." Then he grabbed a cane from a nearby deacon and threatened to bash the head of the first man to try to lay "an unfriendly hand" on the freedwoman. The *St. Anthony Express* quoted his profanity: "G—d d—n you come, kidnappers. Come on, you kidnappers. G—d d—n you come on." He startled the crowd with his outburst and his waving of the cane.[38]

The outburst was not out of character for King, considering his line of work. He published Minneapolis's Republican-leaning newspaper, the *State Atlas*. His work involved finding ways to reach masses of people with his information and opinions. He also had to attract people who were willing to advertise their businesses in his periodical. Winston's hearing was newsworthy enough as the state's first freedom trial, but the editor made the event even more significant by becoming part of the story. In addition, because of his ties to local abolitionists, other newspapers were certain to rely on his coverage and the exclusive information he could provide about Winston and her supporters.

The proslavery crowd was frozen in disbelief. As the mob processed how to react to King, the freedwoman and her allies took advantage of the distraction. They dashed toward a door at the front of the courthouse and rushed out of the building. Such an exit was probably a rare experience for Winston, who had been leaving mansions and hotels through the rear for her entire life. And even inside a facility of justice in the Northwest and during her initial minutes of freedom, she was still African American, only a few moments removed from bondage and possibly on her way back to it.

Fortunately, she and her allies left the building undetected. The Babbitts rushed Winston to their carriage, and they all quickly boarded it. The vehicle swiftly pulled away from the courthouse, and her allies entered their own carriages and followed them. They raced through the beautiful city as fast as their horses could carry them.

King's profane outburst at the courthouse was too strong even for people who did not support local slavery. A church deacon who stood behind him during his tirade later complained, "It was the most awful swearing I ever heard." Nevertheless, however strongly the clergyman disagreed with the substance of King's belligerence, he had to admit to its effectiveness. "I don't believe in doing evil that good may come," the deacon cautiously prefaced, "but if King hadn't sworn that day, we couldn't have saved Eliza Winston."[39]

Christmas's supporters eventually realized that the woman about whom they argued was no longer among them. They could only watch helplessly from the courthouse as Winston and the abolitionists receded farther and farther from view. Eventually, they could no longer see the freedwoman at all.

≋11

An Emancipated Life

Winston spent her first minutes of freedom racing through Minneapolis with the Babbitts, fleeing desperately from people who wanted to return her to captivity. About two dozen of her supporters followed them, offering some protection.[1]

The carriage reached the Babbitts' home, which lay at the intersection of Tenth Street and Russell (later Park) Avenue. The house, like Grey's home, was a safe space for the freedwoman, and her presence made the residence a new station of Hennepin County's Underground Railroad (UGRR). Winston and the Babbitts spent a moment there regaining their composure after the stress from the arrest and the emancipation earlier that day.[2]

The former captive rested in her liberation for only a short while at the Babbitts' house. The proslavery Minnesotans at the courthouse had seen the Babbitts escort her out of the courtroom, and some in the crowd who had also been at the lake house may have seen William Babbitt in the posse there. The Babbitts assumed that Christmas's local allies would be angry enough and desperate enough to go to their home and try to recapture Winston.

William Babbitt and Winston soon climbed into the carriage again and drove through Minneapolis, two to three miles to the east, to the corner of Oak and Walnut Streets (now 630 Twenty-Second Avenue South). This was the home of abolitionist George B. Stone, who ran the city's public school. Stone had attended Winston's hearing, and he was one of the people who congratulated her in the courtroom. He had kept a lower profile than the Babbitts that day, but he immediately accepted his new role as a local UGRR conductor. Stone welcomed Winston into his home and away from her pursuers.[3]

By staying inside the Stone house that night, Winston avoided two different bands of local predators. One group of proslavery Minnesotans marauded through Minneapolis, the other in St. Anthony. These rioters acted as if Winston were legally an enslaved fugitive who had escaped from the Christmases instead of a free African American released from an illegal kidnapping. The mobs specifically targeted the residences of the women who had sat next to Winston in the hearing, on the assumption that one of the women was sheltering her. The gang in St. Anthony broke into the Grey residence and ransacked it while searching for Winston. Meanwhile, the mob in Minneapolis threw rocks at the Babbitts' home and forcibly entered it, but Elizabeth Babbitt fended them off by aiming a shotgun at them.[4]

The crowd retreated but remained at the house, threatening to burn it down. Elizabeth Babbitt, in spite of her pregnancy, stole out of the house and ran for help. She found Sheriff Strout and pleaded for his assistance. He brought two or three men with him to confront the agitators at her residence. The sheriff, whose failure to pacify the crowd at the courthouse earlier in the afternoon had allowed the mayhem to grow, convinced the mob at the Babbitt house to disperse—but he did not arrest any of the vandals. The rioters retreated, and the streets of Minneapolis quieted to an uneasy peace for the rest of the night.[5]

Southerners vacationing in St. Anthony and surrounding communities prepared to immediately leave Minnesota. They did not want their enslaved servants to conspire with abolitionists for freedom and request their own hearings. The enslavers and their captives boarded the first available steamboat, the *Northern Light*, and they retreated downriver to Missouri and other slave states. The Christmases were among the first tourists to leave after the hearing.[6]

Residual anger festered among the proslavery locals, and Winston wisely remained secluded with allies in Minneapolis. The Christmases' allies turned her name into a slur, calling William Babbitt "Eliza" when they saw him in public; they referred to Winston as a "n----- wench." Their anger revealed their anxiety about the rapid and massive departure of their clientele. An employee at Minneapolis's Nicollet House lamented that after Winston's emancipation, "within a week all the Southern families had left."[7]

Some southern newspapers resorted to fiction to portray the Christmases as benevolent victims of northern antislavery hostility. While Eliza's own account noted that Richard Christmas gave her ten dollars before the court proceedings began, some articles reported that he handed money to her *after* their post-trial conversation—fifty dollars from him and at least forty from his wife—and then walked away for the last time from the woman he enslaved. However, none of the affidavits submitted after the hearing mentioned any gift of money from Christmas to her after the hearing ended. Moreover, Winston herself claimed that the exchange never happened. William Babbitt remembered, "On hearing the rumor that he [Christmas] gave her fifty dollars, she denied it but said she wished he had, as he really owed her more than that."[8]

Winston's trunk returned to Mississippi with the Christmases. In October the *St. Cloud Democrat* announced that the abolitionists who had helped Winston "insisted upon her prosecuting the Col. for the wardrobe and taking out a replevin to recover it." But she refused, sending a message via "one of his neighbors who was about to return . . . that she would not prosecute him for the theft of her clothes . . . on account of the little child she had nursed so long, and whom she loved as her own."[9]

For the first three months after Winston's liberation, she remained in hiding, as her allies waited for local proslavery tempers to cool. She emerged from hiding once to speak to her supporters. On October 19 she traveled to Woodman Hall in Minneapolis, where she gave a public address to the Hennepin County Antislavery Society—the same abolitionist organization that had helped to liberate her. Woodman Hall was a theater, but that day it became the newest station of Hennepin County's UGRR. Winston risked confrontation by the Christmases' supporters when making her speech, but she delivered it without incident. According to audience member William King, she "declared herself satisfied with her present condition." Her remarks even won over her listening detractors; King noted that "those who were at first disposed to interest themselves for the owner find their sympathy for Mr. Christmas oozing out and drying up as facts

Woodman Hall, on Hellen Street (now Second Avenue South) in Minneapolis, in 1860. *MNHS*

become more fully known." The speech was Winston's final public appearance in Minnesota.[10]

The group's sponsorship of her address exemplified the local abolition movement's strategy for ending slavery. European American abolitionists throughout the North arranged for freed people to give public speeches about their enslavement. The content of those remarks provided evidence for abolitionists to use when trying to convince the general public of the evil of slavery, as Babbitt thought the movement should do. The activists rarely integrated the formerly enslaved themselves into the movement, except as speakers; they were not allowed to hold leadership positions. Then again, as someone in hiding, Winston could not engage in multiple public activities.[11]

During her seclusion, newspapers nationwide reported her emancipation. Her affidavit allowed reporters to use her own words in their stories, but very few people read the complete document. Only three Minnesota newspapers, all run by abolitionist editors in towns with strong sympathies toward enslavers, printed it in full. On August 28—four days after Hennepin County's justice of the peace filed the affidavit—William S. King of the St. Anthony *Falls Evening News* first published it. Exactly one week later, it appeared in the *Chatfield Republican*. Then on September 6, Jane Grey Swisshelm printed it in the *St. Cloud Democrat*. Their promotion of Winston's statement was consistent with the local abolition movement's resolve to end slavery by "bringing the public mind to see and deplore the evil of it," as Babbitt had put it in his affidavit. King also published Babbitt's affidavit, likewise written a few days after Winston's hearing; it was one of the first public statements to confirm that Winston had instigated her own freedom journey. Babbitt recalled that he had refused to involve himself in her plans until he knew that she sought freedom for herself.[12]

In November Winston's allies arranged for her to leave Minnesota entirely. When Hennepin County's antislavery activists took her to St. Paul, they connected their county's UGRR to the more established and experienced national UGRR. Through the 1850s, conductors in St. Paul had helped enslaved people to escape from enslavers at the city's hotels, sending them to Canada via such points east as Chicago and Detroit. In contrast, the enslaved in Hennepin County did not have access to antislavery resources. The county's activists did not officially organize as an entity until 1859, and the Winslow House's location on a plateau isolated its enslaved people among enslavers and proslavery locals. Fortunately for Winston, Babbitt and his colleagues managed to link Hennepin's UGRR line to the line going from St. Paul to Canada.[13]

> Fall was nearly past, but the river had not yet frozen over. Winston boarded a Mississippi steamboat in St. Paul and sailed downriver. The buildings of urban St. Paul soon gave way to trees shedding the last of their colorful leaves. The vessel's destination was St. Louis, but UGRR conductors near the Iowa–Illinois border helped enslaved fugitives travel eastward to Chicago by train. Winston entered Illinois as an already free African American escaping proslavery kidnappers from a free state farther to the northwest; most UGRR passengers in Illinois had escaped slavery in Missouri. The states of origin did not matter when they arrived in Galena, Illinois. The conductors there directed them all to Canada via the same eastbound trains.[14]

Winston herself headed east to Detroit, where she had settled by later in November. According to some reports, she had gone from Detroit to Canada and then back to Detroit. If so, she would have been one of thousands of African Americans whose journey out of slavery included passage through Detroit to Canada. Over one thousand runaways fled to Canada through Detroit in 1855 alone.[15]

Meanwhile, the freedwoman thought of returning to Memphis. She wrote to her allies in Minneapolis, asking them for money and for her free papers. She required money to travel, and she needed her papers in order to avoid being captured and resold into slavery while there. She still erroneously believed that ownership of her late husband's land in Memphis had transferred to her after his death, and she wanted to return there to claim it. In addition, she expected to find the labor of her choice in a slave state that did not welcome free African Americans. To make ends meet, she planned to work in the field of health care, but she intended to do it for pay instead of for free. "I could get employment as a nurse girl, and could earn from ten to fifteen dollars a month," she had predicted in her affidavit.[16]

As Winston established herself as a northern freedwoman, sectionalism intensified throughout the country. At first, newspapers across the South complained about Winston's emancipation. They referred to her as having been "abducted" from the Thornton House; the *Weekly Mississippian* called her removal from there "capturing" and an "outrage." The writers simply did not consider Minnesota's prohibition of slavery to be applicable to enslavers. Indeed, the reporters described the events as if she had still legally belonged to the Christmases in a free state.[17]

The Christmases' lawyer, John D. Freeman, was livid about Winston's emancipation. He, his family, and his young captive returned to Mississippi, and he wrote that the South should stop submitting to the North's restricting of southerners' enjoyment of slavery. He suggested that the Union dissolve: "I see no serious obstacles to a peaceable severance between the slave and free States—they hate each other cordially and cannot live peaceably together." It did not help that a Republican-leaning Minnesota newspaper had called him "a seedy pettifogger when at home, who hires some decrepit old n—— to lick occasionally, so as to show his devotion to the institution."[18]

Even as 1861 dawned, southern newspapers still followed Winston's fate. They spread a false rumor that she had returned to Shiloh plantation in Tallula. The staff of a newspaper in Sauk Rapids, Minnesota, claimed to have received a letter from Richard Christmas stating that Winston had "begged her way back to her master in Mississippi" ("[she] is again at her old house in the

South, minus everything save a thankful heart"). The newspaper wryly added, "Can any one now tell which Eliza prefers—the South or the North—Slavery or Freedom?" It was a dig at her allies—a suggestion that they never should have interfered with her relationship with her enslavers.[19]

Most readers saw the report as a desperate ruse and refused to believe it. For years Sauk Rapids land baron George W. Sweet had made thousands of dollars selling his land to enslavers, and in March 1860 he had voted as a state legislator in favor of the failed bill to legalize slavery in Minnesota for tourists only. His town was especially invested in making sure southerners were happy. Some southern newspapers reprinted the false rumor.[20]

On January 1, 1861, Winston spent her first post-emancipation New Year's Day in Detroit. No one owned her, and no one could tell her where to live or where to work for that year or any year afterward. She did not have to spend the day in dread, unlike the enslaved people nervously awaiting their fates at Shiloh and Hamilton Place. Whether she celebrated the arrival of 1861 with new friends or whether she kept to herself, she controlled how she observed that day.

When sectionalism erupted into the Civil War three months later, the southern press finally turned its attention away from Winston and Minnesota's abolitionists. Secession statements from Confederate states did not mention the freedwoman or her emancipation but instead expressed determination to protect their right to enslave people in slave states. The South's Confederates engaged in armed conflict against Union men—most of whom were northern men. The anger from southerners concerning the loss of an enslaved person to Minnesota abolitionists suddenly paled in comparison to the Confederacy's commitment to war against the Union. Northern aggression no longer meant Winston's arrest in St. Anthony but rather battles at Antietam, Manassas, and Gettysburg.

The war prevented Winston from returning to Memphis,

because Tennessee seceded from the Union and joined the Confederacy. The state still banned free African Americans and sent people who achieved freedom through manumission to Liberia. She could neither reside in Memphis as a free woman nor attempt to claim the home she and her husband had bought there. Then again, she did not actually own property in Memphis. Whatever real estate she had purchased with her husband had always legally belonged to Thomas Gholson, because he had bought the land in his own name on their behalf.[21]

Winston's exile from Memphis provided some benefits. By staying in Michigan, she remained in a free state, and the war kept southerners from coming to the North to try to find and recapture her. Detroit became her new permanent residence, and she found employment there in the field she preferred—nursing. A letter addressed to her with the Winston surname arrived at the city's post office in November 1861, and a city directory listed her by name, address, and occupation the following year.[22]

She found a strong African American free community in Detroit. As of 1862 she resided at Beaubien Street, between Macomb and Croghan Streets. Just around the corner to the southwest lay Second Baptist Church at 441 Croghan (now Monroe). The church was the last station on the UGRR in the United States for many enslaved fugitives traveling north, just before they crossed into Canada. In addition to sheltering captive runaways, the facility was a major community center for the city's local African American residents.[23]

Winston survived at least two years in her new surroundings. Detroit was not as far north as Minnesota, but she was still hundreds of miles north of Memphis. She experienced her first northern winters in Detroit's snow and ice, which remained on the ground much longer than in Memphis. The summers in the North were like the South's spring seasons but shorter, and she spent more time during the year enduring coolness and cold. But she was willing to bear the North's climate in order to enjoy her freedom.

Winston's relocation to the free urban North did not relieve her of struggles facing African Americans because of racism. Detroit's African American community accounted for only 1,400 of the city's 44,200 residents. In March 1863 European American teenage boys and young men, many of them Irish and German, conducted mob violence against African Americans after an African American's arrest for an alleged rape of two girls. The attackers were working-class residents, upset at their financial struggles while the Union prioritized emancipating enslaved African Americans in rebel states. The rioters hated that President Abraham Lincoln's recent Emancipation Proclamation broadened the Union's conduct of the war to the liberation of those captives—who would compete for jobs.[24]

Winston apparently survived the riot. She made her peace with the city and stayed for the duration. Even as the twentieth century began, newspapers in Minnesota provided updates on her life. According to an article published in the *Mirror* in 1895, one local woman who had helped Winston become free in Minneapolis claimed to have visited the former captive in Detroit during the previous year. If this visit happened, the visitor was likely Emily Grey. She was one of the few women involved in Winston's liberation effort who still lived in Minnesota as of 1894. That article and one from 1907 in the *Minneapolis Tribune* claimed that Winston had realized her dream of marrying a free man and starting a family. However, neither article identified any of her family members by name, and both included many inaccuracies.[25]

Winston's emancipation did not result in any significant legal changes in Minnesota. Judge Vanderburgh's verdict merely affirmed the antislavery law as it had appeared in the state constitution for the previous two years. Minnesota still went without additional legislation that explicitly prohibited tourists from bringing captives with them. The judge's decision applied only to Winston herself and not to the enslaved servants remaining in the district. Nevertheless, it was an important step in eliminating antebellum de facto slavery from Minnesota. The panicked retreat of tourists and their illegally enslaved servants downriver precipitated the demise of slavery in the state, and it allowed locals a buffer of time in adjusting to the loss of clientele before the Civil War erupted. Winston's victory set a precedent, and her abolitionist allies had a record of judicial success.

The longest article about her free status that appeared in the Memphis press originated from outside of Tennessee. "A correspondent of the *Vicksburg Whig*, writing from St. Paul, Minn., on the 2d ult., states that Col. RICHARD CHRISTMAS of Mississippi had a slave girl abducted from him at Lake Harriet, near St. Paul," announced the *Memphis Weekly Bulletin* in September 1860. "She was taken from the house where he was boarding by a posse, headed by the Sheriff, who behaved in a very rude and disorderly manner." The report took the standard southern position of portraying northerners as aggressors, and it cast the enslaver— not the captive kept illegally in a free state—as the victim. The periodical failed to identify Winston by name, and the surviving McLemores in Memphis likely did not know they were reading about the woman their family had enslaved from 1822 to 1848.[26]

The war years were not kind to the McLemores, and many of the family members Winston had served did not survive to the conflict's end. In Virginia in October 1861, A. J. McLemore went out for a walk one dark night, fell into a canal, and drowned. His brother William died in 1863. Patriarch "Mr. Macklemo," having buried half his children at that point, passed away in 1864. His daughter Mary McLemore Walker bore those losses and others. Two of her three children born between 1835 and 1848 died before the start of the war, and her husband was killed in 1863 while defending the Confederacy. She survived him by one decade, succumbing after having her heart broken many times over.[27]

In Maury County, Tennessee, Lucius Polk carried on at Hamilton Place without Eliza but not without his own hardships.

In 1843 Polk, like John C. McLemore, encountered financial calamity—a "hard run for money," as Polk's cousin James K. Polk put it—and had to sell off thirty-five of his captives. His beloved wife Mary Ann Eastin Polk passed away in 1847. He married a second time and had two more children, but his second spouse died in 1858. He later entered the Confederate army and survived the war, but he too had to relinquish ownership of his enslaved people in 1865. He passed away five years later.[28]

The Christmases tried to resume their lives as major planters after returning to Mississippi from Minnesota in August 1860, but they faced several tragedies over the next two decades. The family left their plantation Shiloh during the Civil War. Richard Christmas relocated with his family to Texas. From there he left the country, going first to Cuba and then to England. Perhaps as a reflection of the family's constant absences from Shiloh or their treatment of their enslaved people, none of the captives at Shiloh adopted the Christmas surname when they became emancipated.[29]

The sickly Mary Phillips Christmas had lived for several decades without the unpaid labor of Eliza Winston. When the Civil War ended in 1865, she also had to do without the scores of remaining captives who became emancipated. She outlived her son Richard Jr., and her husband also preceded her in death. He fell from a buggy pulled by a frightened horse in 1880. That same year she and Norma returned to the North, residing at the Victoria Hotel in New York.[30]

Winston's memory survived for a much longer time among the children whom she raised while enslaved. All five of the Polk children she served at Hamilton Place from 1834 to 1842 lived at least into the 1890s. The tragically orphaned Josephine Gholson returned permanently to Memphis during her adolescent years. She graduated from college and married her second cousin once removed; the couple had no children. Meanwhile, Norma Christmas married the Marquis de Suarez d'Aulan in 1886, thus becoming the Marchioness de Suarez d'Aulan. The couple resided in Paris, giving Winston's legacy an international dimension. The marchioness raised two daughters, perhaps imparting lessons from Winston to them; both daughters survived until 1980.[31]

A few people formerly in captivity with Winston in Tennessee survived, and they may have shared their memories of her with their children. As of October 1860 Mary McLemore Walker still enslaved Winston's younger virtual siblings Malinda and Julius. Three of Malinda's children born before Winston's departure from Memphis in 1853 remained in bondage there, and afterward Malinda added three more children to her family. Her youngest daughter at the time was named Mollie—just like Winston's mother.[32]

After John D. Freeman and his family returned to Jackson, Mississippi, their enslaved girl Ann stayed with the family into adulthood. Upon emancipation, she assumed the surname French, and she attended school while working as one of the family's two domestic employees. By 1870, at age seventeen, she knew how to read and write. Within the decade she moved out of the Freeman home to work as the servant for a next-door neighbor. Regardless of whether she ever directly channeled the bravery of Winston's stand at Lake Harriet, that moment remained a part of her history. It must have affected how she conducted the rest of her life.[33]

With southern tourists and their captives absent from Minnesota during the war, the state's abolitionist residents did not encounter any additional African Americans who needed help becoming free. Hennepin County's local Underground Railroad line sat dormant after having connected only one passenger. Winston's safe passage to Canada proved that the Greys, the Babbitts, and the Stones were competent conductors. They showed that they could protect an African American escaping captivity and then take her to people more skilled in guiding escapees to Canada, just as other abolitionists throughout the country had done. However, Hennepin County's UGRR stations started too late in the antebellum era to collectively establish themselves further as part of the national UGRR.

Meanwhile, the coalition that had organized to help free Winston dissolved after its success. Grey continued to reach out to African Americans she met in St. Anthony, but none of them after August 1860 were captives. Within ten years E. F. Bates and William D. Babbitt no longer lived in the state. Judge Vanderburgh received no further applications for writs of habeas corpus on behalf of enslaved locals. The breakup of the group ended a brief but remarkable period in which men conducted activism at the initiative and direction of women.

The coalition's dissolution was a considerable setback for political activism among women across the color line. Winston, Grey, and Bates had been a formidable collective force in confronting Minnesotans for ignoring their own constitutional ban on slavery. Bates's involvement in a scheme that was initiated and directed by African American women was a rare example of a white woman yielding to African American leadership. Throughout the country European American women rarely united with African American women in the name of abolitionism, and even less often did the former submit to the latter. The coalition's success with Winston might have given women across the country a template to follow for their own political organizing, had it been acknowledged and publicized. But the Civil War sapped the momentum for such unity, because women in the Union states redirected their energies toward the war effort. Jane Grey Swisshelm, for example, became a battlefront nurse.[34]

The parting of the ways of women across the color line continued after the war. Although they had worked together to free one African American, they disagreed about extending rights to African Americans en masse. European American women organized increasingly among only themselves. Whenever they conducted campaigns with African American women, they did not honor

African American leadership. They did not work with African American women on the issue of suffrage during the late nineteenth century. Some European American women opposed the extension of suffrage to African American men before its extension to women.[35]

After the dramatic summer of 1860, abolition in Minnesota once again became an abstract issue instead of a pertinent local one. Antislavery journalists like William S. King and Jane Grey Swisshelm continued to call for the end of slavery, but this was in a national context. They referred to Winston's emancipation more as a victory that stopped slavery in Minnesota than as a warning to remain vigilant for other local captives. "Thank God that our air cannot be polluted by the breath of a slave, or rent by the clank of a chain," Swisshelm cheered in October 1860. She declared once and for all that month, "Minnesota is free—her laws and constitution supreme on her own soil; and her hospitality vindicated." In April 1861, seven months after Winston left for Detroit, Minnesotans were consumed by the demands of the Civil War—and, in 1862, by the US–Dakota War. By 1862 the state's antislavery outlets did not mention Winston at all.[36]

Minnesotans remained divided among themselves about slavery during the war. Newspapers sympathetic to the Christmases implied that abolitionists had merely used Winston to advance their own cause in Minnesota, and the pro-Christmas press accused her allies of discarding her after they had accomplished their goal of freeing her. They published unsubstantiated claims that her allies had refused her requests for money. Some reports alleged that her supporters had grown frustrated with her desire to return to the South, but other articles portrayed the abolitionists as feeling satisfied with the assistance they had already given and not wanting to assist further.[37]

The bitterness among Minnesota's southern sympathizers worsened as the war progressed. After President Lincoln's Emancipation Proclamation liberated the enslaved people in

Confederacy-held locations and enabled enslaved men to join the Union Army, some Minnesotans sharply complained that the president had ended the possibility for a negotiated, peaceful end to the war. Also, many Minnesotans did not want to die to free enslaved people. In 1864 a Democrat-leaning newspaper from the town of Chatfield, Minnesota, more bluntly referred to the post-Proclamation conflict as "this abolition n——— war."[38]

Emily Grey outlived nearly all the other primary figures in Winston's liberation, and her longevity allowed her not only more opportunities to tell her story than the others had but also to offer detailed and accurate information about Winston that eventually no one else could dispute. Grey briefly discussed the story in her memoir. Grey's husband Ralph's obituary in 1904 also referred to Winston by name, and it made a point not to identify her as an enslaved person. This exemplified the Greys' recognition of Winston's legal freedom from the moment she set foot onto Minnesota soil. The obituary called her "a colored girl employed as a maid by a Mississippi family spending the summer in [Minneapolis]."[39]

Grey's remembrances were important, because no one else in her immediate family told her story after her passing in 1916. Tragedy struck her repeatedly in the years following Winston's hearing, turning her longevity into a curse of sorts. Together the seamstress and her husband grieved the losses of three of their four children; Ralph then also preceded his wife in death. She survived her husband by a dozen years, but during that time the fourth child died. None of the children had families, so St. Anthony's first free African American family did not regenerate beyond the children whom Grey had raised there.[40]

The formal prose in Winston's affidavit may have kept anti-slavery newspapers outside of Minnesota from publishing it. Many northerners received information about enslaved people primarily through caricatured depictions in blackface minstrel shows and fictional writings, and if the formerly enslaved did not present their stories in the stereotyped dialect, then their audiences were less likely to believe them. Winston's poise and self-expression—honed through years of enslavement by political and wealthy elites—did not fit the caricature. Former captives' accounts written in grammatically correct English were suspected of being fictional stories written by abolitionists, not unlike Harriet Beecher Stowe's novel *Uncle Tom's Cabin*.[41]

One exception—former enslaved woman Harriet Jacobs's memoir *Incidents in the Life of a Slave Girl*—was published to national acclaim in the year following Winston's emancipation. Jacobs wrote to an audience primarily of European American women, and she emphasized her identity as a woman and a mother. In contrast, Winston composed her affidavit not with a mass readership in mind but rather for an audience of one—the justice of the peace in Minneapolis. Also, her account did not give a favorable portrayal of the North; instead, she discussed her preference for Memphis. Nevertheless, both Jacobs's book and Winston's affidavit provided proof in the early 1860s of the determination of formerly enslaved women to define themselves on their own terms.[42]

As for Winston herself, she refrained from attracting public attention in Detroit. She did not exploit her national celebrity as a woman freed from northern slavery, nor did she brag about once having belonged to a sitting US president. Having limited access to Minnesota-based newspapers in Detroit, she did not challenge any of the remembrances of her that appeared in periodicals from that state. Her silence left her acquaintances and contemporary observers to debate among themselves the meaning of her emancipation. She did not need their adulation or their criticism. She had already achieved what she wanted. She was free.

EPILOGUE
The Icon

In 1915, when the United States observed the fiftieth anniversary of the Confederacy's surrender at Appomattox, the nation was actively isolating itself from World War I. After the country entered the war in 1917, newspapers nationwide printed fewer public remembrances of the Civil War. Revisiting the old arguments about slavery and remembering the nation's bloodiest battles on its own soil soon gave way to reports about new battles across the ocean. African Americans serving in Europe saw the relative absence of segregation there, and they became determined to end the practice in the United States. Their celebrations of a half century of freedom transitioned into activism to end discrimination.

At the time, at least one writer in Minnesota wanted to keep Eliza Winston alive in local public memory but not in the hoary binary of either a heroine of emancipation or an opponent of states' rights. Instead, the new observance of her life, picked up by the Associated Negro Press wire service, tried to establish the relevance of her struggle to conditions facing African Americans in 1919, the year after World War I ended. That spring, tensions increased between African American veterans seeking social change and their resistant fellow Americans, and the country was mere weeks away from a summer-long deadly series of lynching and massacres by European Americans against African Americans. The writer saw Winston's ordeal in Minnesota as a reminder of the importance for African Americans to defend themselves from oppressors. The article said, "She was taken away from her master and solicitiously [*sic*] cared for by the women while the men turned out en masse prepared to nullify any forcible attempt to return her to servitude." In terms of current unrest, according to the essay, "Timid ones among the present Colored population here [in Minneapolis] who do not know this incident in the history of this city are inclined to be apprehensive lest the Chicago trouble spread to Minneapolis."[1]

The writer's attempt at making Winston relevant to what became known as the Red Summer also gave the historical figure a brief resurgence of publicity outside Minnesota. The Associated Negro Press picked up the story and made it available to African American newspapers across the country. The article marked one of the first times that the African American press publicized Winston's story. Before 1919, accounts had appeared in newspapers run solely by European Americans, and, when presenting statements from people who knew her, those periodicals largely quoted European Americans. Emily Grey was the sole exception. The Associated Negro Press's decision to distribute Winston's story made its employees the first African Americans since Grey to share the story in print.

On April 23 the article appeared in Texas in the *Dallas Express*. During the Red Summer, European Americans killed African Americans over one hundred miles northeast of Dallas in the city of Longview. The essay became an artifact of the ethnic violence from that year. Despite more mass killings of African Americans in the two years that followed—the lynching in Duluth, Minnesota, in 1920, and the massacre in Tulsa, Oklahoma, in 1921— Winston again receded from national consciousness outside of Minnesota.

When the medium of radio emerged, radio journalism followed. In addition to reading newspapers, people could listen to news broadcasts to remain informed about local, national, and global events. The radio station WTCN in Minneapolis took seriously its responsibility to educate its listeners. In 1934 WTCN aired the latest episode in its series of "historical dramatizations," as *Minnesota History* magazine put it. The broadcast consisted of a reenactment of African American enslaved woman Eliza Winston's quest for freedom in Minnesota in the summer of 1860. WTCN partnered with the *Minneapolis Tribune* for the series. After each broadcast, the newspaper published an article about the historic events portrayed in that most recent episode.[2]

Harry Remington—the periodical's entertainment reporter and movie critic—wrote each of the essays. He conducted solid research for the article about Winston. He gave accurate information about the events concerning her time in Minnesota. He noted that she had come from Mississippi to Minnesota, and he told of how a group of abolitionists had helped her escape from her enslavers. He described her appearance in court and the judge's decision to emancipate her.

On the other hand, Remington added dramatic touches to his portrayal, including unsubstantiated descriptions of events and people. He placed Colonel Christmas at the Thornton House when the sheriff arrived, asserting that Christmas suggested Eliza hide, if she were afraid of the process servers. He identified Winston's husband as "Jim Winston," although Winston herself never did so in the only primary source consisting entirely of her own words—her affidavit from August 1860. Moreover, she never distinguished "Winston" as either her married name or her maiden name; the reporter assumed she had acquired it with her marriage. Remington also gave her a verbal tic of profanity and described her as a hefty "mammy," but no primary sources attributed either quality to her.[3]

Remington's essay, as with the Minnesota-based works that

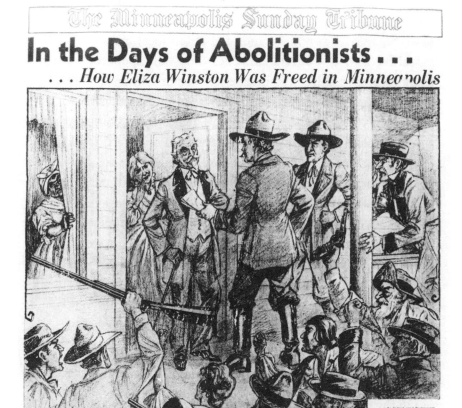

The Minneapolis Sunday Tribune

In the Days of Abolitionists...

...How Eliza Winston Was Freed in Minneapolis

By HARRY REMINGTON.

ABOLITIONISTS had to wait years for a really impressive hold day in Minnesota. These rock-ribbed dogmatists comprised only a scant one-eighth of the population. And no one took them very seriously but themselves.

At first this parcel of holy men and women, fanatically opposed to slavery and all its works and pumps, functioned mainly as a kind of secret brotherhood. The homes of its members were hotbeds of abolition. Grim little meetings were held in lamplit parlors to denounce and condemn slavery and slaveholders.

By 1857, however, the fires of slavery had become more openly and briskly militant. For that was the sleeping. That was comfort enough.

To fill its 82 rooms with the class trade, the Winslow advertised extensively, not only in the local newspapers of Minneapolis, St. Anthony and St. Paul, but also throughout the south. Minnesota was prescribed attractively by the proprietors of the hotel as a summer resort, with the Winslow as the center of hospitality, with the wooded shores of Lakes Calhoun and Harriet, nearby, as cool, sylvan retreats.

It was not long before the southern gentlemen, their families and their slaves began coming to Minnesota in great numbers, to avoid the expenses, especially after the Winslow house was opened. Blithely ignoring the Dred Scott decision, the most rase

of our material interests and our reputation at home and abroad?"

That was the situation in July, neopolis gave the Abolitionists a chance to perform a melodramatic good turn.

realised that life had been unusually rough on her.

Her early years were spent as maid of all work for a Mr. Gholson of Memphis, Tenn. She was well treated, but there was a lot of work, washing, ironing, cooking, scrubbing, taking care of Mr. Gholson's kids and a bit of nursing thrown in. Eliza stood it, stood it because she had to, of course, but principally because she had dreams.

HER dreams were embodied, thru

near to be the first lady of the black republic of freedmen in Liberia.

Jim never came back. He died of fever in Liberia. That was why Eliza cursed softly whenever she could find time to rest and contemplate her situation.

She rented the house in Memphis for $8 a month and put the rent money into the hands of Mr. Gholson as in-ta'lment payments on the $1,000 that would buy her freedom, an opportunity that still was open, even if Jim was dead. Eliza had paid Gholson some $200. Apparently that wasn't enough to stem the overwhelming tide

Harry Remington's article—and its illustration—depicted Eliza Winston as a pawn in her own story. Minneapolis Sunday Tribune, *November 18, 1934* preceded it, did not delve into Winston's life before reaching Minnesota—either with or without embellishments. He started her biography in her adulthood and focused almost entirely on the enslavers who brought her to the Northwest. Although her affidavit mentions previous captors, the author did not develop them as characters for his article. Among Winston's enslavers before the Christmases, Remington mentioned only "Mr. Gholson" and did so merely to explain how Winston came into the possession of the Mississippians.[4]

No witnesses to Winston's ordeal publicly challenged any of Remington's claims. Nearly three-fourths of a century had passed since that fateful summer in Minnesota, and the principal figures were long dead. The promotion of the radio series and the newspaper articles in *Minnesota History*, the membership magazine of the Minnesota Historical Society, gave Remington's work historical legitimacy. His article was later cited in scholarly writings as an unquestioned secondary source—his dramatization treated as a legitimate historical work.

Remington's neglect of Winston's life outside of Minnesota was not corrected by any works of popular culture beyond the state. To date, no newspaper, radio, or television sketches from Tennessee have commemorated her as a native of the state who went on to change Minnesota history. Similarly, no media in Mississippi have explored how her life there with the Christmases influenced her actions when they brought her to Minnesota. As a result, she exists almost solely in Minnesota's popular memory, and only as a figure of the state.

Moreover, by concentrating on Minnesotans, Remington minimized Winston's role in her own story. He went into great detail about the sacrifices and sufferings of the abolitionists who helped to liberate her. He concluded his essay by lamenting that the freeing of "plump, puzzled Eliza Winston" had little significance in the lives of her allies. "That got Abolitionists practically nothing but abuse, ridicule and headaches," he asserted.[5]

Although Remington did not portray the cause of slavery with sympathy, he did not glamorize Eliza and her supporters either. Moreover, he adopted the old Democratic point of view about the ordeal of Eliza's arrest and trial. He depicted her allies as having short memories, claiming that mere months later "the Civil War had made her friends forget there ever was such an unfortunate Negress as Eliza Winston." He chided Winston for having "too much pride" to ask the Christmases to help her as she initially struggled in the North. However, he said that she considered her allies "severe in manner" and "rather ill-tempered." He referred to them as a "besieging army" and "angry mob" when discussing their demeanor at Lake Harriet.[6]

Remington was not the first writer to compare Winston to Dred Scott. However, he explicitly said that Scott had more significance to the abolitionists than Winston did. To be sure, although Scott lost his case in the US Supreme Court, that defeat gave opponents of slavery an issue around which to rally while the verdict remained law. To the reporter, Winston's usefulness to Minnesota's abolitionists ended when she became free; thus, he considered her as relevant to the state for only the forty days that she resided there as a captive.[7]

Also, Remington did not mention the mass exodus of enslavers from Minnesota after Winston's emancipation, which effectively ended the de facto slavery that had existed in the state since 1849. His reduction of the affair to a conflict of abolitionists versus proslavery locals eliminates such nuances.

In recent years, examinations of Winston's time in Minnesota have offered some direct challenges to Remington. None of the works since 1934 have repeated Remington's claims about Winston's profanity. However, they do not replace the refutations with new facts about Winston's life. In addition, the post-Remington authors have portrayed Winston's allies in a much more favorable light, and they depict Christmases' allies more critically because of their rowdy behavior and their support for

Winston's illegal enslavement. Again, the focus on the European American abolitionists presents Winston as a minor figure in her own story, and the focus only on her weeks in Minnesota supports this minimizing.

Since 2000, some notable exceptions to the whitewashing have emerged. William D. Green's groundbreaking article "Eliza Winston and the Politics of Freedom in Minnesota, 1854–60" set the standard for historical study on Winston's life by focusing on her enslavement and the prominence of slavery itself in antebellum Minnesota. In 2004 Twin Cities Public Television produced a short film about Emily Grey, and Winston's story figures prominently in it. Seventeen years later, one author artistically re-centered Winston in her own story. Mary Moore Easter's *Free Papers* is a book of poems inspired by Winston's ordeal, and the author drew primarily from the affidavit to creatively tell the story of the woman's enslavement by the Christmases.

Very little of the architecture that played important roles in Winston's life has survived to the present day. Andrew Jackson's plantation, the Hermitage, and the Polks' plantation, Hamilton Place, still stand in Tennessee. Of course, Jackson's residence

In 2004 Twin Cities PBS's *North Star: Minnesota's Black Pioneers* included a segment that focused on Emily Grey. Myrtis M. Simmons played Eliza Winston. *TPT*

while he claimed Winston during his second presidential term—
the White House—remains in Washington, DC. Worship services
continue at First Presbyterian Church in Memphis and at Second
Baptist Church in Detroit. On the other hand, none of the buildings remain from the Hennepin County stations of the Underground Railroad in Minnesota. No one can see the Winslow
House, the Thornton House, or the Tremont House and the Grey
residence near it; the residences where Winston hid after her trial;
or the theater where she spoke. Secombe's church still exists as a
fellowship, but the First Congregational Church's original building is no more.

The most powerful aspect of Winston's legacy is her ability to
find outlets for agency—and ultimately liberation—amid the multiple changes in her enslavement. Her literacy and her semi-free
life in Memphis, her hard work with her husband, her continued
striving for freedom under the Christmases—all these show that
she was not helpless in pursuing her own liberation, nor a power-
less captive completely deferring to whomever enslaved her. She
prepared herself, and by the time she finally had a chance for
freedom, she both knew what to do and had the courage to do
it. And Eliza Winston's life, when traced through all the states in
which she resided, shows that hers is less a Minnesota story and
more an American story.

ACKNOWLEDGMENTS

Several offices in local governments across the country helped me in my search for information about Eliza Winston's life in the many places where she lived and traveled. I thank Siva Blake of the Civil District Court of Orleans Parish, Louisiana; Kevin Cason of the Tennessee State Library and Archives; Chris Dillingham and Frank Stewart of the Shelby County Archives in Tennessee; and Lacie Petrash of the Hennepin County Recorder's Office in Minnesota. They sent invaluable property deeds, which allowed me to trace Winston's life from enslaver to enslaver, sale to sale.

Some of the personal papers of people who knew Winston presented to me a deeper look into Winston's daily life in the places where she was enslaved. I am grateful to Tim Hodgdon of the Wilson Special Collections Library at the University of North Carolina–Chapel Hill; Marsha Mullin of the Hermitage; and Tom Coens of the Papers of Andrew Jackson at the University of Tennessee.

I thank Ann Regan, Josh Leventhal, and all the staff of the Minnesota Historical Society Press. They took a chance on me for *Slavery's Reach*, and it paid off wonderfully. When I subsequently decided to write a biography of one of the enslaved people mentioned in that book, there was no doubt as to whom I would ask to publish it.

Bill Green mentored my work on this book. He gave advice on my findings and the direction of my writing. His support has meant so much to me, especially considering his pioneering work on Minnesota's history of slavery and Winston's role in it. I offer my thanks to him. I also appreciate the advice from Manisha Sinha and Beth Berila for how to write biographies of women.

My deepest thanks are to my loved ones. I thank my family for supporting my work on this book. I am especially grateful to my wife Sampada for her support, sacrifices, and love.

APPENDIX A

Chronology of
the Enslavement
of Eliza Winston

1817: born, enslaved, to mother Molly

1822, January: sold by Thomas Hopkins of Tennessee to John Christmas McLemore of Nashville, Tennessee

1834, early: seized by Davidson County, Tennessee, sheriff Willoughby Williams

1834, July: auctioned by Sheriff Williams to Lucius Junius Polk of Maury County, Tennessee

1834, July: transferred to Polk and Mary Ann Eastin Polk at Hamilton Place in Maury County, Tennessee

1834, October: purchased by President Andrew Jackson for Polk to hold in trust for the McLemore family

1840s, before 1847: gave birth to a child

1842, September: transferred by Polk to Catherine "Kate" McLemore Gholson in Memphis, Tennessee; a mother of at least one child by then

1842, September: became fully enslaved by Kate

1844, February 25: joined the First Presbyterian Church of Memphis

1846: moved with Kate and family to Louisville, Kentucky

1847: a mother of at least one child in Louisville

1847, November: moved with Kate and family to Nashville

1848, July 2: became enslaved by Thomas Gholson when his wife Kate died

1849: returned with Gholson to Memphis

1850s, early: married; invested in real estate with her husband via Gholson; became widowed

1853, early: brought to New Orleans

1853, March: pawned in New Orleans by Gholson to Richard and Mary Christmas of Tallula, Mississippi

1853, mid: moved with the Christmases to Louisville

1853, late: moved with the Christmases to Tallula

1855, December: became fully enslaved by the Christmases when Gholson died

1860, early July: traveled with the Christmases from Mississippi to Minnesota

1860, July 6: was promised her freedom by the Christmases, who reneged on the promise

1860, July 12: arrived in Minnesota and registered with the Christmases at the Winslow House in St. Anthony

1860, mid-July: met Emily Grey in St. Anthony

1860, mid-August: met with abolitionist women at Grey's house in St. Anthony, the first station of the Underground Railroad (UGRR) in Hennepin County, Minnesota

1860, mid-August: transferred with the Christmases to the Thornton House, by Lake Harriet, Minnesota

1860, August 19: still at the lake house instead of meeting a UGRR conductor at St. Anthony's Congregational Church, as planned by Grey

1860, August 20: visited at the lake house by abolitionist spies

1860, August 21: arrested by the Hennepin County sheriff;

brought to court in Minneapolis; emancipated by Judge Charles
Vanderburgh; left the Christmases and lived first in the Babbitts' home and then the Stones' home in Minneapolis—two
more stations of the local UGRR

1860, October 19: spoke at Woodman Hall to the Hennepin
County Antislavery Society in Minneapolis, thus making the
venue another station of the local UGRR

1860, November: traveled on the national UGRR to Canada; settled in Detroit

APPENDIX B

Documentation of
Eliza Winston's Transfers

Deed, Thomas Hopkins to John C. McLemore
[Warren County, Tennessee Deeds Book D, 215]

Know all men by these present that I Thomas Hopkins of Warren County, Tennessee for and in consideration of the sum of four thousand three hundred and fifty dollars to me in hand paid by John C. McLemore of Nashville, Tennessee, the receipt thereof I hereby acknowledged, I have this day bargained and sold, and I do hereby bargain and sell unto the said John C. McLemore, his heirs, and assigns the following described negro slaves with their increase to wit: Moses a negro fellow about twenty-seven years of age, also Molly a negro woman about twenty-four years of age, also George a negro boy about nine years of age (a son of Molly's), also Matilda a negro girl about seven years of age, also Eliza a negro girl about five years of age, also Sally a negro girl about three years of age (all daughters of Molly), also Judah a negro woman about forty years of age (the mother of Molly), also Burgis a son of Judah's a mulatto boy about twelve years of

age, also Phebe a negro girl about ten years of age (a daughter of
Judah's), also a negro fellow named Dick about twenty-four years
of age. . . . this 18th day of January 1822.

Thomas Hopkins

Deed, Willoughby Williams to Lucius J. Polk
[Davidson County, Tennessee Deeds Book W, 600–601]

Know all men by these presents that I Willoughby Williams, Sheriff of Davidson County, for and in consideration of the sum of
four thousand two hundred dollars to me in hand paid by virtue
of sundry executions from the circuit court of Davidson County,
and the county court of said county against John C. McLemore,
at the instance of Samuel Meek and others, have this day bargained, sold, and delivered to L. J. Polk the following, the following named negroes and other property—Malinda 10 years old,
Julius 8 years old, Gabriel 25 years old, Harriet 22 years old, Eliza
17 years old—one four-wheel carriage and two gray horses, one
sorrel mare, also all the household and kitchen furniture belong-
ing to said McLemore, the items of which are mentioned on the
execution in the circuit court *Meek v. McLemore*. . . . All of which
property was sold by me to satisfy said executions on the 19th day
of July 1834, and the said Polk became the last and highest bidder
for the same. Witness my hand and seal this 20th July 1834.

Willo, Williams, Shff.

Andrew Jackson memorandum, October 2, 1834
[Papers of Andrew Jackson, the Hermitage]

To redeem the furniture & house servants of John C. McLemore.
The property is to be conveyed on the payment of the money to a
trustee for the use of John C. McLemore & his wife during their
life & to their children at their death.

Deed, Lucius J. Polk to Mary Ann Walker
and Catherine Gholson
[*Shelby County, Tennessee Deeds Book N*, 342]

Whereas on the 24th July 1834 there was sold at executor sale in the Town of Nashville on the property of John C. McLemore all his household & kitchen furniture together with the following negro Slaves (viz) One Negro woman named Eliza, One Negro Girl named Linda and one negro boy named Julius, which furniture and negroes was purchased by mc and paid for by General Andrew Jackson with instructions that I convey the same to Mary Ann Walker for her separate use and to Catherine McLemore now Catherine Gholson as follows, (viz) all the household and kitchen furniture, the negro girl Linda and negro boy Julius to Mary Ann Walker for her separate use and the negro woman Eliza to Catherine McLemore now Catherine Gholson for her separate use and whereas said houschold furniture and negro slaves have been removed with my trust[?] to the County of Shelby and is now in the possession of the said Mary Ann Walker and Catherine Gholson as above state now therefore in accordance with the instructions of Genl Jackson and one dollar to me in hand paid by him, I do by these powers to transfer, convey, and deliver to the said Mary Ann Walker for her separate use so as not in any way to be liable for the debts of her husband James M. Walker all of said household and kitchen furniture, Also the said negro girl Linda and negro boy Julius. And I hereby in like manner transfer, convey, and deliver to the said Catherine Gholson the said Negro woman Eliza with her increase. To have and to hold the same to these [?] the said Mary Ann Walker and Catherine Gholson as above state for their separate use.

Witness my hand and seal this 17th day of September 1842

Lucius J. Polk

The Underground Railroad in Hennepin County, Minnesota

Residence of Ralph and Emily Grey, behind Tremont House, Main Street, St. Anthony [H. E. Chamberlin, *Commercial Advertiser Directory for Saint Anthony and Minneapolis* (St. Anthony, MN: Croffut and Clark, 1859), 152]; now Southeast Main Street between Central Avenue Southeast and Southeast Third Avenue in Minneapolis.

Charles Secombe's Congregational Church, Fourth Street between Linden and Bay, St. Anthony [Chamberlin, *Commercial Advertiser Directory*, 162]; now Fourth Street Northeast between First Avenue Northeast and East Hennepin Avenue in Minneapolis.

Residence of W. D. Babbitt, corner of Tenth Street and Russell, Minneapolis [Chamberlin, *Commercial Advertiser Directory*, 33]; now corner of South Tenth Street and Park Avenue in Minneapolis.

Residence of George B. Stone, corner of Oak and Walnut,

Minneapolis [Chamberlin, *Commercial Advertiser Directory*, 122]; now 630 Twenty-Second Avenue South off Riverside Avenue and Twenty-First in Minneapolis.

Woodman Hall, Hellen Street, Minneapolis; now Second Avenue South between South Washington Avenue and South Second Street in Minneapolis.

APPENDIX D

Eliza Winston's Affidavit August 1860

[“Affidavits in the Slave Case,” St. Anthony
Falls Evening News, August 28, 1860, 2]

STATE OF MINNESOTA, HENNEPIN COUNTY
Eliza Winston *being duly sworn, deposes and says*:

My name is Eliza Winston, am 30 years old. I was held as the
slave of Mr. Gholson of Memphis, Tennessee, having been raised
by Mr. Macklemo, father in law of Mr. Gholson. I married a free
man of color who hired my time of my master, who promised
me my freedom upon the payment of $1,000. My husband and
myself worked hard and he invested our savings in a house and
lot in Memphis, which was held for us in Mr. Gholson's name.
This house was rented for $8 per month. My husband by request
went out with a company of emancipated slaves to Liberia, and
was to stay two years. He went out with them because he was
used to travelling, and it was necessary to have some one to assist
and take care of them. When he returned, my master was to take
our house and give me my free papers, my husband paying the
balance due, in money. My husband died in Liberia, and my
master Mr. Gholson got badly broken up in money matters, and

having pawned me to Col. Christmas for $800, died before he could redeem me. I was never sold. I have always been faithful, and no master that I have ever had has found fault with me. Mr. Macklemo my first master always treated me kindly and has tried to buy me of Col. Christmas, a good many times. When Mr. Gholson married Mr. Macklemo's daughter, I went with my young mistress. I became the slave of Mr. Christmas seven years ago last March. They have often told me I should have my freedom and that they promised me that I should have my free papers when their child was seven years old. This time came soon after we left home to come to Minnesota. I had not much confidence that they would keep their promise, for my mistress has always been feeble and she would not be willing to let me go. But I had heard that I should be free by coming to the North, and I had with my colored friends made all the preparations which we thought necessary. I had got a little money and spent it in clothes, my colored friends gave me some good clothing, and I came away with a good supply of clothing in my trunk, sufficient to last me two years and of a kind suitable to what we supposed this climate would be. The trunk containing this clothing was left at the Winslow House when we went to Mrs. Thornton's, I taking only one calico dress, besides an old washing dress. After I got to St. Anthony, I got acquainted with a colored person and asked her if there were any persons who would help me in getting my freedom. I told her my whole story, and she promised to speak with some persons about it. She did so, and a white lady living near met me at the residence of my colored friend. I also told her my story, and she told me there were those who would receive me and protect me. I thought I had a right to my clothes, because they did not come from my master or mistress, and I purposed to carry away at different times when I should not be suspected some portion of them. I fixed upon the coming Sunday when I would leave my master, but before the time came Col. Christmas and his family went out to Mrs. Thornton's and as I understand were not coming back to the Winslow House to stay any more, I thought some one of the servants had made my master suspicious and that he went away on that account. On the day I was taken by the officer, some men came out to Mrs. Thornton's, and I heard them tell them that persons were coming out to carry me off. So whenever any one was seen coming, my mistress would send me into the woods at the back of the house. I minded her, but I did not go very far, hoping they would find me. I was sent into the woods several times during the day, as was the case, at the time when the party came who took me away. I had on my washing dress, and I went in to change it before going with the officer. My mistress asked me why I went off in this way, she said she would give me free papers. I asked her why she did not in St. Louis. She said over again and again that I must not go in this way but that they would give me my free papers. I told her I had rather go now. When my master came into the court room, he came up to me and gave me ten dollars. When I was told I was free, my master asked me if I would go with him, told me not to do wrong. I told him I was not going to do wrong but that I did not wish to go with him. I have been Col. Christmas' slave for more than seven years, and I have always been faithful to him and done my best to please him and my mistress. The latter has always been feeble, and I have waited upon her and taken care of her and the child. During all this time, owing to the poor health of my mistress, I have been closely confined, have had scarcely any time to myself or to see the other slaves, as most house servants can have, but I have never fretted or complained because I thought if I did my very best, they would perhaps give me my freedom. Since my husband died I might have married very happily with a free colored person, but Col. Christmas would not let me marry any one but one of his plantation hands, and I would not marry any one but a free person. I thought if I could not better myself by marrying I would not marry at all, and I know it would be worse for me if I married a slave. I wanted my master to give me free papers so that I could go back to Memphis where I could get employment as a nurse girl, and could earn from ten to fifteen dollars a month, and could marry there as I desire to do, but I despaired of getting my freedom in this way and although I am sorry I must sacrifice so much still I feel that if I cannot have my freedom without, I am ready to make the sacrifice. I will say also that I have never received one cent from my property at Memphis since my husband died.

It was my own free choice and purpose to obtain my freedom, and I applied to my colored friend in St. Anthony, without solicitation on the part of any other person. I have nursed and taken care of the child of my mistress from her birth till the present, and I am so attached to the child that I would be willing to serve Col. Christmas, if I could be assured of my freedom eventually, but with all my attachment to the child, I prefer freedom in Minnesota to life long slavery in Mississippi.

ELIZA X WINSTON
her mark
Subscribed and sworn to before me
this 24th day of Aug. A.D. 1860.
J. F. Bradley, Justice of the Peace.

NOTES

Notes to Introduction. More than a Minnesotan

1. "The Minneapolis 'Slave' Case," *St. Cloud Democrat*, September 6, 1860, 1. On the timing of the affidavit's filing, see page 176.

2. *Winona Republican*, January 1861, 4, as cited in Sydney A. Patchin, "The Development of Banking in Minnesota," *Minnesota History* 2, no. 3 (August 1917): 159.

3. Harry Remington, "In the Days of Abolitionists: How Eliza Winston Was Freed in Minneapolis," *Minneapolis Tribune*, November 18, 1934, magazine section, 2–3.

Notes to Chapter 1. Captive Childhood in Tennessee

1. Annette Gordon-Reed, *The Hemingses of Monticello: An American Family* (New York: W. W. Norton, 2008), 58, 522; Walter Lee Hopkins, *Hopkins of Virginia and Related Families* (Richmond: J. W. Ferguson and Sons, 1931), 29; *Richardson v. Thompson, Administrator*, December 1839, in West H. Humphreys, *Reports and Cases Argued and Determined in the Supreme Court of Tennessee*, vol. 1 (Louisville, KY: Fretter Law Book, 1903), 149; J. Jefferson Looney, *The Papers of Thomas Jefferson: Retirement Series*, vol. 9 (Princeton, NJ: Princeton University Press, 2012), 43; Marcelle Howell, *Meadow Woods: The Beckoning* (Bloomington, IN: AuthorHouse, 2010), 231; James A. Bear Jr. and Lucia C. Stanton, *Jefferson's Memorandum Books: Accounts with Legal Records and Miscellany*,

1767–1826, vol. 1 (Princeton, NJ: Princeton University Press, 1997), 366.

2. Joshua D. Rothman, *The Ledger and the Chain: How Domestic Slave Traders Shaped America* (New York: Basic Books, 2021), 11, 22, 40; *Richardson v. Thompson, Administrator*, December 1839, 149; Hopkins, *Hopkins of Virginia and Related Families*, 29; *Goochland County, Virginia Deeds Book 20*, 52; US 1820 Census, Warren County, Tennessee, 311.

3. *Warren County, Tennessee Deeds Book D*, 215; Jacqueline Jones, *Labor of Love, Labor of Sorrow: Black Women, Work and the Family from Slavery to the Present* (New York: Vintage, 1995), 35. In 1800 the average age at first pregnancy for all women was twenty-three. "Limiting Births in the Early Republic," *Digital History*, https://www.digitalhistory.uh.edu/topic_display.cfm?tcid=134.

4. *Davidson County, Tennessee Deeds Book P*, 87; US 1820 Census, Warren County, Tennessee, 311.

5. Wilma A. Dunaway, *Slavery in the American Mountain South* (Cambridge: Cambridge University Press, 2003), 54.

6. Gordon-Reed, *The Hemingses of Monticello*, 110.

7. *Richardson v. Thompson, Administrator*, December 1839, 149; US 1820 Census, Warren County, Tennessee, 311.

8. "The Minneapolis 'Slave' Case"; *Southern Statesman*, August 4, 1832, 4.

9. John Hope Franklin and Loren Schweninger, *In Search of the Promised Land: A Slave Family in the Old South* (New York: Oxford University Press, 2006), 49.

10. *Warren County, Tennessee Deeds Book C*, 162.

11. *Alabama Supreme Court Cases, Record Book, July 1828*, vol. 22, 507–28.

12. *Warren County, Tennessee Deeds Book D*, 215.

13. *Warren County, Tennessee Deeds Book D*, 215.

14. Bobby L. Lovett, *The African-American History of Nashville, Tennessee, 1780–1930: Elites and Dilemmas* (Fayetteville: University of Arkansas Press, 1999), 1, 8–9.

15. Franklin and Schweninger, *In Search of the Promised Land*, 14.

16. US 1820 Census, Nashville, Davidson County, Tennessee, 135; *Davidson County, Tennessee Deeds Book P*, 48–49.

17. *Davidson County, Tennessee Deeds Book P*, 85, 87, 125, 290; *Obion*

County, Tennessee Deeds Book C, 453; *Davidson County, Tennessee Deeds Book W,* 600.

18. *Davidson County, Tennessee Deeds Book P,* 85, 87; *Henry County, Tennessee Deeds Book A,* 29–33; *Madison County, Tennessee Deeds Book 1,* 164, 172; "The Minneapolis 'Slave' Case"; US 1820 Census, Davidson County, Tennessee, 128; Emily Donelson Walton, *Autobiography of Emily Donelson Walton* ([Nashville, TN]: Methodist Publishing, 1949), 10–11; Betsy Boles Ellison, *Rachel Donelson Jackson: The First Lady Who Never Was* (Jefferson, NC: McFarland, 2020), 176; Jon Meacham, *American Lion: Andrew Jackson in the White House* (New York: Random House, 2008), 6–7.

19. H. W. Brands, *Andrew Jackson: His Life and Times* (New York: Anchor Books, 2005), 376–77; J. M. Keating, *History of the City of Memphis, Tennessee* (Syracuse, NY: Mason and Co., 1888), 124; *Shelby County, Tennessee Deeds Book A,* 260 61; Marvin Downing, "John Christmas McLemore: 19th Century Tennessee Land Speculator," *Tennessee Historical Quarterly* 42 (1983): 257, 259, 262, 264; *Henry County, Tennessee Deeds Book A,* 29–33; *Madison County, Tennessee Deeds Book 1,* 164, 172; *Gibson County, Tennessee Deeds Book A,* 434; *Henry County, Tennessee Deeds Book D,* 169; Robert V. Remini, *The Life of Andrew Jackson* (New York: Harper Perennial, 1988), 146.

20. *Shelby County, Tennessee Deeds Book A,* 521.

21. John C. McLemore, in Ephraim Foster, letter to John Coffee, February 25, 1828, Andrew Jackson Collection, Tennessee Virtual Archive, Tennessee Historical Society, 3, https://teva.contentdm.oclc.org/digital/collection/p15138coll33/id/224/rec/1.

22. Meacham, *American Lion,* 4–7, 51; Brands, *Andrew Jackson,* 404–5; Remini, *The Life of Andrew Jackson,* 169–70, 183. Rachel had first been married to Lewis Robards; in 1791, believing that Robards had finalized a divorce, she married Andrew Jackson. But because the divorce was not completed, they were required to marry a second time. During the presidential campaign, she was accused of adultery and bigamy.

23. *Davidson County, Tennessee Deeds Book T,* 129.

24. US 1820 Census, Nashville, Davidson County, Tennessee, 135; US 1830 Census, Davidson County, Tennessee, 269.

25. Aaron M. Boom, "A Student at the University of Nashville: Correspondence of John Donelson Coffee, 1830–1833," *Tennessee Historical Quarterly* 16, no. 2 (June 1957): 145, 147–50, 152.

26. Brands, *Andrew Jackson*, 422–24; Meacham, *American Lion*, 74–75; Andrew Jackson to John C. McLemore, September 28, 1829, in *The Papers of Andrew Jackson*, vol. 7, ed. Daniel Feller, Harold D. Moser, Laura-Eve Moss, and Thomas Coens (Knoxville: University of Tennessee Press, 2007), 455; Richard Douglas Spence, *Andrew Jackson Donelson: Jacksonian and Unionist* (Nashville, TN: Vanderbilt University Press, 2017), 44; Mark. R. Cheatham, *Old Hickory's Nephew: The Political and Private Struggles of Andrew Jackson Donelson* (Baton Rouge: Louisiana State University Press, 2007), 78–79, 82, 84.

27. John C. McLemore, notice, July 14, 1827, in *North Carolina Star*, August 30, 1827, 4.

28. *The Papers of Andrew Jackson*, vol. 8, ed. Daniel Feller, Thomas Coens, and Laura-Eve Moss (Knoxville: University of Tennessee Press, 2010), 220; James Phelan, *History of Tennessee: The Making of a State* (Boston: Houghton, Mifflin and Co., 1888), 344; *Henry County, Tennessee Deeds Book D*, 169; Andrew Jackson to John C. McLemore, June 27, 1831, in *Correspondence of Andrew Jackson*, ed. John Spencer Bassett (New York: Kraus, 1969), 4:306; Marvin Downing, "An Admiring Nephew-in-Law: John Christmas McLemore and His Relationship to 'Uncle' Andrew Jackson," *West Tennessee Historical Society Papers* 44 (December 1990): 43; John C. McLemore, letter to Andrew Jackson, August 19, 1831, Andrew Jackson Papers, 1775–1874, Library of Congress; *Davidson County, Tennessee Deeds Book 10*, 28–29.

29. Mary Ann Easton to Andrew Jackson, December 5, 1830, in *Papers of Andrew Jackson*, 8:648; Mary Ann Eastin, letter to Andrew Jackson, June 12, 1831, in *The Papers of Andrew Jackson*, digital ed., ed. Daniel Feller (Charlottesville: University of Virginia, Rotunda, 2015–), https://rotunda.upress.virginia.edu/founders/JKSN.

30. Downing, "John Christmas McLemore," 256; Ludwig M. Deppisch, *Women in the Life of Andrew Jackson* (Jefferson, NC: McFarland and Co., 2021), 183; Pauline Wilcox Burke, *Emily Donelson of Tennessee*, ed. Jonathan M. Atkins (Knoxville: University of Tennessee Press, 2001), 224; House of Representatives, *Bank of the United States*, April 30, 1832, 22nd Congress, 1st sess., no. 460, 178, 182; Andrew Jackson to Martin Van Buren, September 5, 1831, *Correspondence of Andrew Jackson*, 4:347; Andrew Jackson to Andrew Jackson Jr., April 23, 1832, in *Andrew Jackson and Early Tennessee History*, vol. 2, 2nd ed., ed. S. G. Heiskell (Nashville, TN: Ambrose, 1920), 396. Mary evidently did not write to her parents as often as they wished. As early as November 1831,

while Mary studied in Pennsylvania, her father asked Jackson, "When did you hear from my daughter? She writes but seldom. Pray write me frequently & let me know what is going on." John C. McLemore, letter to Andrew Jackson, November 9, 1831, *The Papers of Andrew Jackson*, digital ed.

31. *Huntsville Democrat*, August 18, 1831, 3; John Christmas McLemore, letter to Andrew Jackson Donelson, *The Papers of Andrew Jackson*, digital ed.

32. George D. Free, *History of Tennessee from Its Earliest Discoveries and Settlements* (Nashville, TN: G. D. Free, 1896), 231; Harriet A. Washington, *Medical Apartheid: The Dark History of Medical Experimentation on Black Americans from Colonial Times to the Present* (New York: Harlem Moon, 2006), 29–30.

33. Andrew Jackson to Sarah Yorke Jackson, June 21, 1832, *Papers of Andrew Jackson*, vol. 10, ed. Daniel Feller, Thomas Coens, and Laura-Eve Moss (Knoxville: University of Tennessee Press, 2016), 312; Meacham, *American Lion*, 202, 216, 235.

34. Andrew Jackson to Andrew Jackson Jr., October 21, 1832, in *Papers of Andrew Jackson*, 10:536.

35. Andrew Jackson to John Coffee, November 26, 1832, in *Papers of Andrew Jackson*, 10:618; Spence, *Andrew Jackson Donelson*, 68; Robert V. Remini, *Andrew Jackson and the Course of American Democracy, 1833–1845*, vol. 3 (Baltimore, MD: Johns Hopkins University Press, 1984), 49.

36. Spence, *Andrew Jackson Donelson*, 68; Mary Coffee, letter to Mary Polk, January 18, 1833, folder no. 4: "G. W. Polk, 1832–1834," 1–2, Polk and Yeatman Family Papers, series 1.1, Southern Historical Collection, Wilson Library, University of North Carolina at Chapel Hill.

37. Meacham, *American Lion*, 151–52; Brands, *Andrew Jackson*, 489–90; H. Donaldson Jordan, "A Politician of Expansion: Robert J. Walker," *Mississippi Valley Historical Review* 19, no. 3 (December 1932): 364; "List of the Purchases of Land at Columbus and Chocchuma in Mississippi in 1833 and 1834," no. 1263, 23rd Congress, 2nd sess., in *American State Papers: Public Lands*, vol. 7, ed. Asbury Dickins and John W. Forney (Washington, DC: Gales and Seaton, 1860), 437–40; Robert V. Remini, *Andrew Jackson and His Indian Wars* (New York: Viking, 2001), 249.

38. McKay W. Campbell, letter to James K. Polk, November 23, 1833, in *Correspondence of James K. Polk*, vol. 2, ed. Herbert Weaver and Paul H. Bergeron (Nashville, TN: Vanderbilt University Press, 1972),

138. Chocchuma has vanished; the site is about three miles southwest of Holcomb, Mississippi.

39. William Berkeley Lewis to Andrew Jackson, May 1, 1833, in *The Papers of Andrew Jackson*, vol. 11, ed. Daniel Feller, Laura-Eve Moss, and Thomas Coens (Knoxville: University of Tennessee Press, 2019), 286–87; Andrew Jackson to Mary Donelson Coffee, in *The Papers of Andrew Jackson*, 11:356; Daniel Feller, Laura-Eve Moss, and Thomas Coens commentary, in *The Papers of Andrew Jackson*, 11:880; Andrew Jackson to Andrew Jackson Jr., November 25, 1833, in *The Papers of Andrew Jackson*, 11:778.

40. *Davidson County, Tennessee Deeds Book T*, 13, 144–45; *Davidson County, Tennessee Deeds Book W*, 1, 101–2, 184.

41. Meacham, *American Lion*, 65–66, 351.

42. William Berkeley Lewis to Andrew Jackson, April 27, 1833, in *The Papers of Andrew Jackson*, 11:261.

43. Mary Coffee, letter to Mary Polk, January 18, 1833, folder no. 4: "G. W. Polk, 1832–1834," 1–2, Polk and Yeatman Family Papers.

44. Burke, *Emily Donelson of Tennessee*, 258; "Married," *Nashville Banner and Daily Advertiser*, February 21, 1834, 3; Deppisch, *Women in the Life of Andrew Jackson*, 183; Eugene D. Genovese, *Roll, Jordan, Roll: The World the Slaves Made* (New York: Vintage, 1974), 481.

Notes to Chapter 2. Enslaved by President Jackson

1. "List of the Purchases of Land at Columbus and Chocchuma in Mississippi in 1833 and 1834," 383; *Davidson County, Tennessee Deeds Book W*, 600–601.

2. Daina Ramey Berry, *The Price for Their Pound of Flesh: The Value of the Enslaved, from Womb to Grave, in the Building of a Nation* (Boston: Beacon Press, 2017), 79, 84–85; Franklin and Schweninger, *In Search of the Promised Land*, 49, 51.

3. *Davidson County, Tennessee Deeds Book Y*, 523.

4. "The Late Lucius J. Polk," *Nashville Union and American*, October 11, 1870, 1; "Masonic," *Nashville Tennessean*, November 15, 1870, 4.

5. *Davidson County, Tennessee Deeds Book W*, 600–601.

6. "The Minneapolis 'Slave' Case"; Berry, *The Price for Their Pound of Flesh*, 43.

7. *Shelby County, Tennessee Deeds Book N*, 342; Andrew Jackson,

memorandum, October 2, 1834, manuscript collection, the Hermitage, available on microfilm at *The Papers of Andrew Jackson: A Microfilm Supplement* (Wilmington, DE: Scholarly Resources, 1986), reel 26, frame 0473; Stephanie E. Jones-Rogers, *They Were Her Property: White Women as Slave Owners in the American South* (New Haven, CT: Yale University Press, 2019), 4, 20.

8. The paper trail for this transaction is complicated. Andrew Jackson's memorandum of October 2, 1834, provides the specifics as quoted in the previous paragraph, and it demonstrates the depth of his financial support for his Donelson relatives: the total of $10,798.87 included expenses "for AJ Donelson's House, and for Thomas J. Donelson's debts," and $5,000 "for A Jackson Jrs land." The documents depicted on page 37 show how he reimbursed the bank for Hill's draft. Lucius Polk's involvement is clear from other evidence. The October 2 memorandum stipulated "payment of the money to a trustee" for McLemore's captives; because Polk enslaved those people and turned them over to Mary Ann Walker and Catherine Gholson (see Appendix B), he was clearly the trustee who received the money. The bank book page is available at Andrew Jackson Bank Book, 1833–1835, Andrew Jackson Papers, Series 9, Miscellaneous Manuscripts, 1795 to 1856, MSS 27532, Vol. 183, Library of Congress, and at https://www.loc.gov/resource /maj.09183_0136_0188/?sp=19. The check is available at Andrew Jackson Papers, Series 1, General Correspondence and Related Items, 1775 to 1885, MSS 27532, Vol. 87, Library of Congress, and at http://hdl.loc .gov/loc.mss/maj.01087_0415_0415.

9. Mary French Caldwell, *Andrew Jackson's Hermitage* (Nashville, TN: Ladies' Hermitage Association, 1933), 81.

10. US 1830 Census, Davidson County, Tennessee, 266; US 1840 Census, Davidson County, Tennessee, 315; Meacham, *American Lion*, 302; Robert V. Remini, *The Legacy of Andrew Jackson: Essays on Democracy, Indian Removal, and Slavery* (Baton Rouge: Louisiana State University Press, 1988), 90, 97; Remini, *Andrew Jackson and the Course of American Democracy*, 147.

11. Jessie Clay Connors, "The Years Are Kind," *Nashville Tennessean*, July 10, 1949, magazine section, 8.

12. Mrs. Frank M. Angellotti, "The Polks of North Carolina and Tennessee," *New England Historical and Genealogical Register* (October 1923): 253.

13. Andrew Jackson, memorandum, October 2, 1834.

14. Connors, "The Years Are Kind," 10.

15. *Maury County, Tennessee Deeds Book Z*, 449.

16. Mary Polk Branch, *Memoirs of a Southern Woman: Within the Lines* (Chicago: Joseph G. Branch, 1912), 11–12.

17. Branch, *Memoirs of a Southern Woman*, 11–12.

18. *Nashville Union*, August 9, 1847, 2; Meacham, *American Lion*, 107.

19. William M. Polk, *Leonidas Polk: Bishop and General*, vol. 1 (New York: Longmans, Green and Co., 1893), 128, 133, 135.

20. Polk, *Leonidas Polk*, 163–64.

21. James Douglas Anderson, *Making the American Thoroughbred: Especially in Tennessee, 1800–1845* (Norwood, MA: Plimpton Press, 1916), 84, 122, 188.

22. Andrew Jackson to Mrs. Andrew Jackson Jr., January 5, 1834, *Correspondence of Andrew Jackson*, 5:239; William B. Lewis to Andrew Jackson, July 25, 1834, *Correspondence of Andrew Jackson*, 5:275; Andrew Jackson to Andrew Jackson Jr., October 11, 1834, *Correspondence of Andrew Jackson*, 5:293; Remini, *Andrew Jackson and the Course of American Democracy*, 179.

23. Andrew Jackson to Andrew Jackson Jr., December 22, 1833, *Correspondence of Andrew Jackson*, 5:235; Remini, *Andrew Jackson and the Course of American Democracy*, 145–47.

24. Andrew Jackson to Andrew Jackson Jr., September 10, 1834, *Correspondence of Andrew Jackson*, 5:290.

25. Stockley Donelson to Andrew Jackson, October 14, 1834, *Correspondence of Andrew Jackson*, 5:296; Remini, *The Life of Andrew Jackson*, 279.

26. Andrew Jackson to Andrew Jackson Jr., October 23, 1834, *Correspondence of Andrew Jackson*, 5:302; Andrew Jackson to Andrew Jackson Jr., October 30, 1834, *Correspondence of Andrew Jackson*, 5:303.

27. Andrew Jackson, memorandum, October 2, 1834; Andrew Jackson to Andrew Jackson Jr., May 1, 1835, *Correspondence of Andrew Jackson*, 5:342.

28. Richard D. Battery, "St. John's Episcopal Churchyard: Material Culture and Antebellum Class Distinction," *Tennessee Historical Quarterly* (Summer 1994): 97; *Maury County, Tennessee 1836 Tax Book*, 138; *Maury County, Tennessee Deeds Book T*, 195.

29. F. A. Polk, letter to Sarah Polk, April 2, 1836, folder 5: "G. W. Polk, 1835–1838," 3, Polk and Yeatman Family Papers.

30. Andrew Jackson, letter to Mary Polk, March 14, 1836, folder no. 5: "G. W. Polk, 1835–1838," 1–2, Polk and Yeatman Family Papers.

31. Burke, *Emily Donelson of Tennessee*, 293; Andrew Jackson to Francis P. Blair, August 12, 1836, *Correspondence of Andrew Jackson*, 5:418; Deppisch, *Women in the Life of Andrew Jackson*, 182; Remini, *Andrew Jackson and the Course of American Democracy*, 331–32, 337.

32. Meacham, *American Lion*, 325–27; Remini, *Andrew Jackson and the Course of American Democracy*, 333, 336, 348–49.

33. Andrew Jackson to Andrew Jackson Jr., September 22, 1836, *Correspondence of Andrew Jackson*, 5:426–27; Remini, *Andrew Jackson and the Course of American Democracy*, 333.

34. Martin Van Buren, letter to James K. Polk, December 27, 1843, in *Correspondence of James K. Polk*, vol. 6, ed. Wayne Cutler and Carese M. Parker (Nashville, TN: Vanderbilt University Press, 1983), 396; Meacham, *American Lion*, 107–8; Remini, *Andrew Jackson and the Course of American Democracy*, 373–74.

35. Sidney C. Posey, letter to James K. Polk, October 8, 1836, in *Correspondence of James K. Polk*, vol. 3, ed. Herbert Weaver and Kermit L. Hall (Nashville, TN: Vanderbilt University Press, 1975), 755; "The Dinner to Col. Polk at Captain Webster's," *Columbia, Tennessee Democrat*, in *Daily Globe* (Washington, DC), October 18, 1836, 2.

36. Mary Polk, letter to Mary Coffee, December 7, 1837, folder no. 5: "G. W. Polk, 1835–1838," 3, Polk and Yeatman Family Papers.

37. Andrew Jackson to Andrew J. Donelson, December 10, 1836, *Correspondence of Andrew Jackson*, 5:442; Meacham, *American Lion*, 333–35.

38. Branch, *Memoirs of a Southern Woman*, 9; Brands, *Andrew Jackson*, 541.

39. *Maury County, Tennessee Deeds Book 10*, 221.

40. Glenn Robins, *The Bishop of the Old South: The Ministry and Civil War Legacy of Leonidas Polk* (Macon, GA: Mercer University Press, 2006), 47; Polk, *Leonidas Polk*, 134.

41. Robins, *The Bishop of the Old South*, 40; US 1840 Census, Maury County, Tennessee, 325; Jill K. Garrett, "St. John's Church, Ashwood," *Tennessee Historical Quarterly* 29 (Spring 1970): 7.

42. Garrett, "St. John's Church, Ashwood," 7; Trezevant Player Yeatman Jr., "St. John's—A Plantation Church of the Old South," *Tennessee Historical Quarterly* 10, no. 4 (December 1951): 335–36; Angellotti, "The Polks of North Carolina and Tennessee," 253.

43. George W. Freeman, *The Rights and Duties of Slave-Holders: Two Discourses Delivered on Sunday, November 27, 1836* (Charleston, SC: A. L. Miller, 1837), 12–13.

44. Polk, *Leonidas Polk*, 151–52; "APTA Tour in Columbia Announced," *Nashville Tennessean*, April 3, 1860, D19.

45. Mary Eastin, letter to Mary Polk, January 19, 1839, folder no. 6: "G. W. Polk, 1839–1841," 1, Polk and Yeatman Family Papers; Edward E. Baptist, *The Half Has Never Been Told: Slavery and the Making of American Capitalism* (New York: Basic Books, 2014), 361; Rothman, *The Ledger and the Chain*, 265.

46. Robins, *The Bishop of the Old South*, 54; Leonidas Polk, letter to Susan S. Polk, April 7, 1841, box 9, document 4, Polk Family Collection, University Archives and Special Collections, Sewanee: The University of the South, Sewanee, TN.

Notes to Chapter 3. The Young Mistress

1. Jones-Rogers, *They Were Her Property*, 1–2.

2. John C. McLemore, letter to A. J. Donelson, January 1, 1836, Andrew Jackson Papers, 1775–1874, 6–7, Library of Congress; *Davidson County, Tennessee Deeds Book Y*, 523; *Shelby County, Tennessee Deeds Book E*, 79; *Shelby County, Tennessee Deeds Book 41*, 556–57; *Shelby County, Tennessee Deeds Book G*, 71; *Weekly Mississippian*, June 14, 1839, 2; *Mississippi Free Trader*, July 6, 1839, 4; *Weekly Mississippian*, April 3, 1840, 3; *Vicksburg Daily Whig*, May 19, 1840, 4; *Southern Pioneer* (Carrollton, MS), June 26, 1841, 4.

3. "List of the Purchases of Land at Columbus and Chocchuma in Mississippi in 1833 and 1834," 385; *Southern Argus*, December 9, 1840, 4; "List of Letters," *North Carolina Star*, July 28, 1841, 4; John N. Norton, *Life of Bishop Freeman of Arkansas* (New York: General Protestant Episcopal Sunday School Union and Church Book Society, 1867), 109.

4. Meacham, *American Lion*, 289; Brands, *Andrew Jackson*, 530; Michael F. Holt, *The Rise and Fall of the American Whig Party: Jacksonian Politics and the Onset of the Civil War* (New York: Oxford University Press, 1999), xiii, 29–30; "Public Meeting," *Southern Argus*, June 9, 1840, 3; *Raleigh Weekly Standard*, August 5, 1840, 2; Remini, *Andrew Jackson and the Course of American Democracy*, 137; Sean Wilentz, *Andrew Jackson* (New York: Times Books, 2005), 11.

5. *Shelby County, Tennessee Deeds Book N*, 342; US 1840 Census, Shelby County, Tennessee, 200.

6. *Nashville Union*, June 9, 1843, 3.

7. *Lowndes County, Mississippi Tax List 1841*, 13, 43; *Tax Assessment: Western District, Jefferson County, Kentucky, 1847*, 38.

8. *Shelby County, Tennessee Deeds Book N*, 342; Jones-Rogers, *They Were Her Property*, 19, 29, 31.

9. *Shelby County, Tennessee Deeds Book N*, 342.

10. *Memphis Eagle and Enquirer*, April 24, 1853, 3.

11. Beverly G. Bond and Janann Sherman, *Memphis in Black and White* (Charleston, SC: Arcadia, 2003), 26.

12. "The Minneapolis 'Slave' Case."

13. *Nashville Union*, June 9, 1843, 3; Andrew J. McLemore, letter to James G. Martin Jr., March 30, 1843, John Coffee Papers, Tennessee State Library and Archives, Nashville.

14. Will of Mary Ann Walker, October 4, 1860, Shelby County (TN) Probate Court, loose papers, no. 1496, record no. 4; Jones-Rogers, *They Were Her Property*, 104–6.

15. Andrew J. McLemore, letter to James G. Martin Jr., March 30, 1843, 1, 3.

16. Andrew J. McLemore, letter to James G. Martin Jr., March 30, 1843, 2.

17. *Nashville Union*, June 9, 1843, 3; *Nashville Tennessean*, October 6, 1843, 2.

18. *Shelby County, Tennessee Deeds Book O*, 448–50; *Kimball and James Business Directory for the Mississippi Valley: 1844* (Cincinnati, OH: Kendall and Barnard, 1844), 407; *Memphis Appeal*, December 13, 1844.

19. *Shelby County, Tennessee Deeds Book Q*, 200.

20. *Shelby County, Tennessee Deeds Book O*, 133; *Shelby County, Tennessee Deeds Book P*, 386; *Shelby County, Tennessee Deeds Book 3*, 441; *Tri-Weekly Memphis Enquirer*, July 23, 1846, 3; US 1840 Census, Shelby County, Tennessee, 201, 206; Edwin Gholson and Eleanor Gholson Taft, *Notes on the Genealogy of the Gholson Family* (Cincinnati, OH: Cincinnati Law Library Association, 1949), 13.

21. *Ansearchin' News* (Fall 1969): 123. This publication of the Tennessee Genealogical Society reprints the minutes of the First Presbyterian Church of Memphis, Tennessee, which list the "Members in Communion on the 11th Day of September, 1845," followed by a "List of

Colored Members," including Eliza (Gholson)—giving the date each person joined.

22. Adrian Miller, *Soul Food: The Surprising Story of an American Cuisine, One Plate at a Time* (Chapel Hill: University of North Carolina Press, 2013) 20.

23. Freeman, *The Rights and Duties of Slave-Holders*, 30–31.

24. *Minutes of the General Assembly of the Presbyterian Church in the United States of America: A.D. 1842*, vol. 10 (Philadelphia: William B. Martien, 1842), 16; *Minutes of the General Assembly of the Presbyterian Church in the United States of America: A.D. 1844* (Philadelphia: William B. Martien, 1844), 377.

25. George Bourne, *Picture of Slavery in the United States of America* (Boston: Isaac Knapp, 1838), 193.

26. *Ansearchin' News* (Fall 1969): 121–23; US 1840 Census, Shelby County, Tennessee, 206.

27. *Ansearchin' News* (Fall 1969): 121–23; US 1850 Census, Second Ward, Memphis, Shelby County, Tennessee, 20a.

28. *Ansearchin' News* (Fall 1969): 123; US 1850 Census, Fourth Ward, Memphis, Shelby County, Tennessee, 46a; US 1850 Census, Third Ward, Memphis, Shelby County, Tennessee, 34a.

29. Burke, *Emily Donelson of Tennessee*, 303.

30. Gholson and Taft, *Notes on the Genealogy of the Gholson Family*, 13.

31. Brands, *Andrew Jackson*, 533; Meacham, *American Lion*, 345; Remini, *The Legacy of Andrew Jackson*, 90. Jackson paid sixty dollars to Lucius Polk on January 21, 1842, according to "Series 1, General Correspondence and Related Items, 1775–1885," Andrew Jackson Papers, Library of Congress. Polk would have received the money while still enslaving Eliza.

32. Brands, *Andrew Jackson*, 541; Remini, *Andrew Jackson and the Course of American Democracy*, 470–71.

33. Martin Case, *The Relentless Business of Treaties: How Indigenous Land Became US Property* (St. Paul: Minnesota Historical Society Press, 2018), 126.

34. Colonel Talcott, letter to John C. McLemore, August 14, 1845, in *The Territorial Papers of the United States: The Territory of Wisconsin, 1839–1848*, vol. 28, comp. John Porter Bloom (Washington, DC: National Archives, 1975), 870.

35. *Louisville Daily Democrat*, October 14, 1846, 2; *Memphis Enquirer*, December 1, 1846, 1; *Louisville Daily Courier*, December 8, 1846, 1;

Louisville Daily Courier, February 23, 1847, 3; *Tax Assessment: Western District, Jefferson County, Kentucky, 1847*, 38.

36. *Louisville Daily Courier*, June 3, 1847, 2; *Louisville Daily Courier*, June 14, 1847, 2; *Louisville Daily Courier*, June 17, 1847, 2; *Nashville Daily Union*, August 25, 1847, 2; *Louisville Courier-Journal*, January 1, 1847, 4.

37. *Tax Assessment: Western District, Jefferson County, Kentucky, 1847*, 38.

38. *Louisville Daily Courier*, August 27, 1847, 2; "Morse's Telegraph," *Louisville Daily Courier*, October 9, 1847, 2; *Louisville Daily Courier*, December 23, 1847, 2.

39. *Shelby County, Mississippi Deeds Book 3*, 441; *Louisville Daily Courier*, October 27, 1847, 3; *Louisville Daily Courier*, October 28, 1847, 3; *Louisville Daily Courier*, November 1, 1847, 4; *Louisville Daily Courier*, November 25, 1847, 2.

40. *Shelby County, Tennessee Deeds Book Y*, 328; *Louisville Daily Courier*, November 25, 1847, 2; *Louisville Daily Courier*, December 23, 1847, 2.

Notes to Chapter 4. Marriage and Property

1. *Louisville Daily Courier*, November 25, 1847, 2.

2. *Nashville Christian Advocate*, July 21, 1848; *Memphis Daily Eagle*, May 6, 1848, 4; *Memphis Daily Eagle*, July 20, 1849, 4; *Memphis 1849 City Directory*, 49; US 1850 Census, Fourth Ward, Memphis, Shelby County, Tennessee, 88; US 1850 Slave Schedule, Fourth Ward, Memphis, Shelby County, Tennessee, 2; *Memphis Daily Eagle*, November 1, 1847, 3; *Memphis Daily Eagle*, December 8, 1849, 3.

3. US 1850 Census, Northern Division, Marshall County, Mississippi, 154; US 1850 Slave Schedule, Northern Division, Marshall County, Mississippi, 293; *Shelby County, Tennessee Deeds Book 6*, 395; *Shelby County, Tennessee Deeds Book 7*, 555; *Shelby County, Tennessee Deeds Book 8*, 214–16.

4. Will of Mary Ann Walker, October 4, 1860, Shelby County Probate Court, loose papers, no. 1496, record no. 4.

5. *African Repository and Colonial Journal* (September 1848): 272; *Ansearchin' News* (Fall 1969): 121; Caleb Perry Patterson, *The Negro in Tennessee, 1790–1865* (Austin: University of Texas, 1922), 99.

6. "The Minneapolis 'Slave' Case."

7. "The Minneapolis 'Slave' Case"; Freeman, *The Rights and Duties of Slave-Holders*, 25, 27.

8. Freeman, *The Rights and Duties of Slave-Holders*, 9–10, 12; "The Minneapolis 'Slave' Case."

9. *Memphis Tax Records: July 1852 to July 1853*, 90; *Memphis Tax Records: July 1853 to July 1854*, 21—both Shelby County, TN, Archives; "The Minneapolis 'Slave' Case."

10. "The Minneapolis 'Slave' Case"; Jones, *Labor of Love, Labor of Sorrow*, 43, 46.

11. *Weekly Memphis Eagle*, July 26, 1849, 2.

12. *Memphis Tax Records: July 1852 to July 1853*, 90; "The Minneapolis 'Slave' Case."

13. *Shelby County, Tennessee Deeds Book 5*, 442; US 1850 Slave Schedule, Sixth Ward, Memphis, Shelby County, Tennessee, 627.

14. *Shelby County, Tennessee Deeds Book 5*, 420; US 1850 Slave Schedule, Fifth Ward, Memphis, Shelby County, Tennessee, 1; US 1850 Slave Schedule, Sixth Ward, Memphis, Shelby County, Tennessee, 623; Alison M. Parker, *Unceasing Militant: The Life of Mary Church Terrell* (Chapel Hill: University of North Carolina Press, 2020), 7, 9; *Memphis Tax Records: July 1850 to July 1851*, 19; *Memphis Tax Records: July 1851 to July 1852*, 56; *Memphis Tax Records: July 1852 to July 1853*, 90; US 1850 Census, Fifth Ward, Memphis, Shelby County, Tennessee, 1. Eliza—not Genina—was probably Gholson's other enslaved person. In the 1852–53 tax year, his two captives were worth $1,800 together, and Peter's value comprised about half of that amount. Genina was bought for just six hundred dollars in 1849 at age thirty-six, and she would have only lessened in monetary value in the years that followed. In contrast, Gholson pawned Eliza in 1853 for eight hundred dollars. Also, in 1851 Charles B. Church, who sold Peter to Gholson, bought an adolescent boy he had fathered, and years later that enslaved son had a daughter—suffragist Mary Church Terrell.

15. *Memphis Eagle and Enquirer*, November 10, 1852, 2, 3; "From Our New Orleans Correspondent [November 19, 1852]," *Memphis Eagle and Enquirer*, November 28, 1852, 2; Maurie D. McInnis, *Slaves Waiting for Sale: Abolitionist Art and the American Slave Trade* (Chicago: University of Chicago Press, 2011), 164.

16. "From Our New Orleans Correspondent [November 20, 1852]," *Memphis Eagle and Enquirer*, November 28, 1852, 2; "From Our New Orleans Correspondent [November 30, 1852]," *Memphis Eagle and Enquirer*, December 7, 1852, 2; *Memphis Eagle and Enquirer*, November 21, 1852, 2.

17. *Memphis Tax Records: July 1850 to July 1851*, 19; *Memphis Tax Records: July 1851 to July 1852*, 56; *Memphis Tax Records: July 1852 to July 1853*, 90.

18. *New Orleans Times-Picayune*, December 7, 1852, 2; Jerome Loving, *Walt Whitman: The Song of Himself* (Berkeley: University of California Press, 1999), 119; *Routledge's American Handbook and Tourist's Guide through the United States* (London: George Routledge, 1854), 81–82; Jones-Rogers, *They Were Her Property*, 144–45; Richard Tansey, "Bernard Kendig and the New Orleans Slave Trade," *Louisiana History* 23, no. 2 (Spring 1982): 167–68; *Orleans Parish Deeds* 60, 279; "From Our New Orleans Correspondent [December 8, 1852]," *Memphis Eagle and Enquirer*, December 14, 1852, 2.

19. "List of Letters," *Memphis Eagle and Enquirer*, February 16, 1853, 2. It is not clear that Eliza learned to write. The newspaper transcripts of her affidavit show that it is signed with a mark, not a signature.

20. Elizabeth Stordeur Pryor, *Colored Travelers: Mobility and the Fight for Citizenship before the Civil War* (Chapel Hill: University of North Carolina Press, 2016), 57; Mia Bay, *Traveling Black: A Story of Race and Resistance* (Cambridge, MA: Harvard University Press, 2021), 23.

21. Louis C. Hunter, *Steamboats on the Western Rivers: An Economic and Technological History* (Cambridge, MA: Harvard University Press, 1949), 391; Franklin and Schweninger, *In Search of the Promised Land*, 173; Thomas C. Buchanan, *Black Life on the Mississippi: Slaves, Free Blacks, and the Western Steamboat World* (Chapel Hill: University of North Carolina Press, 2004), 11–12; Laura F. Edwards, *Only the Clothes on Her Back: Clothing and the Hidden History of Power in the Nineteenth-Century United States* (New York: Oxford University Press, 2022), 32.

22. *New Orleans Times-Picayune*, February 16, 1853, 2; Jones-Rogers, *They Were Her Property*, 101–2; "From Our New Orleans Correspondent [February 16, 1853]," in *Memphis Eagle and Enquirer*, February 23, 1853, 2; "Burning of the John Swasey," *New Orleans Times-Picayune*, February 16, 1853, 2.

23. "From Our New Orleans Correspondent [February 12, 1853]," in *Memphis Eagle and Enquirer*, February 20, 1853, 2; "The Minneapolis 'Slave' Case."

24. "From Our New Orleans Correspondent [March 7, 1853]," *Memphis Eagle and Enquirer*, March 15, 1853, 2; "The Minneapolis 'Slave' Case."

25. "The Minneapolis 'Slave' Case."

26. US 1850 Census, Second District, Louisville, Jefferson County, Kentucky, 132; US 1850 Slave Schedule, Second District, Louisville, Jefferson County, Kentucky, 794; US 1840 Census, Jefferson County, Kentucky, 169.

27. *Issaquena County, Mississippi Deeds Book B*, 487; *Jefferson County, Kentucky Deeds Book 87*, 491; *Jefferson County, Kentucky Deeds Book 95*, 13.

28. "The Minneapolis 'Slave' Case"; Jones-Rogers, *They Were Her Property*, 104.

29. "The Minneapolis 'Slave' Case"; Jones-Rogers, *They Were Her Property*, 104.

30. "The Minneapolis 'Slave' Case."

31. *Jefferson County, Kentucky Deeds Book 88*, 143.

32. Rothman, *The Ledger and the Chain*, 104; J. D. B. Debow, *The Seventh Census of the United States: 1850* (Washington, DC: Robert Armstrong, 1853), 447.

33. US 1850 Slave Schedule, Issaquena County, Mississippi, 24–25; *Issaquena County, Mississippi Deeds Book A*, 232, 344–45; Martha A. Burnley, "Albert Triplett Burnley," *Texas Historical Association Quarterly* 14, no. 2 (October 1910): 152–53; "Homicide in Issaquena," *Vicksburg Whig*, October 20, 1858, 2; *Issaquena County, Mississippi Deeds Book B*, 611–12; "Biographical Sketch of Countess Annie De Montaigu," *Young Woman's Journal* (December 1896): 107.

34. Baptist, *The Half Has Never Been Told*, 360.

35. "The Minneapolis 'Slave' Case"; Baptist, *The Half Has Never Been Told*, 360–61.

36. Herbert C. Covey and Dwight Eisnach, *What the Slaves Ate: Recollections of African American Foods and Foodways from the Slave Narratives* (Santa Barbara: ABC-CLIO, 2009), 5, 19, 26; Genovese, *Roll, Jordan, Roll*, 331.

37. Joseph Lyon Miller, *The Descendants of Captain Thomas Carter of Barford* (Richmond, VA: Whittet and Shepperson, 1912), 385, 386; *Issaquena County, Mississippi Deeds Book C*, 33, 153; US 1860 Slave Schedule, Issaquena County, Mississippi, 15–16.

38. *Vicksburg Whig*, March 8, 1854, 4; *Vicksburg Whig*, May 31, 1854, 3; *Vicksburg Whig*, September 8, 1854, 3; *Vicksburg Whig*, October 18, 1854, 2; *Vicksburg Whig*, December 15, 1854, 3; *Vicksburg Whig*, July 24, 1855, 2.

39. "$200 Reward," *Vicksburg Whig*, March 3, 1855, 4; *Issaquena County, Mississippi Deeds Book C*, 111.

40. James C. Cobb, *The Most Southern Place on Earth: The Mississippi Delta and the Roots of Regional Identity* (New York: Oxford University Press, 1992), 31.

41. *Issaquena County, Mississippi Deeds Book C*, 89–93; William Kauffman Scarborough, *Masters of the Big House: Elite Slaveholders of the Mid-Nineteenth-Century South* (Baton Rouge: Louisiana State University Press, 2006), 134.

42. *Jefferson County, Kentucky Deeds Book 93*, 570–71.

43. *Shelby County, Tennessee Deeds Book 73*, 16; *Memphis Tax Records: July 1853 to July 1854*, 21.

44. "Died," *Memphis Eagle and Enquirer*, December 6, 1855, 3; *Memphis Tax Records: July 1854 to July 1855*, 22.

45. "Died," *Memphis Eagle and Enquirer*, December 6, 1855, 3.

46. Charles W. Calomiris and Larry Schweikart, "The Panic of 1857: Origins, Transmission, and Containment," *Journal of Economic History* 51, no. 4 (December 1991): 816.

47. US 1860 Slave Schedule, Issaquena County, Mississippi, 4; US 1860 Census, Issaquena County, Mississippi, 1.

48. Joseph C. G. Kennedy, *Population of the United States Census in 1860* (Washington, DC: Government Printing Office, 1864), 270.

Notes to Chapter 5. Manumission Promised and Denied

1. *Bolivar County, Mississippi Deeds Book H*, 365; Franklin and Schweninger, *In Search of the Promised Land*, 173.

2. John W. Blassingame, *Black New Orleans, 1860–1880* (Chicago: University of Chicago Press, 1973), 21; *Christmas v. Russell*, in John William Wallace, *Cases Argued and Adjudged in the Supreme Court of the United States, December Term, 1871*, vol. 4 (New York: Banks and Brothers, 1890), 71.

3. Cobb, *The Most Southern Place on Earth*, 14, 30–31; US 1860 Census, Issaquena County, Mississippi, 1; US 1860 Slave Schedule, Issaquena County, Mississippi, 2–4.

4. Avery F. Gordon, *The Hawthorn Archive: Letters from the Utopian Margins* (New York: Fordham University Press, 2018), 173; "Our St. Paul Correspondence," July 9, 1860, *New York Daily Herald*, July 15,

1860, 3; *St. Paul Pioneer and Democrat*, July 20, 1860, 8; "Death of Miss Mary Shannon," *Vicksburg Whig*, August 1, 1860, 3; William D. Green, "Eliza Winston and the Politics of Freedom in Minnesota, 1854–60," *Minnesota History* 57, no. 3 (Fall 2000): 113–14.

5. *Rochester City Post*, August 4, 1860, 4; *St. Paul Pioneer and Democrat*, July 20, 1860, 8.

6. The *Minnesotian* is quoted in the *Red Wing Sentinel*, September 5, 1860.

7. H. W. Brands, *The Zealot and the Emancipator: John Brown, Abraham Lincoln, and the Struggle for American Freedom* (New York: Doubleday, 2020), 269.

8. Christopher P. Lehman, *Slavery's Reach: Southern Slaveholders in the North Star State* (St. Paul: Minnesota Historical Society Press, 2019), 155–56.

9. "The Minneapolis 'Slave' Case"; Jones, *Labor of Love, Labor of Sorrow*, 34–35, 37.

10. "The Minneapolis 'Slave' Case"; "Mr. Bigelow's Statement," *Falls Evening News* (St. Anthony, MN), August 28, 1860, 2.

11. "The Minneapolis 'Slave' Case"; "Will Not Prosecute," *St. Cloud Democrat*, October 11, 1860, 2; Edwards, *Only the Clothes on Her Back*, 31.

12. David Waldstreicher, "Why Thomas Jefferson and African Americans Wore Their Politics on Their Sleeves: Dress and Mobilization between American Revolutions," in *Beyond the Founders: New Approaches to the Political History of the Early American Republic*, ed. Jeffrey L. Pasley, Andrew W. Robertson, and David Waldstreicher (Chapel Hill: University of North Carolina Press, 2004), 93.

13. "The Minneapolis 'Slave' Case"; Edwards, *Only the Clothes on Her Back*, 2–3.

14. "The Minneapolis 'Slave' Case"; "Will Not Prosecute"; Edwards, *Only the Clothes on Her Back*, 2–3.

15. "The Minneapolis 'Slave' Case"; Buchanan, *Black Life on the Mississippi*, 13.

16. S. W. McMaster, "Pioneer Days on the Mississippi," in *Historic Rock Island County: History of the Settlement of Rock Island County from the Earliest Known Period to the Present Time* (Rock Island, IL: Kramer and Co., 1908), 16; Buchanan, *Black Life on the Mississippi*, 10, 13.

17. Bay, *Traveling Black*, 23.

18. Hunter, *Steamboats on the Western Rivers*, 391.

19. Franklin and Schweninger, *In Search of the Promised Land*, 173.

20. "The Minneapolis 'Slave' Case."

21. "The Minneapolis 'Slave' Case."

22. Franklin and Schweninger, *In Search of the Promised Land*, 171; "The Minneapolis 'Slave' Case."

23. "The Minneapolis 'Slave' Case."

24. *Daily Missouri Democrat*, July 11, 1860, 3; *Daily Missouri Republican*, June 7, 1860, 4; *Daily Missouri Democrat*, June 27, 1860, 3; *Daily Missouri Democrat*, July 6, 1860, 3.

25. Hunter, *Steamboats on the Western Rivers*, 395, 415, 450.

26. Hunter, *Steamboats on the Western Rivers*, 391.

27. Hunter, *Steamboats on the Western Rivers*, 391; George S. Pablis, *Daily Life along the Mississippi* (Westport, CT: Greenwood Press, 2007), 104; "The Minneapolis 'Slave' Case."

28. *Commercial Advertiser* (New York), August 7, 1860, 2.

29. Rae Katherine Eighmey, "TimePieces," *Minnesota History* 59, no. 1 (Spring 2004): 45; George Byron Merrick, *Old Times on the Upper Mississippi: The Recollections of a Steamboat Pilot from 1854 to 1863* (Cleveland, OH: Arthur H. Clark, 1909), 127.

30. "A Journey to the West," *Farmers' Museum*, June 20, 1860, 1.

31. William Kirchner, "Minnesota Revealed as Tourist State in Early Days When California Was Luring Prospectors," *Minneapolis Tribune*, October 8, 1922, magazine section, 8; Bay, *Traveling Black*, 21–22; Pryor, *Colored Travelers*, 149; "Up the Mississippi," *Daily Missouri Republican*, August 21, 1859, 1; Lehman, *Slavery's Reach*, 159; "Editorial Correspondence: The Science of Hotels, Winslow House, St. Anthony," *St. Paul Weekly Minnesotian*, May 28, 1859, 2; "The 'Winslow House,'" *St. Cloud Democrat*, December 9, 1858, 4.

32. *Winslow House Hotel Register*, 103, Hennepin History Museum, Minneapolis, MN.

Notes to Chapter 6. The Hotel and the Seamstress

1. *Commercial Advertiser* (New York), August 8, 1860, 1; Kathryn Strand Koutsky and Linda Koutsky, *Minnesota Eats Out: An Illustrated History* (St. Paul: Minnesota Historical Society Press, 2003), 148; *New Orleans Times-Picayune*, June 10, 1859, 2.

2. Lehman, *Slavery's Reach*, 151, 153; "An Extensive Swindle in St. Louis," *New York Herald*, November 24, 1857, 8; *Louisville Daily Courier*,

May 28, 1852, 3; "Southerners in the Northwest," *Charleston Daily Courier*, September 14, 1860, 1; "Douglas Meeting," *St. Paul Weekly Pioneer and Democrat*, July 20, 1860, 5; *The St. Louis Directory for the Years 1854–5* (St. Louis, MO: Chambers and Knapp, 1854), 121; William L. Montague, *The Saint Louis Business Directory for 1853–4* (St. Louis, MO: E. A. Lewis, 1853), 77.

3. Montague, *The Saint Louis Business Directory for 1853–4*, 77; Richard Edwards, *Edwards' Illustrated Report of the Fourth Annual Fair of the St. Louis Agricultural and Mechanical Association* (St. Louis, MO: Edwards' Monthly, 1860), 234; Jacob N. Taylor and M. O. Crooks, *Sketch Book of Saint Louis* (St. Louis, MO: George Knapp, 1858); 205–6.

4. "Editorial Correspondence: The Science of Hotels, Winslow House, St. Anthony"; "Summer Excursion—Winslow House," *Chicago Tribune*, August 3, 1859, 2; "Letter from Minnesota Territory," *Baltimore Sun*, February 7, 1857, 1; "Notes of Travel," *Mantorville Express*, August 4, 1860, 4.

5. Lehman, *Slavery's Reach*, 157–58.

6. "A Journey to the West," *Farmer's Museum*, June 20, 1860, 1; "Editorial Correspondence [August 19, 1860]," *New Orleans Times-Picayune*, August 26, 1860, 1.

7. David Vassar Taylor, *African Americans in Minnesota* (St. Paul: Minnesota Historical Society Press, 2002), 73–74, 9; *New Orleans Times-Picayune*, June 14, 1859, 2.

8. *Minnesota Weekly Times*, November 24, 1855, 3; Minnesota 1857 Census, St. Anthony, Hennepin County, 439; H. C. Chapin, *Minneapolis Album: A Photographic History of the Early Days in Minneapolis* (Minneapolis, MN: Frank L. Thrasher, 1890); "Minnesota Correspondence," *Cleveland Daily Leader*, October 21, 1858, 2; "Editorial Correspondence: The Science of Hotels, Winslow House, St. Anthony."

9. "Editorial Correspondence: The Science of Hotels, Winslow House, St. Anthony."

10. "Outrageous Proceedings!," *Minnesota Weekly Times*, September 26, 1854, 2.

11. "Outrageous Proceedings!"; Pryor, *Colored Travelers*, 149.

12. "Outrageous Proceedings!"; Koutsky and Koutsky, *Minnesota Eats Out*, 152, 155, 157; Eighmey, "TimePieces"; US 1860 Census, St. Anthony, Hennepin County, Minnesota, 48.

13. Jennifer Jensen Wallach, "What Is the Delta from a Foodways Perspective?," in *Defining the Delta: Multidisciplinary Perspectives on the*

Lower Mississippi River Delta, ed. Janelle Collins (Fayetteville: University of Arkansas Press, 2015), 257.

14. "Outrageous Proceedings!"

15. Lehman, *Slavery's Reach*, 160–62; "Running Off Slaves," *Stillwater Messenger*, July 31, 1860, 2; "The Fugitive Slave," *Falls Evening News*, July 21, 1860, 2.

16. Leon F. Litwack, *Been in the Storm So Long: The Aftermath of Slavery* (New York: Vintage, 1979), 23.

17. Koutsky and Koutsky, *Minnesota Eats Out*, 155.

18. "Degrees of Freedom," *Learning for Life*, October 5, 2020 (William D. Green interviewed by Greg Kaster, Gustavus Adolphus College), https://podcasters.spotify.com/pod/show/gustavus--adolphus-college/episodes/Degrees-of-Freedom-ekl4hm.

19. Kirchner, "Minnesota Revealed as Tourist State."

20. US 1860 Census, St. Anthony, Hennepin County, Minnesota, 4, 47.

21. Kirchner, "Minnesota Revealed as Tourist State."

22. Taylor, *African Americans in Minnesota*, 73–74; Adam Rothman, *Beyond Freedom's Reach: A Kidnapping in the Twilight of Slavery* (Cambridge, MA: Harvard University Press, 2015), 9.

23. Green, "Eliza Winston and the Politics of Freedom," 118.

24. Green, "Eliza Winston and the Politics of Freedom," 118.

25. John Vincent Jazierski, *Enterprising Images: The Goodridge Brothers, African American Photographers, 1847–1922* (Detroit, MI: Wayne State University Press, 2000), 1–3. Because Pennsylvania banned the importing of enslaved people in 1780, it is unclear how Goodridge remained enslaved there after leaving Maryland.

26. Jazierski, *Enterprising Images*, 5, 9.

27. Jazierski, *Enterprising Images*, 17, 18, 19.

28. Emily O. Goodridge Grey, "The Black Community in Territorial St. Anthony: A Memoir," *Minnesota History* 49, no. 2 (Summer 1984): 52.

29. Mary D. Cannon and Patricia C. Harpole, "A Day in the Life: Emily Goodridge Grey," *Minnesota History* 56, no. 4 (Winter 1998–99): 248.

30. US 1860 Census, St. Anthony, Hennepin County, Minnesota, 58.

31. Grey, "The Black Community in Territorial St. Anthony," 47.

32. *Hennepin County, Minnesota Deeds Book F*, 682; Minnesota 1857 Census, St. Anthony, Hennepin County, 432; *Hennepin County, Minnesota Deeds Book O*, 130.

33. Grey, "The Black Community in Territorial St. Anthony," 52.

34. Grey, "The Black Community in Territorial St. Anthony," 52. Winston may have been Eliza's husband's name, but no record has been found to confirm this possibility.

35. "Slavery in Minneapolis," *Minneapolis Tribune,* July 22, 1900, sec. 3, 6.

36. "The Minneapolis 'Slave' Case"; Marion Daniel Shutter, *History of Minneapolis: Gateway to the Northwest,* vol. 1 (Chicago: S. J. Clarke, 1923), 484.

Notes to Chapter 7. The Abolitionists

1. F. A. L., "Editorial Correspondence [August 12, 1860]," *New Orleans Times-Picayune,* August 18, 1860, 2; "Still They Come," *Falls Evening News,* August 16, 1860, 2.

2. Paul Finkelman, "Slaves-in-Transit and the Antebellum Crisis," in *Historic US Court Cases: An Encyclopedia,* vol. 2, 2nd ed., ed. John W. Johnson (New York: Routledge, 2001), 608–9; Jonathan Daniel Wells, *Blind No More: African American Resistance, Free-Soil Politics, and the Coming of the Civil War* (Athens: University of Georgia Press, 2019), 111.

3. *Winslow House Hotel Register,* 116, 122; Lehman, *Slavery's Reach,* 154–56; Burnley, "Albert Triplett Burnley," 153.

4. "Death of Miss Mary Shannon," *Vicksburg Whig,* August 1, 1860, 3; US 1860 Slave Schedule, Vicksburg, Warren County, Mississippi, 3.

5. *Winslow House Hotel Register,* 116.

6. "Police Court," *Falls Evening News,* August 9, 1860, 2; "The Minneapolis 'Slave' Case."

7. Green, "Eliza Winston and the Politics of Freedom," 118; William D. Green, *The Children of Lincoln: White Paternalism and the Limits of Black Opportunity in Minnesota, 1860–1876* (Minneapolis: University of Minnesota Press, 2018), 16–17.

8. Green, "Eliza Winston and the Politics of Freedom," 114.

9. Green, "Eliza Winston and the Politics of Freedom," 114.

10. William Fletcher King, *Reminiscences* (New York: Abingdon Press, 1905), 172.

11. Green, "Eliza Winston and the Politics of Freedom," 118–19.

12. Paul R. Lucas, "The Church and the City: Congregationalism in Minneapolis, 1850–1910," *Minnesota History* 44, no. 2 (Summer 1974): 57; "Slavery in Minneapolis"; Emily Goodridge Grey, letter to William

Goodridge, July 4, 1857, quoted in Cannon and Harpole, "A Day in the Life: Emily Goodridge Grey," 249; Grey, "The Black Community in Territorial St. Anthony."

13. "Slavery in Minneapolis"; "William Dean Babbitt," *Chicago Tribune*, November 1, 1888, 5; Eric Foner, *Gateway to Freedom: The Hidden History of the Underground Railroad* (New York: W. W. Norton, 2015), 58–59, 66; *Proceedings of the National Liberty Convention Held at Buffalo, N.Y., June 14th & 15th, 1848* (Utica, NY: Model Worker, 1848), 3–4, 6.

14. "Anniversary of the West Indian Emancipation," *St. Paul Weekly Minnesotian*, August 14, 1858, 4.

15. "Mr. Babbitt's Statement," *Falls Evening News*, August 28, 1860, 2.

16. "Mr. Bigelow's Statement," *Falls Evening News*, August 28, 1860, 2; *Hennepin County, Minnesota Deeds Book N*, 180.

17. "Mr. Bigelow's Statement."

18. US 1860 Census, Third Ward, St. Anthony, Hennepin County, Minnesota, 58.

19. "Another Nigger Excitement," *Red Wing Sentinel*, September 5, 1860, 1; *Louisville Daily Courier*, June 30, 1860, 4; "The So-Called Kidnapping Case a Schemer to Extort Money," *St. Paul Weekly Pioneer and Democrat*, August 10, 1860, 3; US 1850 Slave Schedule, Vicksburg, Warren County, Mississippi, 3.

20. Lehman, *Slavery's Reach*, 73, 159, 165; "Mr. Babbitt's Statement."

21. "Mr. Bigelow's Statement."

22. "Mr. Bigelow's Statement."

23. "Another Nigger Excitement"; Grey, letter to William Goodridge.

24. Foner, *Gateway to Freedom*, 6, 15.

25. Grey, "The Black Community in Territorial St. Anthony"; "Hayti," *York (PA) Gazette*, May 16, 1843, 1.

26. Freeman Talbot of Cleveland, Minnesota, a Civil War veteran, gave a speech about Winston's bid for freedom at a Fourth of July celebration in Worthington, Minnesota, in 1866. It was excerpted in "The Celebration," *Worthington (MN) Advance*, July 8, 1886, 1.

27. Paula Giddings, *When and Where I Enter: The Impact of Black Women on Race and Sex in America* (New York: Bantam, 1984), 52, 54–55.

28. "The Minneapolis 'Slave' Case."

29. "The Celebration"; "Slavery in Minneapolis"; *Minneapolis Evening Mail*, August 6, 1874, in Ruth Thompson, "Minnesota

Memories: The Eliza Winston Kidnaping," *Minneapolis Tribune*, April 22, 1946, 4.

30. Deborah Swanson, "Joseph Farr Remembers the Underground Railroad in St. Paul," *Minnesota History* 57, no. 3 (Fall 2000): 125–27.

31. Freeman, *The Rights and Duties of Slave-Holders*, 9–10.

32. Lehman, *Slavery's Reach*, 124.

33. *Minneapolis Evening Mail*, August 6, 1874, in Thompson, "Minnesota Memories"; "The Minneapolis 'Slave' Case."

34. *Minneapolis Evening Mail*, August 6, 1874.

35. "The Minneapolis 'Slave' Case."

Notes to Chapter 8. Enslaved at the Lake House

1. "The Minneapolis 'Slave' Case"; Kathleen M. Hilliard, *Masters, Slaves, and Exchange: Power's Purchase in the Old South* (New York: Cambridge University Press, 2014), 86.

2. "Slave Case," *Sauk Rapids New Era*, August 16, 1860, 2.

3. "Slave Case," *Sauk Rapids New Era*, August 16, 1860, 2.

4. A. E. Costello, *History of the Fire and Police Departments of Minneapolis: Their Origin, Progress, and Development* (Minneapolis, MN: Relief Association, 1890), 36.

5. Kirchner, "Minnesota Revealed as Tourist State." The northern boundary of Richfield Township was originally at what is now Lake Street, but much of the township was absorbed into Minneapolis through annexations over many years. Richfield became a city in 1908.

6. King, *Reminiscences*, 172; "Frenzied," *Minneapolis Tribune*, October 15, 1905, 17.

7. King, *Reminiscences*, 172; "Frenzied"; US 1860 Census, Issaquena County, Mississippi, 1; US 1860 Census, Richfield, Hennepin County, Minnesota, 136.

8. US 1860 Census, Richfield, Hennepin County, Minnesota, 136; Horace Bushnell, "Minnesota for the Invalids," *St. Paul Weekly Pioneer and Democrat*, November 23, 1860, 8.

9. "Real Estate," *Minneapolis Daily Tribune*, July 16, 1871, 2; US 1860 Census, Richfield, Hennepin County, Minnesota, 136.

10. *Hennepin County, Minnesota Deeds Book F*, 583–84; *Hennepin County, Minnesota Deeds Book L*, 687.

11. "Dred Scott in Minneapolis," *Minneapolis Tribune*, February 24, 1907, 12.

12. *The Papers of Jefferson Davis*, vol. 2, June 1841–July 1846, ed. James T. McIntosh (Baton Rouge: Louisiana State University Press, 1974), 712.

13. US 1860 Slave Schedule, Hinds County, Mississippi, 13; *The Papers of Jefferson Davis*, 2:712; Jones-Rogers, *They Were Her Property*, 28–29.

14. John D. Freeman, "Gen. Freeman's Alabama Letter," September 17, 1848, in John H. Howard and John D. Freeman, *A Reply to the Arguments of the Hon. A. H. Stephens against the Constitutional Right to Hold Slaves in the Territories of California and New Mexico* (Columbus, GA: Times Office, 1848), 13–14; John D. Freeman, letter, *Weekly Mississippian*, December 19, 1860, 3.

15. US 1860 Census, Hinds County, Mississippi, 43; US 1870 Census, Jackson, Hinds County, Mississippi, 41; "Another Nigger Excitement."

16. F. A. L., "Editorial Correspondence [August 19, 1860]," *New Orleans Times-Picayune*, August 26, 1860, 1.

17. Frank G. O'Brien, *Minnesota Pioneer Sketches: From the Personal Recollections and Observations of a Pioneer Resident* (Minneapolis, MN: H. H. S. Rowell, 1904), 318–19.

18. F. A. L., "Editorial Correspondence [August 19, 1860]," 1; "The Minneapolis 'Slave' Case."

19. George E. Warner, C. M. Foote, Edward D. Neill, and J. Fletcher Williams, *History of Hennepin County and the City of Minneapolis* (Minneapolis, MN: North Star Publishing, 1881), 214–15; "Dred Scott in Minneapolis," 12.

20. "Another Nigger Excitement"; "Outrage upon Southerners" and "Abolition Outrage in Minnesota," *New Orleans Daily Delta*, September 15, 1860, 1.

21. "Another Nigger Excitement"; "Outrage upon Southerners."

22. "Outrage upon Southerners"; Foner, *Gateway to Freedom*, 108, 114, 155.

23. Foner, *Gateway to Freedom*, 113, 132.

24. *St. Paul Weekly Pioneer and Democrat*, August 31, 1860, 2; M. Jane Johnson, "Brig. Gen. Daniel Weisiger Adams," in *Kentuckians in Gray: Confederate Generals and Field Officers of the Bluegrass State*, ed. Bruce S. Allardice and Lawrence Lee Hewitt (Lexington: University Press of Kentucky, 2008), 9.

25. *Minneapolis Evening Mail*, August 6, 1874, in Thompson, "Minnesota Memories."

26. "Another Nigger Excitement"; "Outrage upon Southerners"; "Slavery Days," in *Mirror* (Stillwater, MN), June 27, 1895, 1 (reprinted from the *Penny Press*, a Minneapolis newspaper).

27. "Another Nigger Excitement"; "Outrage upon Southerners"; "Slavery Days," 1.

28. "Another Nigger Excitement"; "Outrage upon Southerners."

29. "Another Nigger Excitement"; "Outrage upon Southerners"; *Minneapolis Evening Mail*, August 6, 1874, in Thompson, "Minnesota Memories."

30. "Another Nigger Excitement"; "Outrage upon Southerners"; "Slavery Days," 5.

31. "Mr. Babbitt's Statement."

Notes to Chapter 9. Rescue by Arrest

1. "Negro Excitement at St. Paul, Minnesota," *Vicksburg Daily Whig*, September 4, 1860, 2; "An Old Settler of St. Paul Dies," *Ashland Weekly News*, April 11, 1888, 7; US 1860 Census, Fourth Ward, St. Paul, Ramsey County, Minnesota, 227; Gene H. Rosenblum, *Jewish Pioneers of Saint Paul, 1849–1874* (Chicago: Arcadia, 2001), 32; W. H. C. Folsom, *Fifty Years in the Northwest* (St. Paul: Pioneer, 1888), 564.

2. "Negro Excitement at St. Paul, Minnesota"; US 1860 Census, Third Ward, St. Paul, Ramsey County, Minnesota, 166; Lehman, *Slavery's Reach*, 85–86, 107; US 1860 Census, Chester County, South Carolina, 181; US 1860 Slave Schedule, Chester County, South Carolina, 128; US 1860 Census, Jackson, Hinds County, Mississippi, 44; US 1860 Slave Schedule, Jackson, Hinds County, Mississippi, 14; *Ramsey County, Minnesota Deeds Book 10*, 98–99.

3. Hiram Fairchild Stevens, *History of the Bench and Bar in Minnesota*, vol. 1 (Minneapolis, MN: Legal Publishing and Engraving Co., 1904), 32; "Mr. Babbitt's Statement."

4. Stevens, *History of the Bench and Bar in Minnesota*, 1:32; Anthony Gregory, *The Power of Habeas Corpus: From the King's Prerogative to the War on Terror* (Cambridge: Cambridge University Press, 2013), 79–80; Foner, *Gateway to Freedom*, 68, 88, 139–40, 167; Thomas D. Morris, *Free Men All: The Personal Liberty Laws of the North, 1780–1861* (Union, NJ: Lawbook Exchange, 1999), ix–x.

5. "The Fugitive Slave at St. Paul," *Falls Evening News*, July 24, 1860, 2; Lehman, *Slavery's Reach*, 161.

6. "Police Court," *Falls Evening News*, August 9, 1860, 2; *Stillwater Messenger*, August 21, 1860, 1; US 1860 Census, Fourth Ward, St. Anthony, Hennepin County, Minnesota, 74.

7. "Veteran Jurist Gone," *St. Paul Globe*, March 4, 1898, 3. In addition, Vanderburgh and Cornell once were business partners, having co-owned real estate in Minnesota. In the summer of 1858, Cornell and his wife allowed Vanderburgh and his wife to co-invest with them in forty acres in Hennepin County. At the end of the year, the two couples sold the land to someone else. Thus, as of August 1860, when Cornell agreed to face Vanderburgh, the former partners no longer owned any property together. See *Hennepin County, Minnesota Deeds Book L*, 310–11; *Hennepin County, Minnesota Deeds Book M*, 58–59.

8. "Veteran Jurist Gone."

9. "Another Nigger Excitement"; Charles Vanderburgh, "An Evening of Great Interest," *Minneapolis Tribune*, November 12, 1895, 4.

10. "Another Nigger Excitement"; *Falls Evening News*, August 16, 1860, 2.

11. "Another Nigger Excitement"; US 1860 Census, Second Ward, Minneapolis, Hennepin County, Minnesota, 200; "Death of Richard Strout," *Emporia Daily Republican*, June 28, 1899, 4.

12. US 1860 Census, Second Ward, Minneapolis, Hennepin County, Minnesota, 200; US 1850 Census, District 30, Lewis County, Virginia, 17; US 1850 Slave Schedule, District 30, Lewis County, Virginia, 1; *St. Cloud Democrat*, August 7, 1862, 3; *Stearns County, Minnesota Deeds Book G*, 59–62; Lehman, *Slavery's Reach*, 55; *Lewis County, Virginia Deeds Book Q*, 241; US 1860 Census, Third Ward, St. Anthony, Hennepin County, Minnesota, 44; Minnesota 1857 Census, St. Anthony, Hennepin County, 73; US 1850 Slave Schedule, District 30, Lewis County, Virginia, 4.

13. Warner et al., *History of Hennepin County and the City of Minneapolis*, 213.

14. "From Minneapolis," *St. Cloud Democrat*, August 30, 1860, 2; "Mr. Babbitt's Statement."

15. "Statement of Deputy Sheriff Canney," *Falls Evening News*, August 28, 1860, 2. Although Quakers opposed slavery, the Quaker community in Hennepin County included the Mendenhalls, who had come from the slave state North Carolina. R. J. Mendenhall was the son of an enslaver, and he sold land in Minnesota to enslavers: see Lehman, *Slavery's Reach*, 144–46.

16. "The Minneapolis 'Slave' Case"; "From Minneapolis," 2; "Slavery Days," 4; "Dred Scott in Minneapolis," 12; US 1850 Census, Eastern District, Monongalia County, Virginia, 525; US 1860 Census, Second Ward, Minneapolis, Hennepin County, Minnesota, 193; "Pioneer Physician Called," *Minneapolis Tribune*, April 30, 1910, 10.

17. "The Minneapolis 'Slave' Case."

18. Jones-Rogers, *They Were Her Property*, 60, 180.

19. "The Minneapolis 'Slave' Case"; Litwack, *Been in the Storm So Long*, 56–57, 106–7.

20. "The Minneapolis 'Slave' Case"; Jones-Rogers, *They Were Her Property*, 61–62.

21. "From Minneapolis," 2; "Mr. Babbitt's Statement"; "The Minneapolis 'Slave' Case."

22. "Another Nigger Excitement"; "Mr. Babbitt's Statement"; "Statement of Deputy Sheriff Canney."

23. "Another Nigger Excitement"; "From Minneapolis," 2; "Mr. Babbitt's Statement."

24. "Another Nigger Excitement"; "Mr. Babbitt's Statement."

25. "Mr. Babbitt's Statement"; David Brion Davis, "Slave Revolts and Abolitionism," in *Who Abolished Slavery? Slave Revolts and Abolitionism: A Debate with João Pedro Marques*, ed. Seymour Drescher and Pieter C. Emmer (New York: Berghahn Books, 2021), 165; David J. Libby, *Slavery and Frontier Mississippi, 1720–1835* (Jackson: University Press of Mississippi, 2004), 53.

26. "Slavery Days," 5; "The Minneapolis 'Slave' Case."

27. "The Minneapolis 'Slave' Case"; "Mr. Babbitt's Statement."

28. "Dred Scott in Minneapolis," 13.

29. Shutter, *History of Minneapolis*, 1:484.

30. "The Minneapolis 'Slave' Case."

31. "Mr. Babbitt's Statement"; "Statement of Deputy Sheriff Canney."

32. "From Minneapolis," 2; "The Minneapolis 'Slave' Case"; "Another Nigger Excitement."

33. "The Minneapolis 'Slave' Case."

34. Hilliard, *Masters, Slaves, and Exchange*, 86.

35. "The Minneapolis 'Slave' Case."

36. "The Minneapolis 'Slave' Case."

37. "The Minneapolis 'Slave' Case."

38. "The Minneapolis 'Slave' Case."

39. "The Minneapolis 'Slave' Case"; "Negro Excitement at St. Paul, Minnesota."

40. Litwack, *Been in the Storm So Long*, 354–55.

Notes to Chapter 10. Freedom Trial in Minnesota

1. "Notes of Travel," *Mantorville Express*, August 4, 1860, 4; Warner et al., *History of Hennepin County and the City of Minneapolis*, 344.

2. Shutter, *History of Minneapolis*, 1:101, 128–29; "Notes of Travel," *Mantorville Express*, August 4, 1860, 4.

3. "Notes of Travel," *Mantorville Express*, August 4, 1860, 4.

4. "From Minneapolis," 3; *Minneapolis Evening Mail*, August 6, 1874, in Thompson, "Minnesota Memories"; "Another Nigger Excitement."

5. "The Minneapolis 'Slave' Case."

6. "Another Nigger Excitement."

7. "Another Nigger Excitement."

8. "Another Nigger Excitement"; "Statement of Deputy Sheriff Canney."

9. Vanderburg, "An Evening of Great Interest."

10. Foner, *Gateway to Freedom*, 44.

11. "Slave Excitement in Minneapolis," *Falls Evening News*, August 23, 1860, 2; Shutter, *History of Minneapolis*, 1:483; "The Minneapolis 'Slave' Case"; "Mr. Babbitt's Statement"; "Statement of Deputy Sheriff Canney."

12. Shutter, *History of Minneapolis*, 1:483; "Mr. Babbitt's Statement"; "Statement of Deputy Sheriff Canney."

13. "The Minneapolis 'Slave' Case," 1; Martha S. Jones, *Birthright Citizens: A History of Race and Rights in Antebellum America* (Cambridge: Cambridge University Press, 2018), 1, 10–11.

14. "The Minneapolis 'Slave' Case."

15. "Statement of Deputy Sheriff Canney."

16. Vanderburg, "An Evening of Great Interest."

17. William D. Green, "The Summer Christmas Came to Minnesota: The Case of Eliza Winston, a Slave," *Minnesota Journal of Law and Inequality* 8, no. 1 (March 1990): 166; Orlin Folwick, "Battered House in City Recalls Slavery Ruling," *Minneapolis Tribune*, March 14, 1926, 8; Paul Finkelman, *Dred Scott v. Sandford: A Brief History with Documents* (Boston: Bedford Books, 1997), 33–34, 59, 76.

18. Freeman, "Gen. Freeman's Alabama Letter," 14, 30. Freeman's argument against Winston's freedom was informed by his recent connection to a case involving slavery in his home state. He had represented a formerly enslaved woman whose own father had enslaved her. Her father took her to Ohio and manumitted her in 1846, and he willed a portion of his property in Mississippi to her two years later. She sued her father's executor in Mississippi in 1857 for her inheritance and won, but the executor then brought the case to an appellate court in that state in 1859. The law was on the woman's side, because a lower court in that state had just ruled in 1858 that another former captive residing in the North could claim an inheritance from his former enslaver. However, Freeman lost the woman's case on appeal. The Mississippi High Court of Errors and Appeals ruled that the woman's freedom in a free state did not permit her to claim property in a slave state. State law prohibited enslaved people from becoming free and from inheriting property. Therefore, if Mississippi would not have permitted her to become free, it was reasoned, the state should not allow her to claim an inheritance there. See Aviam Soifer, "Compromise at the Boundaries of Bondage," *Reviews in American History* 10 (June 1982): 188–89; Jeffory A. Clymer, "Family Money: Race and Economic Rights in Antebellum US Law and Fiction," *American Literary History* 21, no. 2 (Summer 2009): 216; Thomas D. Morris, *Southern Slavery and the Law, 1619–1860* (Chapel Hill: University of North Carolina Press, 1996), 398–99.

19. "Unmanly," *State Atlas* (Minneapolis), August 29, 1860, 2.

20. Green, "The Summer Christmas Came to Minnesota," 166.

21. Folwick, "Battered House in City Recalls Slavery Ruling," 8.

22. Walt Bachman, *Northern Slave, Black Dakota: The Life and Times of Joseph Godfrey* (Bloomington, MN: Pond Dakota Press, 2013), 10, 11.

23. "Outrage upon Southerners."

24. Green, "Eliza Winston and the Politics of Freedom," 109; Jane Grey Swisshelm, *Half a Century* (Chicago: Jansen, McClurg, 1880), 174; "Minnesota News by Telegraph and Mail," *Freeborn County Standard*, February 3, 1881, 7.

25. "Slave Excitement in Minneapolis."

26. "From Minneapolis," 2.

27. "From Minneapolis," 2.

28. "Slave Excitement in Minneapolis"; "Statement of Deputy Sheriff Canney"; "Mr. Babbitt's Statement."

29. "The Minneapolis 'Slave' Case."

30. "The Minneapolis 'Slave' Case."

31. "Slave Case in Minneapolis," *Mantorville (MN) Express,* September 1, 1860, 1; "Statement of Deputy Sheriff Canney"; "Mr. Babbitt's Statement."

32. "Slave Case in Minneapolis"; "Statement of Deputy Sheriff Canney"; "Mr. Babbitt's Statement."

33. "Slave Case in Minneapolis"; "Statement of Deputy Sheriff Canney"; "Mr. Babbitt's Statement."

34. *St. Paul Weekly Pioneer and Democrat,* August 24, 1860, 6.

35. Green, "Eliza Winston and the Politics of Freedom," 110.

36. Lehman, *Slavery's Reach,* 163. Winston's emancipation was personal to McLean for another reason. His maternal uncle Horace P. Woodbridge had died in 1851 in St. Louis, and had enslaved two people at the time of his demise. McLean claimed that Woodbridge had left a will during a brief stay with him in Iowa and that the will granted almost all of the estate—including the captives—to the nephew. On the other hand, McLean's step-uncle said that Woodbridge never made a will and that the deceased did not sign the purported will. Multiple other acquaintances of Woodbridge agreed with the step-uncle about the signature, and ultimately so did a judge. McLean missed his chance to inherit his uncle's captives via a court action, and now the Christmases had lost their servant through another court action. In addition, McLean was defeated because the judge believed the words of Woodbridge's blood relative less than the words of mere acquaintances—outsiders to the family. The Christmases' loss in court similarly came from abolitionist northerners—outsiders to the South's slave culture—finding more favor in court than the enslavers supporting the city with their patronage. It was too late for McLean to retrieve his rightful captives; they were sold away within weeks of the verdict. See probate file of Horace P. Woodbridge, 1851, no. 3560, St. Louis County Probate Court, St. Louis, Missouri.

37. Rothman, *The Ledger and the Chain,* 339.

38. "Col. W. S. King Dead," *Minneapolis Tribune,* February 24, 1900, 1. The *St. Anthony Express* is quoted in the *Red Wing Sentinel,* September 8, 1860, 1.

39. *Minneapolis Evening Mail,* August 6, 1874, in Thompson, "Minnesota Memories," 4.

Notes to Chapter 11. An Emancipated Life

1. "From Minneapolis," 3.

2. H. E. Chamberlin, *Commercial Advertiser Directory for Saint Anthony and Minneapolis* (St. Anthony, MN: Croffut and Clark, 1859), 33.

3. "Eliza Winston," *St. Cloud Democrat*, October 11, 1860, 2; US 1860 Census, Fourth Ward, Minneapolis, Hennepin County, Minnesota, 237; "The Hennepin County Slave Case—Triumph of the 'Freedom Shriekers,'" *St. Paul Weekly Pioneer and Democrat*, August 24, 1860, 6; Chamberlin, *Commercial Advertiser Directory for Saint Anthony and Minneapolis*, 122. Stone's home was on what is now the campus of Augsburg University.

4. Green, "Eliza Winston and the Politics of Freedom," 113.

5. Green, "Eliza Winston and the Politics of Freedom," 113.

6. Lehman, *Slavery's Reach*, 163; advertisement, *Red Wing Sentinel*, August 22, 1860, 5.

7. Green, "Eliza Winston and the Politics of Freedom," 113; "End Comes to Negro Pioneer," *Minneapolis Journal*, December 8, 1904, 6; "Senator Seward's Western Town," *New York Herald*, September 27, 1860, 2.

8. "Southerners in the Northwest," *Charleston (SC) Daily Courier*, September 14, 1860; *Oxford Intelligencer*, September 5, 1860, 3; "Mr. Babbitt's Statement"; Berry, *The Price for Their Pound of Flesh*, 93.

9. "Will Not Prosecute," *St. Cloud Democrat*, October 11, 1860, 2.

10. Green, "The Summer Christmas Came to Minnesota," 171–72; *State Atlas*, October 24, 1860, 2, quoted in Green, "Eliza Winston and the Politics of Freedom," 119.

11. Green, "Eliza Winston and the Politics of Freedom," 119.

12. *Falls Evening News*, August 28, 1860, 2; *Chatfield Republican*, September 4, 1860, 2; *St. Cloud Democrat*, September 6, 1860, 1; Lehman, *Slavery's Reach*, 129–31; "Anniversary of the West Indian Emancipation," 4; "Mr. Babbitt's Statement."

13. Swanson, "Joseph Farr Remembers the Underground Railroad in St. Paul," 124.

14. Robert H. Churchill, *The Underground Railroad and the Geography of Violence in Antebellum America* (Cambridge: Cambridge University Press, 2020), 122.

15. "Slavery Days," 4; "Dred Scott in Minneapolis," 12; Foner, *Gateway to Freedom*, 137, 212.

16. "The Minneapolis 'Slave' Case"; Shutter, *History of Minneapolis*, 1:486.

17. *Memphis Daily Appeal*, October 6, 1860, 2; "Another Abduction Case," *Weekly Mississippian*, September 12, 1860, 1.

18. John D. Freeman, letter, *Weekly Mississippian*, December 19, 1860, 3; "Another Abduction Case," *Weekly Mississippian*, September 12, 1860, 1.

19. "A Slave Enticed from Her Master in Minnesota Begs Her Way Back to Mississippi," *St. Paul Weekly Pioneer and Democrat*, January 25, 1861, 4.

20. Lehman, *Slavery's Reach*, 158; "Loosening the Shackles from the Hands of Eliza Winston," *Minneapolis Tribune*, March 4, 1900, 9.

21. *Memphis Tax Records: July 1854 to July 1855*, 22.

22. "List of Letters," *Detroit Free Press*, December 1, 1861, 4; Richard Edwards, *Charles F. Clark's Annual Directory of the Inhabitants, Incorporated Companies, Business Firms, Etc., in the City of Detroit for 1862–3* (Detroit, MI: Charles F. Clark, 1862), 317.

23. Edwards, *Charles F. Clark's Annual Directory*, 317; Jacqueline L. Tobin and Hettie Jones, *From Midnight to Dawn: The Last Tracks of the Underground Railroad* (New York: Doubleday, 2007), 210, 211.

24. Paul Taylor, *"Old Slow Town": Detroit during the Civil War* (Detroit, MI: Wayne State University Press, 2013), 99–100.

25. "The Celebration"; "Slavery in Minneapolis"; "Slavery Days," 4; "Dred Scott in Minneapolis," 12. On the origins of the "Slavery Days" article, which tells the story of the visit to Detroit in the 1890s, see chapter 8, note 26 (page 256); in spite of the article's many inaccuracies, the specificity of the account of the visit suggests that it may have happened.

26. "Slave Abducted," *Memphis Weekly Bulletin*, September 14, 1860, 4.

27. "Sad Case of Drowning," *Richmond Enquirer*, October 11, 1861, 3.

28. James K. Polk, letter to Sarah C. Polk, October 26, 1843, *Correspondence of James K. Polk*, 6:353; *Maury County, Tennessee Deeds Book Z*, 449, 608.

29. *Christmas v. Russell*, in Wallace, *Cases Argued and Adjudged in the Supreme Court of the United States, December Term, 1871*, 4:71.

30. *Jackson Clarion-Ledger*, September 15, 1880, 2; US 1880 Census, District 281, New York City, New York County, New York, 10.

31. *New Orleans Times-Picayune*, February 26, 1888, 13.

32. Will of Mary Ann Walker, October 4, 1860, Shelby County Probate Court, loose papers, no. 1496, record no. 4.

33. US 1870 Census, Jackson, Hinds County, Mississippi, 41; US 1880 Census, Beat 1, Liberty Grove Precinct, Hinds County, Mississippi, 18.

34. Giddings, *When and Where I Enter*, 55.

35. Green, *The Children of Lincoln*, 270–71.

36. "Eliza Winston," *St. Cloud Democrat*, October 11, 1860, 2; Green, *The Children of Lincoln*, 7.

37. Green, "Eliza Winston and the Politics of Freedom," 119–20; "St. Anthony Slave Rescue Case," *Red Wing Sentinel*, January 23, 1861, 2.

38. *Chatfield Democrat*, June 18, 1864, 2.

39. "End Comes to Negro Pioneer," *Minneapolis Journal*, December 8, 1904, 6.

40. "End Comes to Negro Pioneer," *Minneapolis Journal*, December 8, 1904, 6.

41. Green, "Eliza Winston and the Politics of Freedom," 119; "The Minneapolis 'Slave' Case."

42. "The Minneapolis 'Slave' Case"; Valerie Smith, "Form and Ideology in Three Slave Narratives," in *Incidents in the Life of a Slave Girl: Authoritative Text, Contexts, Criticism*, 2nd ed., ed. Frances Smith Foster and Richard Yarborough (New York: W. W. Norton, 2019), 228.

Notes to Epilogue. The Icon

1. Associated Negro Press, "Some Racial History of Minneapolis," *Dallas (TX) Express*, August 23, 1919, 1.

2. "News and Comment," *Minnesota History* 16, no. 1 (March 1935): 116.

3. Remington, "In the Days of Abolitionists."

4. Remington, "In the Days of Abolitionists."

5. Remington, "In the Days of Abolitionists."

6. Remington, "In the Days of Abolitionists."

7. Remington, "In the Days of Abolitionists."

INDEX

Page numbers in *italics* refer to illustrations.

It Took Courage was designed and set in type
by Judy Gilats in Saint Paul, Minnesota.
The text face is Plantin and the display faces
are Abolition and IM Fells English Pro.